Directory of
Building and Equipment Grants

Third Edition

An Innovative Reference Directory Pinpointing
Building, Renovation, and Equipment Grants
Available to Nonprofit Organizations

RICHARD M. ECKSTEIN
Editor

Research Grant Guides, Inc.
P.O. Box 1214
Loxahatchee, Florida 33470

To Jared Burton Tosner

THIRD EDITION

Printed in the U.S.A.

ISSN 1062-6492
ISBN 0-945078-08-0

Table of Contents

Preface

The third edition of the *Directory of Building and Equipment Grants* will assist fund-raisers seeking grants for building, renovation and equipment grants.

The following subject areas are profiled in the directory: community development, cultural organizations, disabled, education, elderly, environment, health organizations, higher education, hospitals, libraries, minorities, recreation, religion, social welfare, women and youth organizations.

Funding sources may change their priorities and expenditure levels. Corporate foundations frequently respond to the general economy and may curtail their grant-making programs until profits reach a satisfactory level. Don't be discouraged if your proposal is not funded on the first try.

To get started, use the Directory to research funding agencies supporting your type of organization. Be careful to remember that many foundations award grants only in their own geographic area. Next, send a brief letter to the funding agency and request a copy of their most recent grant guidelines, if they publish them. Guidelines issued by the funder should always be followed. Before writing a grant proposal, read the guidelines listed in *The Realist's Guide to Foundation and Corporate Grants* beginning on page 15.

Several elements in a successful grant proposal include:

1) Uniqueness of proposal subject matter

2) A clear, well-written application

3) A realistic budget

4) Qualifications of the Project Director

5) Issues of concern to the proposed sponsor

If the proposal warrants, there should be a table of contents to guide the reviewer. A timetable depicting your proposed progress also may be helpful. Try to present a readable, professional-looking proposal written in clear language that avoids jargon.

Successful Strategies for Winning Building and Equipment Grants

by
Andrew J. Grant, Ph.D.
and Suzy D. Sonenberg, M.S.W.

Introduction

Applicants seeking grants for construction and equipment face greater challenges than grant seekers in general. Construction projects and equipment purchases tend to be more expensive than other types of undertakings. Sponsors may look upon capital projects as less attractive because they do not appear to deliver services directly to the at-risk constituencies served by nonprofit organizations. Success in this area of grantsmanship depends on careful research and planning and requires a broad vision of the needs served by the project. More than for most other types of funding, searches for capital grants require systematic, strategic approaches that may span several years. The approach may be toward a project grant for a single purpose, or it may be part of a multifaceted capital campaign. This article will describe such strategies and offer a few examples of successful results.

Building a Project Matrix to Plan the Strategy

In order to plan appropriate strategies and maximize prospects for success, nonprofit organizations must develop clear, sharply focused profiles of their projects. They must have an unambiguous understanding of what they plan to do and why they are doing it. The type of organization applying for funding, the type of project and the reasons for the project all will have an impact on the funding strategy. Building an APPLICANT-PROJECT-REASON matrix will define the project and guide the applicant toward a realistic funding strategy. These three factors will help determine which type of sponsor organization and which type of funding instrument will be most appropriate.

Andrew J. Grant, Ph.D. is Director of Grants at Baruch College/CUNY. He also teaches a graduate course on grants administration at Hofstra University, Hempstead, New York. Dr. Grant has been involved with sponsored project administration for twenty years.

Dr. Grant has written grant proposals that were successfully funded from corporations, foundations and government agencies. He conducts workshops and publishes articles on varied topics in fund-raising. He received his Ph.D. in Public Administration from New York University. His e-mail address is agrbb@cunyvm.cuny.edu. Dr. Grant and his wife Mindy are principals in the consulting firm Grant Services Corp.

Suzy Sonenberg has been Executive Director of the Long Island Community Foundation (an affiliate of The New York Community Trust) since March, 1988.

After receiving a Master's Degree in Social Work from Adelphi University in 1976, Ms. Sonenberg spent 8 years as a non-profit administrator and grant seeker before joining the funding community. She has taught social policy on the graduate and undergraduate levels at Adelphi School of Social Work, and often appears as a guest lecturer on "fundraising from foundations" at various institutions of higher learning in the New York Metropolitan area.

In order to develop such a matrix, the applicant organization must perform a simple self-study or evaluation to specify its goals, catalog its resources and characterize its mission. The following model can be used to get the process going. The applicant needs to select one item from each of the following lists for every component of its project. The resulting combinations will help structure an approach and begin to suggest potential sponsors.

Nonprofit organizations fall into one or more of many categories. The following list is illustrative, but by no means exhaustive:

- small nonprofit;
- medium nonprofit;
- large nonprofit;
- hospital or health services;
- long-term care;
- elementary or secondary education;
- postsecondary education;
- social services;
- transportation;
- serving people with disabilities.

Projects for capital needs fall into several categories. Typical situations can be illustrated as follows:

- an organization intends to build a brand new facility;
- an organization intends to modify or renovate an existing facility;
- an organization requires maintenance on its facilities;
- an organization intends to buy an existing facility;
- an organization needs brand new equipment to begin a new project;
- an organization needs to repair or replace much of its existing equipment.

Reasons for undertaking a capital project are equally varied and may be among the following:

- the organization needs space to initiate a new project or service;
- the organization has experienced an increase in the number of clients it serves;
- the facilities occupied by the organization no longer meet its needs or those of its clients;
- the organization has determined it is more economical to purchase a building it has been leasing;
- the organization needs to modernize its equipment in order to remain competitive;
- the organization needs specialized equipment to conduct a new project;
- the organization does not have sufficient funds to perform necessary maintenance on its equipment and facilities;
- the organization needs to renovate its facilities in order to comply with new codes or requirements;
- the organization has suffered damage or loss to its facilities because of a natural disaster.

Using the Matrix to Structure the Project

The matrix approach provides organizations with a planning tool designed to bring the project into sharp focus. It lends structure to the assessment of need underlying the justification for the project. The matrix takes three essential questions, separates them and presents them as separate modules to be developed individually. They form the rationale for any project. As we have already suggested they are:

Who are we (the APPLICANT)?

What do we want to do (the PROJECT)?

Why is it important (the REASON)?

In most cases, answering the first question is easy, but nonetheless essential. Most nonprofit organizations have clear visions about their mission and purposes in the community, be it a single neighborhood or the entire world. Some organizations have a more difficult time answering the "who are we" question. These include organizations with multiple missions, or nonprofit organizations with changing client bases who may be in the process of redefining their mission, or part of it, and are seeking grant support to assist in that process. Often, the process of applying for funding, especially its requirement for a clear statement of organizational identity, can bring attention to ambiguous or changing goals or a loss of clarity regarding the mission. In such cases, the leadership is well advised to deal with these issues before proceeding with the funding search.

"Who are we?" is important because it defines the organization in terms of its mission, its clients and its expertise. Organizational leaders who experience difficulty answering this question must first determine why. As noted above, there are various reasons for a less than crystal clear identity. A health organization, for example, may provide health education services. If such an organization were seeking funds for a new education facility, it would be logical for it to approach sponsors interested in both health and education. It must answer the "who are we?" question in terms of its expertise in both areas, emphasizing one or the other or their convergence depending on the sponsor's interests. Regardless of the merit of a project, an organization without a strong, focused description of its mission, clients and expertise, as these relate to the proposal, will not be competitive for funding.

"What do we want to do?", separated from "why?", describes the project substance. The "what" in building and equipment projects is simply the means for providing service, conducting research or performing training. This component of the matrix defines the magnitude of the grant being sought. It also defines the focus or orientation of the project. A request for equipment needed to conduct a research or training program focuses more on the project itself than on the clients served by the organization. A request for funds to construct a new building to house an organization's operations focuses more on the clientele than on any specific project.

This is an important distinction. Some sponsors support capital projects without requiring much detail about the activities to be conducted. For example, a university seeking funds to construct a new classroom building may structure its proposal by describing itself in terms of its history, student body and need for the building to upgrade its physical plant to provide the newest technology. Some sponsors, although not many, make grants for large construction or equipment projects in the context of broad guidelines. What sells the proposal is the reputation or importance to the community of the organization (the WHO) as well as the justification for the new or expanded facilities.

Contrast this with the hospital seeking funds for an AIDS care unit. Here the WHO is still vital to the success of the proposal, but the WHAT assumes greater importance. The activities to be conducted in the new facility are the central focus of the proposal, and the organization's reputation, as well as a profile of the clients it serves, provide additional support for the funding appeal. The latter, however, appears as background information.

In an appeal from a research university to a pharmaceutical firm for upgrading laboratory equipment in the chemistry department, the proposal may focus almost exclusively on the activities to be conducted in the newly outfitted lab. The sponsor will be interested in specific results that promise to enhance its own market position with the development of new compounds. Certainly, the applicant's reputation is vital, but the proposal focuses on the project itself, not necessarily on the potential benefit to students or faculty.

A final example is that of the small community social services organization with a need to refurbish its badly deteriorated building. Its appeal will focus on the clients it serves and the consequences to them of the conditions in the building. The organization will specify its importance in the community and detail the services it provides to an at-risk client population. The focus of the proposal is on the clients and their needs, rather than on the project or the applicant itself. Again, the WHO is still important, but the approach centers on the beneficiaries of the services provided by the applicant organization.

"Why is it important?" provides the rationale for undertaking the project. The specific REASON can be as varied as the types of projects, but in general the "why" of building and equipment proposals falls into one or more of several categories. They are noted above by way of example and can be categorized as follows:

- initiation;
- expansion;
- modernization;
- community needs (e.g. economic development);
- client specific or changing client needs;
- project specific needs (e.g. laboratory research equipment);
- maintenance;
- disaster relief.

Our matrix approach helps define the proposal. It makes it easier to visualize the different components common to most projects. The applicant organization can use the matrix to identify and develop the specifics of each of the APPLICANT-PROJECT-REASON modules of the proposal. Each element should be seen as distinct from the others and then combined to form a unified proposal. The process will focus the project for the applicant and guide the way to a potentially successful funding campaign.

Developing Strategies and Identifying Sponsors

The matrix model facilitates sponsor identification because it assists the applicant with the important, but frequently neglected, task of forming a precise definition of every aspect of the project. So armed, the organization can narrow the field of sponsors, categorize them into groups and rank each group in terms of its suitability, likelihood of support and potential magnitude of support. This exercise also helps in assembling a diversified base of funders for large projects whose scope exceeds the possibility of full support from a single source.

Getting started with the search requires access to a library of government, foundation and corporate funding directories, including the *Directory of Building and Equipment Grants*, or access to a computer data base of sponsors. Access to both is the ideal situation. Using the APPLICANT-PROJECT-REASON matrix for the project, the organization would develop lists of sponsors interested in supporting projects from like applicants. This will be a large list and will be narrowed by limiting it to potential funders who support similar applicants and who have an interest in the particular type of project being proposed. This is a good place to start, although the list may be narrowed further by cross matching the first two categories with the reason category.

For example, a community health organization may be interested in remodeling part of its facility to start a new AIDS education program. The search first would identify sponsors with a history of support for community health organizations - focused on the local geographic region for foundation and corporate sponsors - and then restrict the list by eliminating those who don't support building, start-up or AIDS projects. It is a tedious process of elimination which can be made much more efficient by using a computer search tool. The matrix helps focus the search by providing clear criteria against which to match the interests of potential sponsors.

A matrix would look like the following table.

	APPLICANT	PROJECT	REASON
Sponsor 1	✓	✓	
Sponsor 2	✓	✓	✓
Sponsor 3	✓		
Sponsor 4		✓	✓
etc...			

Sponsor 2 is the obvious first choice among this group. Listing all identified sponsors and checking off the matrix boxes as shown above will provide a strong visualization of the most promising. This method forces the applicant into the discipline of analyzing each component of the proposal in terms of the sponsor's priorities.

Depending on the project, an initial list of possible sources can range from zero to several hundred. A first cut longer than three to four hundred means the search is too broad. That first list needs to be narrowed down to those with a closer fit. A condensed list of from twenty to fifty is about right. These should be analyzed using the matrix to identify the short list of "best fit" sponsors.

What if there are no potential sponsors to be found? We'll deal with that problem in a later section. Let's now examine some of the grant making agencies that may show up on our list of possibilities.

Nirvana - Or Finding the Perfect Government Source

Some capital projects are ideally suited to large government sponsors. Most nonprofit organizations qualify for many government funding programs. The APPLICANT part of the matrix must fit the eligibility criteria for the particular program. Some are quite broad while others are narrow. The range could go from any nonprofit organization to, for example, school districts enrolling children of specific socio-economic and educational characteristics. The applicant organization must ascertain that it is included in such criteria.

Most government programs are more specific about the type of PROJECT they will fund. This *Directory* lists many of them. Fortunate is the applicant who finds a government agency with a program designed to fund exactly the kind of project under consideration, and for the whole amount. It's not impossible. Let's consider some of the categories.

Instrumentation - Several programs from the National Science Foundation, National Institutes of Health and US Department of Energy make grants specifically for the purchase of equipment to upgrade laboratories in universities, hospitals and research institutions. There also are programs specifically targeted at improving animal laboratories. Applicants can include equipment as part of budgets for larger research or training projects. All such programs are highly competitive, but they provide an avenue for support of such purchases. Some of these programs are listed in this *Directory*, and many others are described in the *Directory of Computer and High Technology Grants*, also published by Research Grant Guides.

Housing and Urban Development - The US Department of Housing and Urban Development (HUD) is a major source of funding for construction projects. Some of their programs are listed in this *Directory*. HUD funds primarily through block grant programs. Large "blocks" of federal funds are allocated to the states by means of formulae. States and local units of government then distribute the funds within their jurisdictions.

Block grants often require that applicants do some detective work to locate which state or local agency has federal money to spend. Then it's a matter of accessing the local political process to get on the list of organizations or agencies who will receive funding. One example is that of a private university that received a $100,000 grant toward the cost of constructing a child care center. University officials worked closely with local leaders over several years to plan the project and do their political homework in order to secure the funding. This type of grant almost always comes with "strings attached". In this case, a stipulation of the funding required that the university accept a percentage of low-income children from the surrounding community for placement in day care.

State Pass-Through Programs - Many federal programs are similar to block grants in that they make grants to state agencies who then use these funds to support projects within the state. The federal money "passes through" the states to grantees on the local level. Transportation and disaster relief programs are two examples.

Organizations frequently seek funds to help transport clients to and from their facilities. The Urban Mass Transportation Administration (UMTA) has a program that supports vehicle acquisition for just this purpose. Applicants must locate the state official in charge of the program to obtain an application. The program is listed in the *Catalog of Federal Domestic Assistance*, but in order to get an application potential grantees must call the state department of transportation. The best resource is the telephone directory or information operator for the individual state capitals.

The federal government reacts quickly in times of such natural disasters as earthquakes, hurricanes and other major weather related problems. Destruction from urban riots also brings these agencies into action. Organizations in areas affected by such occurrences may be eligible for grants to help with relief efforts or to repair damage to their own facilities. The Federal Emergency Management Agency (FEMA) is the organization that handles these matters. When disaster strikes, FEMA personnel travel to the affected area and set up local offices and hot lines to help deal with the problems.

School Programs - The US Department of Education has a program of long standing that assists with school construction in areas where federal activities cause substantial increases in school enrollment. The program, named *Impact Aid-Construction*, traditionally funded districts near military bases. It has a reduced role to play as the result of decreases in military spending and base closings.

Other Miscellaneous Categories - The federal listings in this *Directory* offer many other, smaller sources of funds for such projects as health facilities and housing programs. Some basic research may uncover just the right federal agency. Also not to be overlooked are the state agency counterparts to these federal programs. Many states use their own funds to support similar activities. There is no central information source regarding state funding programs. Applicants need to research their own states to find out about the opportunities for grants.

Foundations and Corporations

Foundations and Corporations represent a small amount of grant making activity when compared to government sources. Foundation giving represents only about 5% of total annual giving in the United States. Of that, very little goes to the direct support of capital grants. Corporations represent an even smaller proportion. Other than the well known programs of the Hayden, Kresge and Olin Foundations, foundation and corporate dollars for capital projects are scarce. As we previously noted, some applicants may not find any sources when they do a search for a construction project, even with a well developed proposal.

In such cases, the funding approach must be broad based rather than focused on individual grant prospects. The same foundations and corporations that participate in capital campaigns, may be much less likely to make direct grants for similar projects that are not part of a larger campaign. Capital campaigns are large, organization-wide multiyear undertakings that require meticulous planning, often with the assistance of professional consulting firms brought in to supplement development and grants office efforts. Good campaigns can help organizations meet their goals and diversify their funding sources.

In capital campaign strategies, foundation, corporate and even some government grants become part of a mix of funds raised primarily from major donors and smaller contributors. Every now and then, a major gift such as the multimillion dollar contribution made by Walter Annenberg to his alma mater the Peddie School because he was grateful for his education, comes as a complete surprise to the organization. Such gifts can motivate other donors, especially in the context of a campaign. We've interviewed several grant seekers and grant makers to illuminate some effective grant seeking strategies. Although we don't use individual or organization names, each of the following success stories is based on actual experience.

Winning Capital Grants - Success Stories

One nonprofit was conducting a $3 million capital campaign to build a new facility. An individual donor from whom they sought a gift offered them a $150,000 challenge grant requiring a one-to-one match. At around the same time they were contacted by an out-of-town foundation, previously unknown to them, interested in making a grant toward the campaign. Hoping to make the match, the nonprofit asked whether the foundation would consider a gift of $150,000. The foundation responded that it was more likely to give in the $50,000 range. The campaign director explained that the organization had been offered a challenge grant and that a gift of $150,000 from the foundation would actually add $300,000 to the fund. Two days later the foundation called them back and agreed to the $150,000 match. This entire transaction took place over the phone with no individual contact. The nonprofit is currently going back to the foundation to ask for an additional gift in order to meet a condition imposed by another foundation as outlined below:

This same organization approached a large national foundation through the normal proposal process using no special connections, but knowing that the foundation had given capital gifts to similar organizations (THE APPLICANT module of our matrix). After submitting the proposal, nonprofit staff called the foundation to speak with a program officer. After some discussion, the program officer expressed willingness to meet. The director, campaign chair, and a board member of the nonprofit flew out to spend half a day with the program officer and make their case.

They learned that in order to qualify for a grant they must have already raised a certain amount of money, be in the last third of their campaign, and have a good plan for reaching the goal. They met those requirements. The foundation had many conditions and additional requirements that it laid out, but offered to make a $350,000 grant to complete the campaign once all the other money had been raised and the conditions met. The foundation also shortened the campaign cut-off by several months, urging the nonprofit to end the campaign before moving into the new quarters (claiming once they had moved in, it would be more difficult to raise the funds). Finally, the foundation insisted that the goal be upgraded in order to include a $300,000 operating endowment to help support the building once it was completed.

Each of the foundation's suggestions proved to be helpful to the nonprofit, enabling it to raise money in ways not previously considered, and improving the quality of their planning. According to the nonprofit director, the foundation wanted to be convinced that the campaign would be successful and that the end product would be viable. They further wanted to see that a gift from their foundation would make a big difference. According to the organization's executive director, whether or not they make the goal and receive the grant, the foundation's intervention has already made that difference.

In another success story, a nonprofit organization applied for a foundation grant to help build a new nursing home and was turned down. The moral of this story is not to take "no" for an answer. A board member played golf with the foundation president and talked with him about the project. The president suggested resubmitting the proposal. The program officer, compelled to make a site visit, did so with reluctance - but was completely won over by the time it ended.

The proposal to build a nursing home did not appeal to the program officer and didn't seem to meet the guidelines. During the site visit, however, she learned about the broadened impact of the project. Not only would it create a beautiful and much needed facility in a devastated inner-city environment, but there was a commitment to hire and use local contractors. There would be expanded long-term job possibilities. It wasn't just the grant to build the nursing home. Here the PROJECT was much less important than the REASON.

We need to offer a word of caution about using personal contacts. It worked out very well in this example, but such personal interventions can just as easily work to the disadvantage of the applicant. The program officer may not have overcome her resentment at being forced to reevaluate the project. Not only might the project have been turned down again, but the resentment may have spilled over to future projects. It's also well to remember that foundation, corporate and government grant making organizations and their staff form a close professional community. They compare notes about grantees and applicants. A negative experience with one sponsor is likely to become known in the larger funding community.

Another foundation we spoke with had exclusively awarded bricks and mortar grants but has recently expanded into program grants. They didn't feel that they were getting enough good capital grant requests. They considered most of them to be nothing more than deferred maintenance: letting things die and then replacing them, rather than maintaining them adequately (bad REASON). They felt that a big part of the problem was groups not establishing reserve funds; now they require them. They think of replacement grants as bailing out poor management. They are much more interested in expansion and in new development (good REASON).

Still another foundation says their grants are always part of a bigger picture. This foundation's average grant is $5,000 to $20,000. Most are for equipment and renovations, vans, office equipment and furniture. They get approximately 800 to 900 appeals a year, in response to which they make 200 grants. There clearly are not enough foundations making these kinds of grants. Since they never have enough money to fund all the good requests that come in, it helps to have a contact. It's also worth applying more than once (until it's finally your turn).

They like making capital grants (focus is on the PROJECT) because they don't get locked into the repetition of operating grants which they believe fosters dependency. Because they tend to be in and out (with one-time grants) they don't get as close to agencies. This makes it all the more important that the funders of the agency's programmatic activities be available and willing to attest to the organization's value in the community. In fact, referrals from program funders are very effective.

They look carefully at who the agency is serving, who is running the agency, and what kind of track record they have - both in service statistics and in relationship to funders (again - focus on the APPLICANT). They prefer not to be approached at the beginning of a project, but rather toward the end when it looks as though there is a good chance that the project is going to happen.

Finally, we offer a few thoughts from a successful development officer. The development staff of a nonprofit organization that is unusually successful at raising money for its capital needs says that the single most important ingredient in securing building and equipment grants (or any kind of grant) is relationship with the funder. When they have capital needs, they call each of their program funders and ask whether they can come in to seek some advice and assistance. They meet with the funder and discuss what they intend to build or purchase with constant direct references to the impact on the program that they operate and the lives of their clients. In their experience, many funders who do not generally fund building and equipment grants will make exceptions if they believe in the work of the organization and have a good and trusting relationship with the development staff. If the funder really can't make such a grant, then they seek advice from the funder regarding who might be able to offer the support they need.

They have discovered that it pays to write foundations a thank-you note after they receive a decline. They thank the staff for taking the time to consider their proposal and express understanding for the pressures the funder must be under to select a few grant possibilities from so many applicants. This usually opens the door to their making a personal call later and getting to know the funder. They try very hard to meet with the funder several times before asking for money and to try to understand his or her interests. In one instance a funder that focused on wildlife made a grant outside its priorities to an organization involved with children with disabilities. The grant was for purchasing computers for the educational program operated by the organization. Education of children with disabilities was a special interest of the foundation program officer - the development staff had picked this up in conversation, and they were able to follow up effectively.

Conclusions

The authors collectively have more than thirty-five years experience in the grants business, both as applicants and grant makers. After all that, we can state only one rule with absolute certainty - "If you don't apply, you won't get a grant." As our success stories attest, every other rule and guideline has exceptions. Deviating from "the book" requires judgment and experience, but it often has good results. These success stories fit well into our matrix approach. In each case, the applicant had a well thought out proposal. In some, a change in emphasis among APPLICANT-PROJECT-REASON made the difference between success and rejection.

The Realist's Guide to Foundation and Corporate Grants
by
Andrew J. Grant, Ph.D.

Seeking grant support is often frustrating. It can seem that rejection is the most frequent reward for hard work on behalf of the most compelling causes. It is the rare grant seeker who cannot recite some long list of proposals that were rejected despite their engaging content and structural perfection.

A great deal has already been written about proposal writing and how to succeed in winning grants. There is no shortage of books, articles and training courses offering advice to applicants on how to persuade funders to support their causes. Yet, despite every effort to follow such advice, most proposals are rejected.

This essay also contains some advice. In addition, however, it endeavors to add a realistic perspective to the literature on grant seeking by discussing the nature of grants and the role played by personal contacts. It is designed to help the applicant approach the task with a broader understanding of how things actually work in the world of grant programs.

What are Grants?

Although this is a very basic question, many applicants do not possess an accurate answer. Grants are not gifts or charity. The relationship between grantor and grantee is an exchange relationship. It is important to understand that the funder gets something back for the support he or she provides. The exchange varies with the type of grant making organization.

The role of many government grants in our federal system is to serve as an incentive to induce state and local jurisdictions to behave in ways consistent with the national policy agenda. Linking the twenty-one year minimum drinking age to federal highway funds is one recent example. Such grants and the restrictions attached to them are intended to stimulate state activity where none had been contemplated.

Foundations also make grants on the basis of a policy agenda. Foundation priorities and interests may be determined by charter or by the action of the board of directors. Their grants are designed to promote interests of importance to the foundation. The return to the foundation is seeing its agenda set into motion through the work of nonprofit organizations. A foundation with an interest in equal access for people with disabilities, for example, advances its own mission when it underwrites the construction of facilities that include special aids to individuals with disabilities.

Unlike foundations, corporations exist to make money, not give it away. Corporate contributions, therefore, are said to be based on the concept of enlightened self-interest. The corporate grant usually is made with the company's business agenda in mind. Much corporate giving is restricted to locations where the company operates. It receives a benefit when its employees and customers identify it with the positive work its funds helped to make possible. Corporate support of local arts groups serves as a good example.

Knowing What to Exchange

Keeping the concept of the exchange relationship prominent is essential to gaining the opportunity to participate in grant programs. The applicant must offer the funder something of value. The value, of course, is determined by the funder's interest. Failure to take this concept into account results in the rejection of many otherwise worthy projects.

Proposal writing starts with research. In order to approach the funder from the perspective of its interests, the applicant must devote much effort to learning everything possible about the foundation or corporation.

The most important categories of information regarding foundations include the following:

1. Priorities and interests
2. Geographic preferences
3. Size of assets
4. Range of and average grant sizes
5. Applicant type preferences
6. Project type preferences
7. Name and telephone number of contact person
8. List of recent grantees
9. List of projects recently funded
10. Composition of board of trustees

Information about corporations also includes the categories listed above. In addition to these, a potential applicant would want to know the following:

1. Corporate foundation or direct giving program
2. Major subsidiaries
3. Operating locations
4. Corporate officers
5. Major products or services

Unfortunately, this information representing such a large investment of time and effort is only the starting point. Nor is there any assurance that the information is accurate, up-to-date or consistent with the foundation or corporation's actual behavior.

The activities of government grant programs are determined by legislation and regulations. While many people resent the bureaucratic structure and excessive paperwork associated with federal grants, it is true in most cases that government programs can be held accountable for adherence to articulated priorities.

No such accountability mechanism exists for foundation and corporate grant programs. Although held fiscally accountable for their actions through the Internal Revenue Service, foundations and corporations are free to change or deviate from their published priorities. Sometimes the public is not informed of changes.

The potential applicant, therefore, must go far beyond the information found in the directories. Direct contact is extremely important. Many foundations publish guidelines, annual reports and application forms. The Foundation Center has available the tax returns of the foundations, including corporate foundations (but not direct corporate giving programs). The applicant should obtain as much information as is available. This should be supplemented with a phone call or personal visit, where possible.

All this information helps in identifying those funding sources whose interests most closely coincide with the applicant's. Only by concentrating on funders who share mutual concerns will there be the possibility of a grant. There is, however, one notable exception to this rule; it will be discussed in a subsequent section. Once the research is complete, resulting in a short list of very appropriate foundations and corporations, the proposal writing process can begin.

The Proposal...Or How to Offer to Make an Exchange

The most common error in proposal writing is failing to identify the request with the funder's interest. Many applicants become so involved with their causes or projects, they assume that everyone else will recognize the merit of the proposal. Proposal writing involves the art of persuasion. Winning proposals present well conceived projects in clear, simple English. They link their cause with the funder's agenda. They make no assumptions.

A proposal assuming the reader will identify with the project simply because of the severity of the need will surely be rejected. Rather, the proposal must demonstrate why it is in the funder's interest to support it.

There is much too much competition for funding to assume that projects will sell themselves. The linkages between applicant and funder interests have to be established in the proposal's first paragraphs.

Once this context of common interest, or potential for exchange, has been established, many other items of information must be addressed. Since most corporate and foundation proposals are contained in letters of two to three pages, clarity of thought and brevity of language are essential. The following questions will serve as a guide to the information that should be contained in a proposal letter.

1. Who is the applicant?
2. Why is the applicant the most able to conduct the project?
3. What is the project?
4. How much will it cost?
5. Who are the beneficiaries?
6. What lasting benefits will be realized through the project?
7. Who will do the work?
8. Where will it take place?
9. Why is it important to conduct this project?
10. Who else, if anybody, is supporting it?

That's a large amount of information to get into two or three pages, but it can be done. Applicants should consult any of a number of available proposal writing manuals. It's also not a bad idea to keep a general style manual and guide to writing close at hand. My favorite is the fifth edition of William K. Zinsser's, *On Writing Well*.

The Value of Contacts

The competition for grants is intense. Government funding of domestic social programs is diminishing. Foundations and corporations have become the focus of many fund-raising organizations. The needs of nonprofit organizations greatly exceed the capacity of the philanthropic community. Applicants have become much more sophisticated in seeking funds. Instructional materials and seminars have sharply reduced the number of inadequate proposals. Funders are finding it increasingly more difficult to differentiate among equally good proposals presenting worthy projects.

To complicate the scenario, the community of organizations representing similar populations compete with each other. Rather than presenting a unified approach, groups with common interests appear balkanized in their fund-raising strategies. Funders face the problem of choosing one over another.

Why is it that some of these groups achieve funding success and others of equal merit, can't seem to get a hearing? The answer, assuming all other factors to be equal, lies in the contact base of the successful organizations. The difference between successful and unsuccessful applicants often resides in the board room rather than with the fund-raising or proposal writing staff.

If a foundation or corporation is considering two proposals of equal interest, it will fund the one that has a contact. The use of personal contacts helps the funder to make difficult choices. An organization that is known is less of a risk than one that makes a "cold" approach.

These are high-level contacts among board members, not contacts made between applicant and funder staff members. Board members of grant making organizations usually are people of social position. They may be from prominent families or be executives and/or trustees of large corporations. Generally, they will support organizations known to them or to people whom they know and respect.

Nonprofit organizations often overlook development of their own boards as a fund-raising strategy. If one of the applicant's board members is on or knows someone on the board of a grant making organization, his or her support of the proposal will play a significant role in obtaining funding. This can be true even where the proposal falls outside the funder's articulated areas of interest, and represents the exception noted above.

It is exceptionally important, therefore, to survey the board of trustees to see if they have relationships with people associated with grant making organizations. Developing the nonprofit organization's board to include such individuals is a vital, albeit difficult, task. Without such contacts, even the best proposals are disadvantaged. Although the system of personal contacts may violate the concepts of equity and objectivity, it is unrealistic to disregard or dismiss it. While not all contacts produce results and not all funders can be influenced this way, the organizations with strong contacts generally will win more grants than the organization making a cold approach.

Even with a strong contact, however, it is important to submit a compelling proposal that describes a good project. The last thing an applicant should do is to embarrass a board member by submitting a poor proposal. In fact, project planning and proposal writing are more important when a prominent contact is involved.

Organizations without strong contacts might consider becoming members of consortia. A more unified approach will help reduce fragmentation among organizations representing similar populations. It also increases the possibility that a contact exists among the members of the group.

Some Random Thoughts In Closing

This essay deviates from the traditional advice found in books about funding. It is less optimistic than the frequent pep talks presented at the beginning of funding directories. It seeks to present a realistic perspective and set expectations at a generally low level. It may be more helpful in the long run by focusing attention on the important area of contacts. Grant making and seeking is serious business. Responsible grant seekers are those who understand the factors influencing how funds are distributed. They use that understanding to win grants that can be applied to the solution of problems. These people help formulate and implement the nation's social agenda.

My aim is not to be discouraging, but realistic. Most proposals are rejected, even good ones. This does not mean that organizations should not seek grants. They should, however, focus their efforts on the most productive means of approaching funders. This may mean expanding their boards and/or cooperating with other organizations. Working with grant funds to reach common goals is an exciting and rewarding enterprise. Approaching it with a measure of realism will make the rejections less frustrating.

Ten Tips For More Competitive Grant Proposals
by
Luke A. Cermola

We all want to win. Everyone who writes a grant proposal wants it to be funded. Here are ten simple, easy to use tips that can give you a competitive edge and dramatically increase your chances of success. The key is using a marketing driven strategy throughout the grant seeking process.

For our purposes as grant seekers, marketing means simply looking at the proposal from the frame of reference of the consumer of the proposal — the granting organization — and letting this perspective guide every aspect of your approach.

We know competition for the philanthropic dollar is intense. The number of appeals received by grant making institutions is increasing while resources available to fund proposals are not always keeping pace.

Let's assume your agency is needed by the community and that your proposal contains an adequate plan to meet a community need. This puts your proposal on a roughly equal footing with any number of other good proposals a foundation may receive. The problem is to clearly meet the needs of funding institutions and to differentiate your proposal in some way to win funding. Effectively marketing your proposal may well be the answer.

I urge you to follow all the usual guidelines for writing of grant proposals that are recommended by the Grantsmanship Center (see page 216) and in the many good books and articles on the subject. However, be aware of marketing considerations. Weave these elements into your project whenever possible and appropriate for a more competitive grant proposal.

Use the *Directory of Building and Equipment Grants* to narrow your search to favorably predisposed prospective funders. Most foundations have preferences based on field of interest and geographical areas. This information is provided for many foundations listed in the *Directory of Building and Equipment Grants*. Supplement the information in the guide by calling foundations and requesting a copy of their annual report, application forms and policy guidelines if they publish them. This is an easy, simple and remarkably effective way to prospect for grants.

Once you've identified your target foundations, here are a number of marketing tips that will help your proposal win funding. They apply to a variety of situations — including capital and equipment grants where using a marketing driven strategy is especially important.

Some of these ideas are not widely mentioned in other publications on writing grant proposals. Others are rather basic but can be decisive. They are all based on the principal of marketing to the ultimate consumer of your product.

Place these ideas in your fund-raising tool box and pull them out and use them to strengthen your grant proposals. They will work for you.

Tip 1 - Maintain A "Consumer" Orientation

It is so very easy in our hectic, work-a-day world of providing vital services, to lose sight of the simple fact... that we and our agency do not have needs... but rather the community has needs. The community service organizations we represent are in reality community problem solvers.

In the eyes of foundations, we are the mechanism through which community leaders and philanthropists address community priorities. Of course, we tend to see our financial requirements as overshadowing all other considerations. But foundations have needs too. Because they are the donors in the grant making process we must always focus on how we can help foundations meet their own needs.

Foundations need to find the best available agencies to provide services and implement social change according to their unique policies and mission. This must be our perspective as well if we wish to establish the best possible working relationship with funding institutions. If grant funding organizations see us in the role of community problem solvers then this is the way we must see ourselves in order to establish a common frame of reference.

A consumer orientation is the very essence of the marketing concept. It has revolution-ized the way business is done worldwide. As fund development professionals, we can use this powerful approach too.

Tip 2 - Plan Your Capital Request For Success

You may have heard the old saying among fund-raising professionals that "no one wants to give money to bail out the Titanic". Well it's true... and no one wants to build the Titanic either.

A critical area of concern for funders of brick and mortar projects is "will the agency be able to pay to run an expanded facility if they succeed in building it?" If additional funds will be needed to operate a larger building, where will the funds come from?

Earn the confidence of funders on this issue in three key ways:

1. Show that your project is in line with what has been done in other comparable communities recently. Survey similar agencies in your state or around the nation and collect data to support your planned expansion or refurbishing as prudent.

2. Prepare a five-year projected budget showing how much the new facility will cost to operate. Be as accurate as you can. Take inflation, population growth, demand for services and economic factors into account with clearly stated assumptions in the introduction to your budget projections. Have accountants and bankers look over it and provide input. When it is drafted, get their endorsement of the budget projections to bolster credibility.

3. If new sources of revenue will be necessary to keep the doors of your new building open, demonstrate specifically where the funds will come from. Do you now have a positive trend of increasing revenues which can be projected to continue? What new activities will you undertake to provide new revenues? Inspire confidence in your agency and your proposal by answering these questions in your proposal.

Tip 3 - Position Your Organization Relative To The Competition

Show the funder your agency or service is unique in some way. Is your agency the first of its kind in the community, state, region or country? If so, this helps position you as unique and worthy of high-level consideration.

Was your institution the first to develop new methods of addressing specific problems? We always remember the first person in space, the first to invent the electric light or telephone. No matter what, if you're first in some way, you'll always be first. There can never be another first that would take your place someday.

Being first is a tremendously powerful way to differentiate your agency from the others that may be similar in the minds of the funders. Large corporations do this all the time as they clamor for our attention as consumers. Positioning can strengthen your proposal's appeal to the decision makers. From the funders point of view, they're looking for reasons to single out a proposal from the others. Help them pick your proposal by positioning yourself at the top, apart from the others.

Tip 4 - Be Clear In Communication

Clarity of communication is absolutely essential to marketing your proposal. Bored or confused readers tend to reject proposals that may be otherwise acceptable. Keep jargon to an absolute minimum. If you must use technical terms unique to your field of work, by all means define your terms early in the proposal. Put yourself in the place of the person reading your proposal who may know nothing about the details of how services are provided by your agency. Often there is a whole vocabulary of words available which translate your technical jargon into readily understandable language for general consumption. Stick to everyday words whenever possible. You'll be glad you did.

To check for clarity you can use a test I call the "10 year old kid test." Give a few pages of your proposal to a school child and ask him or her to read it and tell you what it said. If the kid is able to tell you the general idea of the material, then you have succeeded in communicating. If not, go back and rewrite with the 10 year old kid in mind. Most newspapers are written on the sixth grade reading level. Don't fall into a trap of writing to impress yourself or your colleagues when it is non-technical people you truly need to reach with your message.

Tip 5 - Package Your Proposal For Maximum Appeal

There is a noticeable trend among smaller foundations and institutions to give more — but smaller — grants than ever before. Packaging your proposal to attract matching grants is an excellent way to overcome this trend and increase the appeal of your proposal. To some extent this trend may be due to a desire of foundation trustees to avoid making a major error in funding an agency that can't really administer the grant. Another possibility may be a desire to "spread the wealth" around to more agencies in an effort to help the largest number of agencies possible and to minimize the number of rejections they must make. Market to the decision makers by alleviating their fear of making a poor decision and helping them enjoy funding the maximum number of proposals possible.

This is especially true for agencies with little or no grant seeking and grant administration experience. Funders like to feel they are not alone in taking a chance on a new, small or inexperienced agency. Show them how their gift, even a small one, will help you attract other funds by packaging several funding sources together in one proposal.

Tip 6 - "People" Your Proposal

Personalization can mean more than simply typing an individual cover letter for your proposal. In the news media, reporters and editors often talk of a need to "people" a story. By this they mean showing a specific personal account of how a news event has affected a real person's life.

You can use this same technique to enhance your grant proposals. Along with all your facts and figures, be sure to show how the funders can change lives by funding your proposal. Foundations need to effect social change. Show clearly how they can change lives by investing in your proposal.

Tip 7 - Summarize For Busy Readers

Always assume the trustees or committee members serving as the screening panel for your proposal are highly successful people whose time is in great demand. If your proposal is 10 pages or longer, market to your audience by helping them read and understand your proposal quickly and easily by including an Executive Summary of one or two pages. They will appreciate your consideration for their time and may be more inclined to reward your efforts by approval of your request.

Tip 8 - Track Your Funding Request Through The Foundation Maze

Weekly calls to a foundation office which is considering a grant proposal are not out of line. You may legitimately ask who is reviewing your proposal, what the time schedule is for the review process and whether it is advisable to place a phone call or to personally visit the decision makers. Simple phone calls may result in a wealth of helpful information from foundation professionals or support staff, or volunteer officers. There's no harm in what advertising executives would call "top of mind awareness" for your pending grant proposal.

Tip 9 - Lobbying Can Make The Difference

Like it or not, on occasion factors beyond our skills and abilities as grant seekers can play a significant role in the success of a proposal. One of them is high level lobbying for a proposal. On occasion, contacts between your organization's board of directors and the funder's decision makers can pave the way for a proposal. If your board or campaign volunteers have access to foundation trustees, by all means use this influence to improve your chances of being funded. "Lobbying" does occur and you might as well benefit from it.

One example comes to mind of a capital campaign where the requesting agency's board members were personally acquainted with two of five trustees of a foundation that was being approached for a grant in the six to seven figure range. A written proposal was requested as a matter of form and procedure. However, the decision had already been made based on personal contacts and discussions. A capital grant of seven figures was secured!

Foundation trustees have a comfort zone like anyone else. If your agency is within their comfort zone, so much the better.

Tip 10 - Benefit From Positive Rejection

One might well ask, "what is so positive about rejection?" Believe it or not, rejection of a grant proposal can be just another step through the complicated maze of seeking and ultimately receiving a grant. After failing 995 times to find the correct material to be the filament for the electric light bulb, Thomas Edison once said, that he was "all the closer to knowing what would work because he definitely knew 995 things that didn't work."

Being turned down isn't the end to your grant seeking efforts. In fact it is a new beginning as you identify exactly why your proposal was rejected. Knowing this you can then set about removing the obstacles between you and success.

Ask questions if your proposal is rejected. Call or write the foundation and ask for a specific explanation as to why your proposal was not funded. It's acceptable to ask questions about the rejection as long as you don't appear to debate the rejection or become argumentative.

Many times proposals are turned down simply because there is not enough money to fund all the worthy proposals received. If this is the case, keep trying and focus on any characteristics you have in common with the agencies that did receive funds. Perhaps you can package or position your proposal more like the winners next time.

When lack of available funds is given as the reason for rejection, this actually means they ran out of money before they got far enough down the priority list to fund your proposal. This presents an opportunity to move up the list by using marketing and positioning to your advantage.

By asking for help improving your proposals for the future you may also build a rapport with foundation staff and decision makers. This may position you as an "insider" when your next proposal is reviewed.

If on the other hand, your proposal is rejected because it does not meet a specific criterion or guidelines of the funder, be sure to ask the funder a key question which often gets a surprising response. Explain that you understand they have turned down the proposal as it was presented, but that you would like to know "under what circumstances would they be able to provide financial support for your project." Listen carefully to the answer. It may contain clues as to how to package or position future proposals. Also there may be exceptions to the rules which knocked your proposal out of contention. Rules do have some exceptions, and foundation guidelines may as well.

Most proposals are written from a "defensive" posture by aiming to "avoid being eliminated" from consideration. This is good as far as it goes. But in the face of ever increasing competition, why not carry this a step further? Be positive in your approach by using marketing and positioning to place your proposal at the top of the priority funding list.

Consumer orientation, planning for success and positioning can be done in advance of submitting a proposal. Clarity of communication, packaging, personalizing and summarizing will give you an advantage in the preparation of the proposal itself. Tracking, lobbying and handling rejection in a positive manner by learning and growing will give you a leg up on the competition after the proposal has been submitted.

A famous football coach once said, "success is when preparation meets opportunity." This is also true when searching for grants. Use these time tested tips before, during and after your next proposal is created for better results!

FOUNDATIONS

ALABAMA

1
Blount Foundation, Inc.
4520 Executive Park Drive
Montgomery, AL 36116
(205) 244-4348

Building and equipment grants. Health
organizations; higher education; cultural
organizations

Typical grant range: $2,000 to $75,000

2
**Estes H. and Florence Parker Hargis
Charitable Foundation**
317 20th Street North
Birmingham, AL 35203
(205) 251-2881

Building grants. Higher education; youth
organizations; Sheriff's Boys Ranch
(building funds); Ministry (building
funds); Childhaven (building funds)

Typical grant range: $1,000 to $12,000

3
Hill Crest Foundation, Inc.
310 N. 19th Street
Bessemer, AL 35020
(205) 425-5800

Building and equipment grants. Mental
health; community development; youth
organizations; cultural organizations;
social welfare; hospitals; higher education
(building funds); Alcohol and Drug Abuse
Council (building funds); Methodist
Homes for the Aging (building funds);
Family and Child Services (building
funds); United Community Centers
(building funds); Alabama Symphony
(building funds)

Grants awarded to organizations located
in Alabama.

Typical grant range: $3,000 to $25,000

4
Robert R. Meyer Foundation
c/o AmSouth Bank, N.A. Trust Dept.
P.O. Box 11426
Birmingham, AL 35202
(205) 326-5396

Building and equipment grants. Social
welfare; health organizations; cultural
organizations; mentally disabled

Grants awarded to organizations located
in the Birmingham vicinity.

Typical grant range: $10,000 to $50,000

5
Sonat Foundation, Inc.
1900 Fifth Avenue North
P.O. Box 2563
Birmingham, AL 35202
(205) 325-7460

Building grants. Cultural organizations;
social welfare; colleges and universities;
community development; minorities;
youth organizations; hospitals; health
organizations

Grants awarded to organizations located
in areas of company operations.

Typical grant range: $3,000 to $20,000

6
Susan Mott Webb Charitable Trust
c/o AmSouth Bank, N.A.
P.O. Box 11426
Birmingham, AL 35202
(205) 326-5396

Building and equipment grants. Higher
education; social welfare; disabled;
health organizations; elderly; cultural
organizations; Christian organizations

Most grants awarded to organizations
located in the Birmingham vicinity.

Typical grant range: $2,000 to $25,000

ALASKA

7
Z.J. Loussac Trust
c/o National Bank of Alaska
P.O. Box 100600
Anchorage, AK 99510

Building and equipment grants.
Performing arts; disabled; higher
education; social welfare; St. Mary's
School (renovation); Catholic Charities
(office equipment); Alaska Library
Association (books)

Most grants awarded to organizations
located in the Anchorage vicinity.

Typical grant range: $1,000 to $7,000

8
Rasmuson Foundation
c/o National Bank of Alaska
P.O. Box 100600
Anchorage, AK 99510

Building and equipment grants. Social
welfare; elderly; abused women; youth
organizations; disabled; culture; Food
Bank (equipment); Historical Society
(building funds); renovation grants

Most grants awarded to organizations
located in the Anchorage vicinity.

Typical grant range: $400 to $5,000

ARIZONA

9
Arizona Community Foundation
2122 E. Highland Avenue, Suite 400
Phoenix, AZ 85016
(602) 381-1400

Building and equipment grants. Social
welfare; disabled; health organizations;
cultural organizations; minorities;
community development

Grants awarded to organizations located
in Arizona.

Typical grant range: $500 to $14,000

10
J.W. Kieckhefer Foundation
116 E. Gurley Street
P.O. Box 750
Prescott, AZ 86302
(602) 445-4010

Building and equipment grants. Social
welfare; health organizations; disabled;
youth organizations; culture; Forest
Resource Center (building funds);
Bible Institute (building funds)

Typical grant range: $2,000 to $20,000

11
Margaret T. Morris Foundation
P.O. Box 592
Prescott, AZ 86302
(602) 445-4010

Building and equipment grants. Youth
organizations; museums; disabled;
elderly; higher education; social welfare;
health organizations; animal welfare;
Foundation for Blind Children (building
funds); Planned Parenthood (building
funds); Children's Center (renovation);
Volunteer Fire Department (building
funds); Humane Society (building funds);
renovation grants

Grants awarded to organizations located
in Arizona.

Typical grant range: $1,000 to $21,000

12
Mulcahy Foundation
80 W. Franklin Street
Tucson, AZ 85701
(602) 622-6414

Building and equipment grants. Higher
education; youth organizations; cultural
organizations

Grants awarded to organizations located
in Arizona, with an emphasis in Tucson.

13
Steele Foundation, Inc.
702 E. Osborn Road
Phoenix, AZ 85014
(602) 230-2038

Building grants. Social welfare; health
organizations

Grants awarded to organizations located
in Phoenix.

Typical grant range: $5,000 to $100,000

14
Tucson Community Foundation
6601 E. Grant Road, Suite 111
Tucson, AZ 85715
(602) 772-1707

Building and equipment grants. Cultural
organizations; health organizations;
community development; social welfare;
disabled; youth organizations

Most grants awarded to organizations
located in the Tucson vicinity.

15
Del E. Webb Foundation
2023 W. Wickenburg Way
P.O. Box 20519
Wickenburg, AZ 85358
(602) 684-7223

Building and equipment grants. Hospitals;
health organizations; disabled; higher
education (building funds for a scientific
lab); Navajo Nation (equipment); Arizona
Historical Society (building funds for a
museum)

Typical grant range: $5,000 to $75,000

ARKANSAS

16
**De Queen General Hospital
Foundation, Inc.**
P.O. Box 674
De Queen, AR 71832

Equipment grants. County (ambulance)

Grants awarded to organizations located
in Sevier County.

17
Murphy Foundation
200 N. Jefferson Ave., Suite 400
El Dorado, AR 71730

Building grants. Salvation Army (building
funds)

18
**William C. and Theodosia Murphy
Nolan Foundation**
200 N. Jefferson, Suite 308
El Dorado, AR 71730
(501) 863-7118

Building and equipment grants. Social
welfare; historical societies; Salvation
Army (building funds)

Grants awarded to organizations located
in Arkansas.

Typical grant range: $500 to $8,000

19
Ross Foundation
1039 Henderson Street
Arkadelphia, AR 71923
(501) 246-9881

Building and equipment grants. Social
welfare; disabled; health organizations;
community development; public schools
(playground improvement); American
Red Cross (office equipment); Fire
Department (equipment)

Grants awarded to organizations located
in the Arkadelphia vicinity.

Typical grant range: $2,500 to $10,000

20
Harold S. Seabrook Charitable Trust
c/o Worthen Trust Co.
P.O. Box 6208
Pine Bluff, AR 71611

Building and equipment grants.
Beautification Committee (equipment);
Women's Shelter (building funds)

Grants awarded to organizations located
in Arkansas.

CALIFORNIA

21
Ahmanson Foundation
9215 Wilshire Blvd.
Beverly Hills, CA 90210
(310) 278-0770

Building and equipment grants. Youth organizations; health organizations; hospitals; social welfare; homeless; disabled; cultural organizations; all levels of education; renovation grants

Grants awarded to organizations located in the Los Angeles vicinity.

Typical grant range: $8,000 to $45,000

22
American Honda Foundation
P.O. Box 2205
Torrance, CA 90509
(310) 781-4090

Building grants. Higher education; scientific education; San Diego Space and Science Foundation (building funds)

Typical grant range: $15,000 to $75,000

23
ARCO Foundation
515 S. Flower Street
Los Angeles, CA 90071
(213) 486-3342

Building and equipment grants. Higher education; disabled; social welfare; minorities; Girl Scouts of America (renovation)

Grants awarded to organizations located in areas of company operations.

24
Atkinson Foundation
1100 Grundy Lane, Suite 140
San Bruno, CA 94066
(415) 876-1359

Building and equipment grants. Social welfare; disabled; youth organizations; elderly; museums; performing arts; higher education; Wildlife Center (building funds); Habitat for Humanity (building funds); Church (building funds); renovation grants

Grants awarded to San Mateo County organizations.

Typical grant range: $2,000 to $12,000

25
Myrtle L. Atkinson Foundation
101 Alma Street, Suite 1207
Palo Alto, CA 94301

Building and equipment grants. Christian organizations; social welfare; hospice; Coyote Point Museum (building funds for a wildlife center); San Mateo Performing Arts Center (building funds); Mental Health Association of San Mateo (furniture and equipment)

Most grants awarded to organizations located in California.

26
R.C. Baker Foundation
P.O. Box 6150
Orange, CA 92613
(714) 750-8987

Building and equipment grants. Hospitals; health organizations; social welfare; youth organizations; higher education; cultural organizations; animal welfare; disabled

Typical grant range: $500 to $30,000

27
BankAmerica Foundation
Bank of America Center, Dept. 3246
P.O. Box 37000
San Francisco, CA 94137
(415) 953-3175

Building grants. Health organizations;
disabled; community development;
cultural organizations

Grants awarded to organizations located in
areas of company operations.

Typical grant range: $1,000 to $15,000

28
William C. Bannerman Foundation
4720 Lincoln Blvd., Suite 250
Marina del Rey, CA 90292

Building grants. Environment; social
welfare; disabled

Grants awarded to organizations located in
the Los Angeles vicinity.

Typical grant range: $2,000 to $15,000

29
Donald R. Barker Foundation
11661 San Vicente Blvd., Suite 300
Los Angeles, CA 90049

Building and equipment grants. Secondary
education; elderly; recreation; disabled;
health organizations; Animal Samaritans,
S.P.C.A. (building funds); Art Center
(building funds); Eugene Mission, Inc.
(building funds); Mental Health for
Children (building funds); renovation
grants

Typical grant range: $2,000 to $11,000

30
Arnold and Mabel Beckman Foundation
100 Academy Drive
Irvine, CA 92715
(714) 721-2222

Building and equipment grants. Scientific
organizations; higher education; Friends of
Library (building funds)

Typical grant range: $100,000 to
$1,000,000

31
Bothin Foundation
873 Sutter Street, Suite B
San Francisco, CA 94109
(415) 771-4300

Building and equipment grants. Elderly;
performing arts; disabled; California
Programs for the Autistic (van); Wildlife
Center (building funds); Food Bank (van);
National Audubon Society (renovation of
historic building); Boys and Girls Club
(equipment); renovation grants

Typical grant range: $1,000 to $20,000

32
Clorox Company Foundation
1221 Broadway
Oakland, CA 94612
(510) 271-7747

Building grants. Social welfare; youth
organizations; disabled; elderly; health
organizations; hospitals; cultural
organizations; Lincoln Child Center
Foundation (building funds); East Bay
Zoological Society (renovation)

Grants awarded to organizations located
in areas of company operations, with an
emphasis in the Oakland vicinity.

Typical grant range: $2,000 to $8,000

33
**Community Foundation for
Monterey County**
P.O. Box 1384
Monterey, CA 93942
(408) 375-9712

Building and equipment grants. Health
organizations; disabled; social welfare;
youth organizations; recreation; cultural
organizations; Food Bank (equipment);
renovation grants

Grants awarded to organizations located
in Monterey County.

34

James S. Copley Foundation
7776 Ivanhoe Avenue
P.O. Box 1530
La Jolla, CA 92038
(619) 454-0411

Building and equipment grants. Cultural
organizations; social welfare; health
organizations; hospitals; child welfare;
disabled; all levels of education

Typical grant range: $1,000 to $8,000

35

S.H. Cowell Foundation
260 California, Suite 501
San Francisco, CA 94111
(415) 397-0285

Building and equipment grants. Elderly;
child welfare; abused women; cultural
organizations; youth organizations;
homeless; Food Bank (renovation,
equipment); Alcohol and Drug Abuse
Council (renovation, equipment);
Association for Retarded Citizens
(renovation); Catholic Charities
(renovation); Community Housing
(building funds); Fine Arts Museum
(renovation); Planned Parenthood
(renovation, building funds); St. Elizabeth
Youth Employment (equipment); Day
Nursery (renovation, building funds);
YWCA/YMCA (building funds,
renovation)

Typical grant range: $15,000 to $70,000

36

Dean Witter Foundation
57 Post St., Suite 510
San Francisco, CA 94104
(415) 981-2966

Building grants. Environment (building
funds)

Grants awarded to organizations located
in Northern California.

Typical grant range: $1,000 to $65,000

37

Joseph Drown Foundation
1999 Ave. of the Stars, Suite 1930
Los Angeles, CA 90067
(213) 277-4488

Equipment grants. Hospital (equipment);
University Theatre and Radio Station
(video equipment)

Grants awarded to organizations located
in California.

Typical grant range: $10,000 to $75,000

38

East Bay Community Foundation
501 Wickson Avenue
Oakland, CA 94610
(510) 836-3223

Equipment grants. Fire Department
(equipment)

Grants awarded to organizations located
in Alameda and Contra Costa Counties.

Few equipment grants awarded.

Typical grant range: $500 to $10,000

39

Exchange Bank Foundation
c/o Exchange Bank
545 Fourth Street, P.O. Box 403
Santa Rosa, CA 95402
(707) 545-6220

Building and equipment grants. Hospitals;
youth organizations; elderly; community
development

Grants awarded to organizations located
in Sonoma County.

40
Freeman E. Fairfield Foundation
3610 Long Beach Blvd.
P.O. Box 7798
Long Beach, CA 90807
(213) 427-7219

Building and equipment grants.
Disabled; hospitals; social welfare;
youth organizations; Goodwill Industries
(renovation); Long Beach Community
Band (renovation); Day Nursery
(renovation); Boys and Girls Club
(renovation); YMCA (renovation,
equipment)

Grants awarded to organizations located
in the Long Beach vicinity.

Typical grant range: $4,000 to $25,000

41
Fireman's Fund Foundation
777 San Marin Drive
P.O. Box 777
Novato, CA 94998
(415) 899-2757

Equipment grants. Disabled; elderly;
social welfare; community development;
cultural organizations

Typical grant range: $1,000 to $5,000

42
**First Interstate Bank of California
Foundation**
633 W. Fifth Street
707 Wilshire Blvd., 15th Floor
Los Angeles, CA 90017
(213) 614-3068

Building and equipment grants. Social
welfare; hospitals; hospice; homeless;
child welfare; community development;
American Red Cross (building funds);
Armory Center for the Arts (renovation);
Boys and Girls Club (building funds for
a recreation center)

Grants awarded to organizations located
in areas of company operations
(California).

Typical grant range: $2,000 to $30,000

43
Fluor Foundation
3333 Michelson Drive
Irvine, CA 92730
(714) 975-6797

Building grants. Health organizations;
community development; disabled;
cultural organizations; social welfare;
colleges and universities; Public Library
(building funds); Providence Speech and
Hearing Center (equipment)

Grants awarded to organizations located
in areas of company operations.

44
Carl Gellert Foundation
2222 Nineteenth Avenue
San Francisco, CA 94116
(415) 566-4420

Building and equipment grants. All levels
of education; elderly; social welfare;
hospitals; City of Daly (renovation);
Holy Angels School (building funds
for kindergarten); Church (renovation);
Jesuit Retreat House (renovation);
Center for the Blind and Handicapped
(equipment); Medical Center (renovation);
Historical Association (equipment)

Grants awarded to organizations located
in the San Francisco vicinity.

Typical grant range: $1,500 to $9,000

45
Fred Gellert Foundation
One Embarcadero Center, Suite 2480
San Francisco, CA 94111
(415) 433-6174

Building and equipment grants.
Social welfare; youth organizations;
elderly; cultural organizations; disabled;
High School (building funds for a science
center and auditorium); YMCA (building
funds)

Typical grant range: $2,000 to $8,000

46
Evelyn and Walter Haas, Jr. Fund
One Lombard Street, Suite 305
San Francisco, CA 94111
(415) 398-3744

Building and equipment grants. Elderly;
health organizations; social welfare;
cultural organizations

Typical grant range: $3,000 to $30,000

47
Walter and Elise Haas Fund
One Lombard Street, Suite 305
San Francisco, CA 94111
(415) 398-4474

Building grants. Social welfare; youth
organizations; health organizations;
Museum of Modern Art (renovation);
Teen Kickoff (van); Temple (renovation
funds); Marin Academy (building funds)

Grants awarded to organizations located
in the San Francisco vicinity.

Typical grant range: $2,000 to $60,000

48
Luke B. Hancock Foundation
360 Bryant Street
Palo Alto, CA 94301
(415) 321-5536

Equipment grants. High School (van)

Grants awarded to organizations located
in the San Francisco vicinity.

Typical grant range: $2,000 to $25,000

49
Harden Foundation
P.O. Box 779
Salinas, CA 93902
(408) 442-3005

Building and equipment grants. Animal
welfare (building and renovation funds);
Affordable Housing (renovation);
American Cancer Society (tables, chairs);
Youth Center (renovation); Planned
Parenthood (renovation); Project Teen
Center (equipment, renovation grant)

Grants awarded to organizations located
in the Salinas vicinity.

Typical grant range: $8,000 to $40,000

50
Hedco Foundation
c/o Fitzgerald, Abbott & Beardsley
1221 Broadway, 21st Floor
Oakland, CA 94612

Building and equipment grants. Social
welfare; health organizations; cultural
organizations; youth organizations;
renovation grants

Grants awarded to organizations located
in California.

51
Herbst Foundation, Inc.
Three Embarcadero Center., 21st Fl.
San Francisco, CA 94111
(415) 951-7508

Building grants. California Academy
of Science (building funds); Children's
Home Society (building funds); French-
American Intern School (building funds);
Library Foundation of San Francisco
(building funds); Recreation Center for
the Handicapped (renovation); Salvation
Army (building funds); Senior Services
(building funds)

Grants awarded to organizations located
in the San Francisco vicinity.

Typical grant range: $5,000 to $45,000

52
William Knox Holt Foundation
505 Sansome Street, Suite 1001
San Francisco, CA 94111
(415) 981-3455

Building and equipment grants. Scientific organizations; University Pacific (building funds); Trinity University (building funds for an education center)

53
Margaret W. and Herbert Hoover, Jr. Foundation
200 S. Los Robles Ave., Suite 520
Pasadena, CA 91101
(818) 796-4014

Building and equipment grants. Medical and scientific organizations; Stanford University (building funds)

Typical grant range: $10,000 to $100,000

54
Humboldt Area Foundation
P.O. Box 632
Eureka, CA 95502
(707) 442-2993

Building and equipment grants. Health organizations; hospitals; disabled; youth organizations; recreation; elementary and secondary education; Humboldt Arts Council (office equipment); After School Program (educational equipment); University Pacific (building funds); Trinity University (building funds for an education center)

Typical grant range: $1,000 to $11,000

55
James Irvine Foundation
One Market Plaza
Spear Tower, Suite 1715
San Francisco, CA 94105
(415) 777-2244

Building and equipment grants. Monterey Peninsula Museum of Art Association (renovation); San Francisco Art Institute (renovation); South Coast Repertory (building funds for a production center); Boys Club of Venice (building funds)

Grants awarded to organizations located in California.

Typical grant range: $20,000 to $100,000

56
William G. Irwin Charity Foundation
711 Russ Building
235 Montgomery Street
San Francisco, CA 94104
(415) 362-6954

Building and equipment grants. Hospital (building funds); St. Vincent de Paul Society (renovation); Girls and Boys Club (van); Peninsula Volunteers (renovate senior center kitchen); Catholic Charities (renovation); Legal Foundation (purchase a building); Salvation Army (equipment); University (building and equipment funds for the Art Center)

Typical grant range: $15,000 to $90,000

57
George Frederick Jewett Foundation
The Russ Building
235 Montgomery Street
San Francisco, CA 94104
(415) 421-1351

Building and equipment grants. Health organizations; hospitals; disabled; cultural organizations; higher education

Typical grant range: $1,000 to $20,000

58
Fletcher Jones Foundation
One Wilshire Building, Suite 1210
624 S. Grand Avenue
Los Angeles, CA 90017
(213) 689-9292

Building and equipment grants. Higher education; health organizations; hospitals; disabled; Food Bank (equipment); renovation grants

Grants awarded to organizations located in California.

Typical grant range: $12,000 to $165,000

59
W.M. Keck Foundation
555 S. Flower Street, Suite 3230
Los Angeles, CA 90071
(213) 680-3833

Building and equipment grants. Higher education; health organizations; disabled; cultural organizations; social welfare; youth organizations; Science Laboratory (renovation, equipment); Food Bank (equipment); University of California (building funds); California Institute of Technology (building funds); renovation grants

Typical grant range: $150,000 to $700,000

60
Karl Kirchgessner Foundation
c/o Greenberg, Glusker, Fields, Claman & Machtinger
1900 Ave. of the Stars, Suite 2100
Los Angeles, CA 90067
(213) 553-3610

Building and equipment grants. Medical institutions; elderly; disabled

Grants awarded to organizations located in the Southern California vicinity.

Typical grant range: $5,000 to $40,000

61
Koret Foundation
33 New Montgomery Street, Suite 1090
San Francisco, CA 94105
(415) 882-7740

Building and equipment grants. Cultural organizations; health organizations; women; elderly; youth organizations; social welfare; Library (building funds); Jewish Home for the Aged (building funds); Mt. Zion Institute on Aging (equipment); Hebrew Union College (building funds); renovation grants

Typical grant range: $1,000 to $50,000

62
Thomas and Dorothy Leavey Foundation
4680 Wilshire Blvd.
Los Angeles, CA 90010
(213) 930-4252

Equipment grants. Hospitals; health organizations

Grants awarded to organizations located in the Los Angeles vicinity.

Typical grant range: $5,000 to $125,000

63
Miranda Lux Foundation
57 Post Street
San Francisco, CA 94104
(415) 981-2966

Equipment grants. San Francisco Boys and Girls Club (equipment)

Grants awarded to organizations located in San Francisco.

Typical grant range: $1,000 to $20,000

64
General and Mrs. William Lyon Family Foundation
P.O. Box 8858
Newport Beach, CA 92658
(714) 833-3600

Building grants. Social welfare; youth organizations; performing arts; Ronald Reagan Presidential Foundation (building funds); St. Andrews Presbyterian Church (building funds)

Typical grant range: $5,000 to $150,000

65
Bertha Ross Lytel Foundation
P.O. Box 893
Ferndale, CA 95536
(707) 786-4682

Building and equipment grants. Disabled; hospitals; social welfare; recreation; secondary education; Open Door Clinic (dental equipment); Fire Department (equipment); 4-H Trail (building funds); Child Abuse Prevention (office supplies); Bay Youth (equipment); Public Library (equipment); Community Services (kitchen equipment)

Grants awarded to organizations located in Humboldt County.

Typical grant range: $500 to $25,000

66
Marin Community Foundation
17 E. Sir Francis Drake Blvd., Suite 200
Larkspur, CA 94939
(415) 461-3333

Building and equipment grants. Social welfare; environment; youth organizations; community development; elderly; Easter Seal Society (building funds); Boy Scouts (building funds, renovation); Catholic Charities of Marin (building funds); Bird Observatory (renovation)

Grants awarded to organizations located in Marin County.

Typical grant range: $5,000 to $200,000

67
McCone Foundation
P.O. Box 1499
Pebble Beach, CA 93953

Building grants. University of California at Berkeley (renovation grants)

Typical grant range: $50,000 to $500,000

68
McConnell Foundation
P.O. Box 991870
Redding, CA 96099
(916) 222-0696

Building and equipment grants. Environment; community development; social welfare; elderly; disabled; recreation; cultural organizations; health organizations; recreation; Public Library; Catholic Social Service (equipment); Youth Shelter (van); Southeast Asian Christian Ministry (furniture, equipment); renovation grants

Typical grant range: $3,000 to $80,000

69
McKesson Foundation, Inc.
One Post Street
San Francisco, CA 94104
(415) 983-8673

Building and equipment grants. Social welfare; disabled; cultural organizations; recreation; youth organizations; elementary and secondary schools; renovation grants

Grants awarded to organizations located in the San Francisco vicinity.

Typical grant range: $1,000 to $20,000

70
Mericos Foundation
1260 Huntington Drive, Suite 204
South Pasadena, CA 91030
(213) 259-0484

Building and equipment grants. Health
organizations; hospitals; elderly; youth
organizations; cultural organizations;
secondary education; Boys and Girls Club
(building funds); Battered Women's
Network (building funds)

Grants awarded to organizations located
in California, with an emphasis in Santa
Barbara.

Typical grant range: $5,000 to $85,000

71
**Kenneth T. and Eileen L. Norris
Foundation**
11 Golden Shore
Long Beach, CA 90802

Building and equipment grants. Social
welfare; disabled; cultural organizations;
hospitals; health organizations; colleges
and universities

Grants awarded to organizations located
in Los Angeles County.

Typical grant range: $10,000 to $100,000

72
**Robert Stewart Odell and Helen
Pfeiffer Odell Fund**
c/o Wells Fargo Bank
P.O. Box 63002
San Francisco, CA 94163
(415) 396-3226

Building and equipment grants. Elderly;
youth; disabled; Children's Hospital
(equipment); St. Vincent's Day Home
(building funds)

Grants awarded to organizations located
in the San Francisco vicinity.

Typical grant range: $3,000 to $20,000

73
Pacific Telesis Foundation
Pacific Telesis Center
130 Kearny Street, Suite 3309
San Francisco, CA 94108
(415) 394-3769

Building and equipment grants. Disabled;
elderly; cultural organizations; minorities;
women; AIDS; Little League (building
funds, equipment)

Grants awarded to organizations located
in areas of company operations.

Typical grant range: $2,000 to $40,000

74
David and Lucile Packard Foundation
300 Second Street, Suite 200
Los Altos, CA 94022
(415) 948-7658

Building and equipment grants. Social
welfare; disabled; minorities; child
welfare; performing arts; environment;
Planned Parenthood; renovation grants

Typical grant range: $5,000 to $100,000

75
Parker Foundation
1200 Prospect Street, Suite 575
La Jolla, CA 92037
(619) 456-3038

Building and equipment grants. Cultural
organizations; social welfare; disabled;
community development; health
organizations; hospitals; youth
organizations; renovation grants

Grants awarded to organizations located
in San Diego County.

Typical grant range: $2,000 to $15,000

76
Ralph M. Parsons Foundation
1055 Wilshire Blvd., Suite 1701
Los Angeles, CA 90017
(213) 482-3185

Building and equipment grants. Health
organizations; performing arts; social
welfare; homeless; disabled; women;
higher education; youth organizations;
Los Angeles Chamber Ballet (equipment);
renovation grants

Grants awarded to organizations located
in the Los Angeles vicinity.

Typical grant range: $15,000 to $85,000

77
Pasadena Foundation
16 N. Marengo Avenue
Pasadena, CA 91101
(818) 796-2097

Building and equipment grants. Health
organizations; hospitals; community
development; recreation; elderly; culture;
social welfare; child welfare; disabled;
renovation grants

Grants awarded to organizations located
in Pasadena.

Typical grant range: $1,500 to $30,000

78
Peninsula Community Foundation
1700 S. El Camino Real, Suite 300
San Mateo, CA 94402
(415) 358-9369

Equipment grants. Social welfare;
homeless; cultural organizations;
elderly; disabled; youth organizations

Typical grant range: $1,000 to $20,000

79
Ann Peppers Foundation
P.O. Box 50146
Pasadena, CA 91105
(818) 449-0793

Building and equipment grants. Social
welfare; disabled; youth organizations;
higher education; Boys Republic
(basketball court); Children's Training
Society (renovation); Valley Learning
Center (equipment); Dogs for the Deaf
(building funds); renovation grants

Grants awarded to organizations located
in the Los Angeles vicinity.

Typical grant range: $2,000 to $11,000

80
**Gustavus and Louise Pfeiffer
Research Foundation**
P.O. Box 1153
Redlands, CA 92373
(714) 792-6269

Building grants. University Library
(building funds)

Typical grant range: $10,000 to $50,000

81
Sacramento Regional Foundation
1610 Arden Way, Suite 298
Sacramento, CA 95815
(916) 927-2241

Building and equipment grants.
Performing arts; culture; disabled;
social welfare; youth organizations;
Public Library (renovation)

Grants awarded in the following counties:
El Dorado, Placer, Sacramento, and Yolo.

Typical grant range: $500 to $9,000

82
San Diego Community Foundation
Wells Fargo Bank Building
101 W. Broadway, Suite 1120
San Diego, CA 92101
(619) 239-8815

Building and equipment grants. Cultural
organizations; disabled; minorities;
elderly; youth organizations; social
welfare; alcohol and drug abuse; health
organizations; child welfare; community
development; AIDS; renovation grants

Grants awarded to organizations located
in San Diego County.

Typical grant range: $1,000 to $15,000

83
Santa Barbara Foundation
15 E. Carrillo Street
Santa Barbara, CA 93101
(805) 963-1873

Building and equipment grants. Social
welfare; disabled; performing arts;
museums; child welfare; health
organizations; minorities; elderly;
libraries; Santa Barbara Zoological
Gardens (renovation)

Grants awarded to organizations located
in Santa Barbara County.

Typical grant range: $5,000 to $25,000

84
**L.J. Skaggs and Mary C. Skaggs
Foundation**
1221 Broadway, 21st Floor
Oakland, CA 94612
(510) 451-3300

Building and equipment grants.
Environment; cultural organizations;
Historical Association (renovation);
Committee to Preserve Rocky Shores
(purchase land); renovation grants

Typical grant range: $5,000 to $25,000

85
John and Beverly Stauffer Foundation
P.O. Box 2246
Los Angeles, CA 90028

Building and equipment grants.
Hospitals; social welfare; colleges
and universities; youth organizations;
culture; Christian organizations

Typical grant range: $500 to $7,000

86
John Stauffer Charitable Trust
301 N. Lake Avenue
Pasadena, CA 91101
(818) 793-9400

Building and equipment grants.
Children's Hospital (renovation grant);
University of California, Berkeley (law
school renovation); UCLA Law School
(building funds for the law library);
Stanford University (renovation of
scientific labs)

Grants awarded to organizations located
in California.

Typical grant range: $30,000 to $120,000

87
Harry and Grace Steele Foundation
441 Old Newport Blvd., Suite 301
Newport Beach, CA 92663
(714) 631-9158

Building and equipment grants. Higher
education; secondary schools; social
welfare; hospitals; cultural organizations;
recreation; youth organizations; Public
Library (building funds); Children's
Foundation (building funds); Union
Rescue Mission (building funds)

Grants awarded to organizations located
in Orange County.

Typical grant range: $10,000 to $125,000

88
Jules and Doris Stein Foundation
P.O. Box 30
Beverly Hills, CA 90213
(310) 276-2101

Building and equipment grants. Cultural organizations; social welfare; disabled; health organizations; Jewish Community Campus (building funds)

Typical grant range: $2,000 to $15,000

89
Sidney Stern Memorial Trust
P.O. Box 893
Pacific Palisades, CA 90272

Building and equipment grants. Social welfare; disabled; cultural organizations; hospitals; health organizations; colleges and universities; child welfare

Grants awarded to organizations located in California.

Typical grant range: $1,000 to $8,000

90
Glen and Dorothy Stillwell Charitable Trust
301 N. Lake Avenue
Pasadena, CA 91101
(818) 793-9400

Building and equipment grants. Social welfare; alcohol and drug rehabilitation; disabled; Florence Crittenton Services (equipment for kitchen)

Typical grant range: $7,000 to $12,000

91
Morris Stulsaft Foundation
100 Bush Street
San Francisco, CA 94104
(415) 986-7117

Building and equipment grants. Youth organizations; social welfare; child welfare; health organizations; renovation grants

Typical grant range: $3,000 to $15,000

92
Times Mirror Foundation
Times Mirror Square
Los Angeles, CA 90053
(213) 237-3945

Building and equipment grants. Cultural organizations; social welfare; higher education; Immaculate Heart High School (furnish a computer room); Food Bank (building funds for a warehouse); San Diego Symphony Orchestra Association (renovation funds)

Grants awarded to organizations located in areas of company operations, with an emphasis in Southern California.

Typical grant range: $7,000 to $75,000

93
Alice Tweed Tuohy Foundation
205 E. Carrillo Street
Santa Barbara, CA 93101
(805) 962-6430

Building and equipment grants. Youth organizations; health organizations; community development; Parent/Child Workshop (building funds); Theatre Foundation (renovation); Community Medical Center (medical and office equipment); Council on Alcoholism and Drugs (office equipment); Public Library (purchase books and rebuild bookmobile); Cancer Foundation (equipment and purchase building); Family Service Agency (equipment); Park Foundation (building funds); Visiting Nurses Association (building funds); Botanical Gardens (tractor and equipment); Legal Aid Society (building funds); Music Academy (van)

Grants awarded to organizations located in the Santa Barbara vicinity.

Typical grant range: $1,000 to $15,000

94
Valley Foundation
333 W. Santa Clara Street
San Jose, CA 95113
(508) 292-1124

Building grants. Health organizations;
hospitals; disabled; Food Bank (building
funds)

Typical grant range: $15,000 to $85,000

95
Wayne and Gladys Valley Foundation
4000 Executive Parkway, Suite 535
San Ramon, CA 94583
(510) 275-9330

Building grants. All levels of education;
health organizations; hospitals; youth
organizations; higher education (building
funds for the science department)

96
**Ventura County Community
Foundation**
1355 Del Norte Road
Camarillo, CA 93010
(805) 988-0196

Building and equipment grants. Youth
organizations; social welfare; cultural
organizations

Grants awarded to organizations located
in Ventura County.

Typical grant range: $500 to $7,000

97
Weingart Foundation
1055 W. Seventh Street, Suite 3050
Los Angeles, CA 90017
(213) 688-7799

Building and equipment grants. Hospitals;
youth organizations; higher education;
Discovery Museum (building funds);
Girls Inc. (building funds); Angel View
Crippled Children's Foundation (building
funds, purchase land); Union Rescue
Mission (building funds); Salvation Army
(building funds); Visually Handicapped
Adults of the Valley (vehicles);
renovation grants

Grants awarded to organizations located
in Southern California.

Typical grant range: $5,000 to $150,000

COLORADO

98
Aspen Foundation
400 East Main Street
Aspen, CO 81611
(303) 925-9300

Building and equipment grants. Cultural
organizations; social welfare; youth
organizations; recreation; renovation
grants

Typical grant range: $2,000 to $65,000

99
Boettcher Foundation
600 17th Street, Suite 2210 South
Denver, CO 80202
(303) 534-1937

Building and equipment grants. Cultural
organizations; historical society; hospitals;
health organizations; homeless; child
welfare; higher education; Regis Jesuit
High School (building funds); Ministry
(building funds); renovation grants

Grants awarded to organizations located
in Colorado.

Typical grant range: $5,000 to $45,000

100
Bonfils-Stanton Foundation
1601 Arapahoe Street, Suite 5
Denver, CO 80202
(303) 825-3774

Building and equipment grants. Hospitals; health organizations; disabled; community development; cultural organizations; Lung Institute (equipment); Rehabilitation Hospital (equipment); renovation grants

Grants awarded to organizations located in Colorado.

Typical grant range: $2,000 to $25,000

101
Collins Foundation
c/o Norwest Bank, Boulder
P.O. Box 299
Boulder, CO 80306
(303) 441-0309

Building and equipment grants. Hospitals; health organizations; performing arts; museums; youth organizations; social welfare; renovation grants

Typical grant range: $500 to $3,500

102
Adolph Coors Foundation
350-C Clayton Street
Denver, CO 80206
(303) 388-1636

Building and equipment grants. Disabled; social welfare; museum; performing arts; youth organizations; health organizations; Salvation Army (renovation); Colorado Springs Fine Arts Center (building funds)

Grants awarded to organizations located in Colorado.

Typical grant range: $5,000 to $45,000

103
Denver Foundation
455 Sherman Street, Suite 220
Denver, CO 80203
(303) 778-7587

Building and equipment grants. Health organizations; social welfare; cultural organizations; renovation grants

Grants awarded to organizations located in the Denver vicinity.

Typical grant range: $2,000 to $20,000

104
El Pomar Foundation
Ten Lake Circle
P.O. Box 158
Colorado Springs, CO 80901
(719) 633-7733

Building and equipment grants. Youth organizations; health organizations; community development; abused women; elderly; cultural organizations; Goodwill Industries (building funds, renovation); Community Affordable Residences Enterprise (construct apartments for low-income families)

Grants awarded to organizations located in Colorado.

Typical grant range: $3,000 to $50,000

105
Gates Foundation
3200 Cherry Creek South Dr., #630
Denver, CO 80209
(303) 722-1881

Building and equipment grants. Museums; performing arts; historical society; social welfare; youth organizations; Public Library; Volunteers of America (building funds); renovation grants

Grants awarded to organizations located in Colorado.

Typical grant range: $5,000 to $30,000

106
Will E. Heginbotham Trust
P.O. Box 245
Holyoke, CO 80734
(303) 854-2497

Building and equipment grants.
Community development; social welfare;
elderly; County Courthouse (renovation);
Melissa Memorial Hospital (ambulance);
School District (renovation); Town of
Haxtun (fire truck)

Typical grant range: $1,000 to $45,000

107
Mabel Y. Hughes Charitable Trust
c/o The First Interstate Bank of Denver
Terminal Annex, Box 5825
Denver, CO 80217
(303) 293-5324

Building and equipment grants. Health
organizations; hospitals; community
development; cultural organizations

Grants awarded to organizations located
in Colorado, with an emphasis in Denver.

Typical grant range: $3,000 to $20,000

108
**Helen K. and Arthur E. Johnson
Foundation**
1700 Broadway, Room 2302
Denver, CO 80290
(303) 861-4127

Building and equipment grants. Social
welfare; elderly; youth organizations;
Colorado College (building funds for the
science department); National Kidney
Foundation (equipment); renovation
grants

Grants awarded to organizations located
in Colorado.

Typical grant range: $12,000 to $100,000

109
Needmor Fund
1730 15th St.
Boulder, CO 80302
(303) 449-5801

Building and equipment grants.
Community development; cultural
organizations; environment; Community
School (playground equipment, truck)

Typical grant range: $2,000 to $20,000

110
Carl A. Norgren Foundation
2696 S. Colorado Blvd., Suite 585
Denver, CO 80222
(303) 758-8393

Building and equipment grants. Health
organizations; community development;
culture; youth organizations

Grants awarded to organizations located
in the Denver vicinity.

Typical grant range: $500 to $3,000

111
**Martin J. and Mary Anne O'Fallon
Trust**
2800 S. University Blvd., #61
Denver, CO 80210
(303) 753-1727

Building and equipment grants. Social
welfare; cultural organizations; recreation;
elderly

Grants awarded to organizations located
in Colorado, with an emphasis in Denver.

Typical grant range: $1,000 to $6,000

112
St. John's Foundation
1419 Pine Street
Boulder, CO 80302

Equipment grants. Elderly; social welfare;
health organizations

Grants awarded to organizations located
in Boulder County.

113
H. Chase Stone Trust
c/o Bank One
P.O. Box 1699
Colorado Springs, CO 80942
(719) 471-5000

Building and equipment grants. Health organizations; youth organizations; cultural organizations; secondary education; American Red Cross (van); Lung Institute (equipment); Boys and Girls Club (renovation); Valley School (renovation); renovation grants

Grants awarded to organizations located in El Paso County.

114
Ruth and Vernon Taylor Foundation
1670 Denver Club Building
Denver, CO 80202
(303) 893-5284

Building grants. Cultural organizations; secondary education; higher education; hospice; hospitals; social welfare; environment

Typical grant range: $3,500 to $65,000

115
US WEST Foundation
7800 E. Orchard Road, Suite 300
Englewood, CO 80111
(303) 793-6648

Building grants. Youth organizations; Social welfare; disabled; cultural organizations; health organizations; community development; renovation grants

Grants awarded to organizations located in areas of company operations.

Typical grant range: $3,000 to $20,000

CONNECTICUT

116
Beatrice Fox Auerbach Foundation
25 Brookside Blvd.
West Hartford, CT 06107
(203) 232-5854

Building and equipment grants. Cultural organizations; health organizations; social welfare; YWCA (building funds); Food Bank (truck)

Grants awarded to organizations located in the Hartford vicinity.

Typical grant range: $2,000 to $60,000

117
Community Foundation of Greater New Haven
70 Audubon Street
New Haven, CT 06510
(203) 777-2386

Building and equipment grants. Social welfare; cultural organizations; health organizations; community development; women; youth organizations

Grants awarded to organizations located in the New Haven vicinity.

Typical grant range: $2,000 to $40,000

118
Community Foundation of Southeastern Connecticut
302 State Street
P.O. Box 769
New London, CT 06320
(203) 442-3572

Building and equipment grants. Disabled; hospital; elderly; YMCA (bicycles); Music School (piano); Youth Service Bureau (renovate restroom for people with disabilities); Public Library (equipment)

Grants awarded to organizations located in Southeastern Connecticut.

Typical grant range: $1,000 to $25,000

119
**Connecticut Mutual Life
Foundation, Inc.**
140 Garden Street
Hartford, CT 06154
(203) 727-6500

Building grants. Social welfare; hospitals;
health organizations; renovation grants

Grants awarded to organizations located
in the Hartford vicinity.

Typical grant range: $1,000 to $20,000

120
Charles E. Culpeper Foundation, Inc.
Financial Centre
695 E. Main Street, Suite 404
Stamford, CT 06901
(203) 975-1240

Building and equipment grants. Cultural
organizations; higher education; health
organizations; disabled

Typical grant range: $3,000 to $55,000

121
**Daphne Seybolt Culpeper Memorial
Foundation, Inc.**
129 Musket Ridge Road
Norwalk, CT 06850
(203) 762-3984

Building and equipment grants.
Health organizations; disabled;
youth organizations

122
Marie G. Dennett Foundation
c/o Whitman & Ransom
Two Greenwich Plaza, P.O. Box 2250
Greenwich, CT 06836
(203) 862-2361

Building grants. Churches

Typical grant range: $1,000 to $7,000

123
Sidney and Arthur Eder Foundation
P.O. Box 949
New Haven, CT 06504
(203) 934-8381

Building grants. Health organizations;
cultural organizations; Jewish related
organizations

Grants awarded to organizations located
in Connecticut.

124
EIS Foundation, Inc.
19 West Walk
Clinton, CT 06413
(203) 669-5367

Building grants. Social welfare; disabled;
YMCA (building funds)

Typical grant range: $500 to $7,000

125
Sherman Fairchild Foundation, Inc.
71 Arch Street
Greenwich, CT 06830
(203) 661-9360

Building and equipment grants. Higher
education (building and equipment funds
for the science department); cultural
organizations; hospitals; social welfare;
Union Theological Seminary (building
funds)

Typical grant range: $50,000 to $500,000

126
**Hartford Courant Foundation,
Incorporated**
285 Broad Street
Hartford, CT 06115

Building and equipment grants. Performing
arts; museums; disabled; women; social
welfare; health organizations; hospitals;
community development; Public Library;
Trinity College (building funds);
renovation grants

Grants awarded to organizations located
in Central Connecticut.

Typical grant range: $3,000 to $12,000

127
Hartford Foundation for Public Giving
85 Gillett Street
Hartford, CT 06105
(203) 548-1888

Building and equipment grants. Social welfare; disabled; hospitals; cultural organizations; Nature Center (equipment); Historical Society (building funds); Community Health Services, Inc. (renovation); renovation grants

Grants awarded to organizations located in the Hartford vicinity.

128
ITT Hartford Insurance Group Foundation, Inc.
Hartford Plaza
Hartford, CT 06115
(203) 547-5000

Building and equipment grants. Health organizations; hospitals; social welfare; community development

Most grants awarded to organizations located in Hartford.

Typical grant range: $1,000 to $15,000

129
Koopman Fund, Inc.
17 Brookside Blvd.
W. Hartford, CT 06107
(203) 232-6406

Building and equipment grants. Social welfare; health organizations

Most grants awarded to organizations located in Connecticut.

130
Olin Corporation Charitable Trust
120 Long Ridge Road
Stamford, CT 06904
(203) 356-3301

Building and equipment grants. Social welfare; health organizations; youth organizations; community development; environment

Grants awarded to organizations located in areas of company operations.

131
Panwy Foundation, Inc.
Greenwich Office Park IX
10 Valley Drive
Greenwich, CT 06831
(203) 661-6616

Building and equipment grants. Hospitals; cultural organizations; Christian related organizations

Small value grants.

132
Alix W. Stanley Charitable Foundation
c/o Shawmut Bank, N.A.
One Exchange Place
Waterbury, CT 06721
(203) 548-3125

Building grants. Community development; cultural organizations; youth organizations

133
Stanley Works Foundation
New Connecticut Bank & Trust Co., N.A.
P.O. Box 567
Hartford, CT 06141
(203) 225-5111

Building and equipment grants. Hospitals; health organizations; social welfare; cultural organizations

Grants awarded to organizations located in areas of company operations.

Typical grant range: $1,000 to $50,000

134
Stone Foundation, Inc.
25 Ford Road, Suite 200
Westport, CT 06880
(203) 227-2000

Building and equipment grants. Medicine;
cultural organizations; Norwalk Maritime
Center (van); New Canaan Country
School (building funds)

Typical grant range: $1,000 to $85,000

135
Swindells Charitable Foundation Trust
c/o Shawmut Bank, N.A.
777 Main Street
Hartford, CT 06115
(203) 728-2274

Equipment grants. Community Health
Center (equipment); Easter Seals
Rehabilitation Center (equipment);
Children's Home (medical supplies)

Grants awarded to organizations located
in Connecticut.

136
Travelers Companies Foundation
One Tower Square
Hartford, CT 06183
(203) 277-2303

Building and equipment grants. Cultural
organizations; community development;
Community Renewal Team (kitchen
equipment for Head-Start Program)

Typical grant range: $15,000 to $120,000

137
R.T. Vanderbilt Trust
30 Winfield Street
Norwalk, CT 06855

Building grants. Hospitals; cultural
organizations

Typical grant range: $250 to $7,000

138
Waterbury Foundation
P.O. Box 252
Waterbury, CT 06720
(203) 753-1315

Building and equipment grants.
Community development; social welfare;
youth organizations; culture; renovation
grants

Grants awarded to organizations located
in the Waterbury vicinity.

Typical grant range: $2,500 to $45,000

DELAWARE

139
Beneficial Foundation
P.O. Box 911
Wilmington, DE 19899
(301) 798-0800

Building and equipment grants. Cultural
organizations; hospitals; higher education;
Medical Center Foundation (building
funds for a pediatric unit)

Typical grant range: $1,000 to $20,000

140
Borkee-Hagley Foundation, Inc.
P.O. Box 230
Wilmington, DE 19899
(302) 652-8616

Building and equipment grants. Elderly;
community development; education;
YMCA (building funds)

Grants awarded to organizations located
in Delaware.

Typical grant range: $1,000 to $5,000

141
Chichester duPont Foundation, Inc.
3120 Kennett Pike
Wilmington, DE 19807
(302) 658-5244

Building and equipment grants.
Community development; youth
organizations; hospitals; health
organizations; Parish (new sidewalk);
Children's Museum (building funds);
YMCA (equipment)

Typical grant range: $10,000 to $44,000

142
Crestlea Foundation, Inc.
1004 Wilmington Trust Center
Wilmington, DE 19801
(302) 654-2489

Building and equipment grants. Health
organizations; hospitals; social welfare;
environment; cultural organizations;
disabled; community development

Grants awarded to organizations located
in Delaware.

143
Crystal Trust
1088 DuPont Building
Wilmington, DE 19898
(302) 774-8421

Building and equipment grants.
Community development; cultural
organizations; disabled; youth
organizations; social welfare; child
welfare; elderly; health organizations;
Youth for Christ (renovation)

Grants awarded to organizations located
in Delaware, with an emphasis in
Wilmington.

Typical grant range: $5,000 to $75,000

144
Delaware Community Foundation
P.O. Box 25207
Wilmington, DE 19899
(302) 571-8004

Building grants. Social welfare;
environment; youth organizations; health
organizations; Public Library; renovation
grants

Grants awarded to organizations located
in Delaware.

Typical grant range: $2,000 to $15,000

145
Laffey-McHugh Foundation
1220 Market Building
P.O. Box 2207
Wilmington, DE 19899
(302) 658-9141

Building and equipment grants. Roman
Catholic organizations; social welfare;
disabled; hospitals; community
development; cultural organizations

Grants awarded to organizations located
in Delaware, with an emphasis in
Wilmington.

Typical grant range: $4,000 to $40,000

146
Longwood Foundation, Inc.
1004 Wilmington Trust Center
Wilmington, DE 19801
(302) 654-2477

Building and equipment grants. Health
organizations; hospitals; environment;
youth organizations; social welfare;
community development; elderly;
recreation; renovation grants

Grants awarded to organizations located
in Delaware, with an emphasis in
Wilmington.

Typical grant range: $20,000 to $325,000

147
Marmot Foundation
1004 Wilmington Trust Center
Wilmington, DE 19801
(302) 654-2477

Building and equipment grants.
Community development; cultural
organizations; social welfare; hospitals;
health organizations; youth organizations

148
**Raskob Foundation for Catholic
Activities, Inc.**
P.O. Box 4019
Wilmington, DE 19807
(302) 655-4440

Building and equipment grants. Roman
Catholic organizations.

Typical grant range: $3,000 to $15,000

149
Welfare Foundation, Inc.
1004 Wilmington Trust Center
Wilmington, DE 19801
(302) 654-2489

Building and equipment grants.
Community development; social welfare;
health organizations; hospitals

Grants awarded to organizations located
in Delaware, with an emphasis in
Wilmington.

DISTRICT OF COLUMBIA

150
**Morris and Gwendolyn Cafritz
Foundation**
1825 K Street, N.W., 14th Floor
Washington, DC 20006
(202) 223-3100

Equipment grants. Disabled; hospitals

Grants awarded to organizations located
in the Washington, DC vicinity.

Typical grant range: $15,000 to $60,000

151
Queene Ferry Coonley Foundation, Inc.
P.O. Box 3722
Washington, DC 20007
(202) 333-3046

Building and equipment grants. Hospital
(renovation); Theatre Company (storm
windows); City Lights (renovate buildings
for schools); Ministries United (materials
and equipment to build a playground);
Planned Parenthood (renovation)

Grants awarded to organizations located
in the Washington, DC vicinity.

Typical grant range: $500 to $6,000

152
**John Edward Fowler Memorial
Foundation**
1725 K Street N.W., Suite 1201
Washington, DC 20006
(202) 728-9080

Building and equipment grants. Disabled;
elderly; social welfare; women; homeless;
child welfare; AIDS; Salvation Army
(building funds); Habitat for Humanity
(building funds); renovation grants

Grants awarded to organizations located
in the Washington, DC vicinity.

Typical grant range: $4,000 to $15,000

153
Philip L. Graham Fund
c/o The Washington Post Co.
1150 Fifteenth Street, N.W.
Washington, DC 20071
(202) 334-6640

Building and equipment grants. Social
welfare; museums; performing arts; youth
organizations; elderly; women; minorities;
disabled; community development;
renovation grants

Grants awarded to organizations located
in the Washington, DC vicinity.

Typical grant range: $10,000 to $40,000

154

Kiplinger Foundation
1729 H Street, N.W.
Washington, DC 20006
(202) 887-6559

Building grants. Cultural organizations;
health organizations; social welfare;
community development

Grants awarded to organizations located
in Washington, DC.

Typical grant range: $1,000 to $3,000

155

**Eugene and Agnes E. Meyer
Foundation**
1400 Sixteenth Street, N.W., Suite 360
Washington, DC 20036
(202) 483-8294

Building grants. Social welfare; homeless;
disabled; youth organizations; renovation
grants

Grants awarded to organizations located
in the Washington, DC vicinity.

Typical grant range: $12,000 to $35,000

156

Public Welfare Foundation, Inc.
2600 Virginia Ave., N.W., Room 505
Washington, DC 20037
(202) 965-1800

Building grants. Child welfare; elderly;
low-income housing; renovation grants

157

Walter G. Ross Foundation
c/o ASB Capital Management Inc.
1101 Pennsylvania Avenue, N.W.
Washington, DC 20004

Building grants. Hospital (building funds,
renovation); Girl Scouts (renovation)

Most grants awarded to organizations
located in the Washington, DC vicinity.

Typical grant range: $10,000 to $65,000

158

**Alexander and Margaret Stewart Trust
u/w of the late Helen S. Devore**
First American Bank, N.A., Trust Dept.
740 Fifteenth Street, N.W.
Washington, DC 20005
(202) 637-7887

Equipment grants. Hospitals; health
organizations; Episcopal Center for
Children (equipment for therapy program)

Grants awarded to organizations located
in the Washington, DC vicinity.

Typical grant range: $15,000 to $100,000

159

Helen Parker Willard Foundation
P.O. Box 4989
Washington, DC 20008
(202) 337-1381

Building grants. Youth organizations;
health organizations; hospitals; disabled

Grants awarded to organizations located
in Washington, DC.

Typical grant range: $2,000 to $9,000

FLORIDA

160

Cordelia Lee Beattie Foundation Trust
P.O. Box 267
Sarasota, FL 34230
(813) 951-7241

Building and equipment grants. Sarasota
Opera Association (equipment); Friends
of the Library (building and equipment
funds); Performing Arts Center (piano and
flooring); Sarasota Community Orchestra
(instruments); Venice Area Middle School
(instruments); renovation grants

Grants awarded to organizations located
in Sarasota County.

161
Broward Community Foundation, Inc.
2601 E. Oakland Park Blvd., Suite 202
Ft. Lauderdale, FL 33306
(305) 563-4483

Building and equipment grants. Child
welfare; elderly; disabled; animal welfare;
cultural organizations; AIDS; Food Bank
(equipment); Museum of Art (equipment);
renovation grants

Grants awarded to organizations located in
Broward County.

Typical grant range: $2,000 to $6,000

162
Edyth Bush Charitable Foundation, Inc.
199 E. Welbourne Avenue
P.O. Box 1967
Winter Park, FL 32790
(407) 647-4322

Building and equipment grants. Disabled;
social welfare; animal welfare; child
welfare; health organizations; women;
cultural organizations; higher education;
youth organizations; renovation grants

Grants awarded to organizations located in
Central Florida.

Typical grant range: $15,000 to $65,000

163
Chatlos Foundation
P.O. Box 915048
Longwood, FL 32791
(407) 862-5077

Building and equipment grants. Emphasis
on Christian organizations; social welfare;
higher education; disabled; homeless;
health organizations; Food for the Poor
(equipment); St. Christopher's Childcare
Services (repair chapel); renovation grants

Typical grant range: $3,000 to $30,000

164
**Community Foundation for Palm Beach
and Martin Counties**
324 Datura Street, Suite 340
West Palm Beach, FL 33401
(407) 659-6800

Building and equipment grants.
Performing arts (equipment); Habitat for
Humanity (building funds); Child Care
Center (equipment)

Grants awarded to organizations located
in Palm Beach, Martin, and Hendry
Counties.

Typical grant range: $1,000 to $12,000

165
**Community Foundation of
Collier County**
4949 Tamiami Trail North, Suite 202
Naples, FL 33940
(813) 649-5000

Building and equipment grants. Health
organizations; social welfare; women;
disabled; youth organizations; Habitat
for Humanity (van); Meals on Wheels
(equipment); Christian Migrant
Association (building funds); Home
for Retired Farm Workers (laundry
equipment); renovation grants

Grants awarded to organizations located
in Collier County.

166
**Community Foundation of Sarasota
County, Inc.**
P.O. Box 49587
Sarasota, FL 34230
(813) 955-3000

Building and equipment grants. Cultural
organizations; social welfare; disabled;
women; youth organizations; Women's
Resource Center (building funds); Rape
Crisis Center (equipment); American Red
Cross (equipment); Southwest Florida
Center for the Handicapped (renovation)

Grants awarded to organizations located
in Sarasota County.

Typical grant range: $500 to $5,000

167
Conn Memorial Foundation, Inc.
220 E. Madison Street, Suite 822
P.O. Box 229
Tampa, FL 33601
(813) 223-3838

Building and equipment grants. Health organizations; hospice; disabled; cultural organizations; youth organizations; Girls Club and Boys Club (building funds); Christian Helplines (renovation); Crisis Center (building funds); Meals on Wheels (equipment, building funds)

Grants awarded to organizations located in the Tampa vicinity.

Typical grant range: $2,000 to $20,000

168
Elizabeth Cope Trust
P.O. Box 215
Ormond Beach, FL 32175

Equipment grants. Libraries; disabled

Grants awarded to organizations located in Florida.

169
Dade Community Foundation
200 S. Biscayne Blvd., Suite 4770
Miami, FL 33131
(305) 371-2711

Building and equipment grants. Social welfare; disabled; elderly; women; community development; cultural organizations; youth organizations; health organizations; hospitals

Grants awarded to organizations located in Dade County.

Typical grant range: $1,000 to $20,000

170
Arthur Vining Davis Foundations
111 Riverside Avenue, Suite 130
Jacksonville, FL 32202
(904) 359-0670

Building and equipment grants. Hospitals; health organizations; public television; College (equipment, building funds for the science department); Mount Angel Seminary (library renovation); School of Theology (equipment, building funds for a library); Nature Conservancy (purchase land)

Typical grant range: $35,000 to $150,000

171
Jessie Ball duPont Fund
225 Water Street, Suite 1200
Jacksonville, FL 32202
(904) 353-0890

Building and equipment grants. Social welfare; health organizations; hospitals; elderly; disabled; AIDS; American Lung Association (equipment); Archdiocese of Miami (building funds); YWCA (building funds); Church (renovation); Oak Grove Assembly of God (bus)

Only previous grant recipients from this foundation are eligible to apply for another grant.

Typical grant range: $5,000 to $85,000

172
Jack Eckerd Corporation Foundation
P.O. Box 4689
Clearwater, FL 34618
(813) 398-8318

Building grants. Hospitals; health organizations

Grants awarded to organizations located in areas of company operations.

173
Charles A. Frueauff Foundation, Inc.
307 E. Seventh Avenue
Tallahassee, FL 32303
(904) 561-3508

Building and equipment grants. Social
welfare; child welfare; disabled; health
organizations; hospitals; higher education;
museum (renovation); Boy Scouts
(renovation); YWCA (renovation)

Typical grant range: $10,000 to $35,000

174
Gore Family Memorial Foundation
4747 N. Ocean Drive, Suite 204
Fort Lauderdale, FL 33302

Building and equipment grants. Paralyzed
Veterans (tires for vehicle); Medical
Depot (equipment); Church (renovation)

Most grants awarded to organizations
located in Broward County.

175
Grace Foundation, Inc.
One Town Center Road
Boca Raton, FL 33486
(407) 362-1487

Building and equipment grants. Social
welfare; higher education; health
organizations; hospitals; community
development; minorities; cultural
organizations; youth organizations

Grants awarded to organizations located
in areas of company operations (W.R.
Grace & Co.).

Typical grant range: $1,000 to $15,000

176
**William M. & Nina B. Hollis
Foundation, Inc.**
P.O. Box 8847
Lakeland, FL 33806
(813) 646-3980

Building and equipment grants. Social
welfare; cultural organizations

Most grants awarded to organizations
located in Lakeland.

Typical grant range: $2,000 to $40,000

177
**John S. and James L. Knight
Foundation**
One Biscayne Tower, Suite 3800
2 S. Biscayne Blvd.
Miami, FL 33131
(305) 539-0009

Building and equipment grants. Child
welfare; social welfare; disabled; elderly;
abused women; health organizations;
hospitals; community development;
Food Bank (truck); American Red Cross
(vehicle); Boy Scouts (building funds);
United Way (building funds); Free
Medical Clinic (building funds); Habitat
for Humanity (building funds, renovation)

Grants awarded to organizations located
in areas of company operations (Knight-
Ridder Newspapers).

Typical grant range: $10,000 to $125,000

178
Koch Foundation
2830 N.W. 41st Street, Suite H
Gainesville, FL 32606
(904) 373-7491

Building and equipment grants. Roman
Catholic related organizations (higher
education; disabled; social welfare;
Churches); renovation grants

Typical grant range: $5,000 to $75,000

179
Mary E. Parker Foundation
1215 Manatee Avenue West
Bradenton, FL 34205
(813) 748-3666

Building grants. Youth organizations

Grants awarded to organizations located in Florida.

Typical grant range: $1,000 to $25,000

180
Dr. P. Phillips Foundation
60 W. Robinson Street
P.O. Box 3753
Orlando, FL 32802
(407) 422-6105

Building and equipment grants. Social welfare; youth organizations; community development

Grants awarded to organizations located in Orange County.

Typical grant range: $1,000 to $30,000

181
Paul E. & Klare N. Reinhold Foundation, Inc.
225 Water Street, Suite 2175
Jacksonville, FL 32202
(904) 354-2359

Building and equipment grants. Health organizations; hospitals; animal welfare; social welfare; cultural organizations

Typical grant range: $1,000 to $20,000

182
M.E. Rinker, Sr., Foundation, Inc.
310 Okeechobee Blvd.
West Palm Beach, FL 33401

Building grants. Higher education (building funds); Boy Scouts (building funds); Church (building funds); Kings Academy (building funds)

Grants awarded to organizations located in Florida.

Typical grant range: $15,000 to $125,000

183
William G. Selby and Marie Selby Foundation
Southeast Bank
P.O. Box 267
Sarasota, FL 34230
(813) 957-0442

Building and equipment grants. Social welfare; disabled; elderly; women; health organizations; all levels of education; Boys and Girls Club (renovation); Child Development Center (equipment); Rape Crisis Center (building funds); YMCA (building funds); School of Art and Design (renovation); Public School Foundation (equipment); renovation grants

Typical grant range: $5,000 to $45,000

184
Hugh and Mary Wilson Foundation, Inc.
7188 Beneva Road South
Sarasota, FL 34238
(813) 921-2856

Building and equipment grants. Social welfare; youth organizations; minorities; women; elderly; recreation; Food Bank (equipment); Child Development Center (furniture); Sheriff's Youth Ranches (truck); Habitat for Humanity (building funds); renovation grants

Grants awarded to organizations located in Florida.

Typical grant range: $1,000 to $20,000

185
Winn-Dixie Stores Foundation
5050 Edgewood Court
Jacksonville, FL 32254
(904) 783-5000

Building and equipment grants. Social welfare; health organizations; youth organizations

Grants awarded to organizations located in areas of company operations.

Typical grant range: $2,000 to $25,000

GEORGIA

186
Atlanta Foundation
c/o Wachovia Bank of Georgia, N.A.
191 Peachtree Street, Suite 1503
Atlanta, GA 30303
(404) 332-6677

Building and equipment grants. Cultural
organizations; community development;
hospitals

187
Callaway Foundation, Inc.
209 Broome Street
P.O. Box 790
LaGrange, GA 30241
(706) 884-7348

Building and equipment grants. All levels
of education; community development;
hospitals; health organizations; disabled;
animal welfare; women; child welfare;
Churches (building funds); Habitat for
Humanity (building funds); American
Red Cross (renovation); Salvation Army
(building funds); Literacy Volunteers
(equipment); Valley Art Association
(building funds); Sheriff's Department
(equipment); LaGrange College
(equipment); renovation grants

Grants awarded to organizations located
in the La Grange vicinity.

Typical grant range: $1,000 to $85,000

188
Fuller E. Callaway Foundation
209 Broome Street
P.O. Box 790
LaGrange, GA 30241
(404) 884-7348

Building and equipment grants. Social
welfare; health organizations; community
development; Churches

Most grants awarded to organizations
located in the La Grange vicinity.

Typical grant range: $500 to $9,500

189
J. Bulow Campbell Foundation
1401 Trust Co. Tower
25 Park Place, N.E.
Atlanta, GA 30303
(404) 658-9066

Building and equipment grants. Social
welfare; health organizations; abused
women; cultural organizations; Churches;
renovation grants

Most grants awarded to organizations
located in Georgia.

Typical grant range: $75,000 to $400,000

190
Equifax Foundation
c/o Equifax Inc.
1600 Peachtree Street, N.W.
Atlanta, GA 30309
(404) 885-8301

Building grants. Social welfare; health
organizations

Grants awarded to organizations located
in Georgia.

191
Lettie Pate Evans Foundation, Inc.
50 Hurt Plaza, Suite 1200
Atlanta, GA 30303
(404) 522-6755

Building and equipment grants. Higher
education; cultural organizations; social
welfare; disabled; youth organizations;
women; Theological Seminary (building
campaign); renovation grants

Grants awarded to organizations located
in the Atlanta vicinity.

Typical grant range: $75,000 to $300,000

192
John and Mary Franklin Foundation
c/o Bank South, N.A.
P.O. Box 4956
Atlanta, GA 30302
(404) 521-7397

Building grants. Hospitals; cultural
organizations; youth organizations

Typical grant range: $4,000 to $65,000

193
**John H. and Wilhelmina D. Harland
Charitable Foundation, Inc.**
Two Piedmont Center, Suite 106
Atlanta, GA 30305
(404) 264-9912

Building and equipment grants. Social
welfare; community development; youth
organizations

Grants awarded to organizations located
in Georgia, with an emphasis in Atlanta.

Typical grant range: $5,000 to $35,000

194
**John P. and Dorothy S. Illges
Foundation, Inc.**
945 Broadway
Columbus, GA 31901

Building grants. Social welfare; health
organizations; youth organizations;
Churches

Typical grant range: $2,000 to $15,000

195
**Ray M. and Mary Elizabeth Lee
Foundation, Inc.**
c/o NationsBank
P.O. Box 4446
Atlanta, GA 30302
(404) 607-4530

Building and equipment grants.
Hospitals; health organizations;
cultural organizations

Most grants awarded to organizations
located in the Atlanta vicinity.

Typical grant range: $2,000 to $25,000

196
**Metropolitan Atlanta Community
Foundation, Inc.**
The Hurt Building, Suite 449
Atlanta, GA 30303
(404) 688-5525

Building and equipment grants. Health
organizations; community development;
cultural organizations; disabled; social
welfare; renovation grants

Grants awarded to organizations located
in the Atlanta vicinity.

Typical grant range: $2,000 to $15,000

197
Roy C. Moore Foundation
First National Bank of Gainesville
P.O. Box 937
Gainesville, GA 30503
(404) 535-5562

Building and equipment grants. Youth
organizations; all levels of education;
cultural organizations

198
**William I.H. and Lula E. Pitts
Foundation**
c/o Trust Co. Bank
P.O. Box 4655
Atlanta, GA 30302
(404) 588-8449

Building grants. Social welfare; elderly

Grants awarded to organizations located
in Georgia.

All organizations awarded grants must be
affiliated with a Church (Methodist).

199
James Hyde Porter Testamentary Trust
Trust Co. Bank of Middle Georgia, N.A.
606 Cherry Street, P.O. Box 4248
Macon, GA 31208
(912) 741-2265

Building and equipment grants.
Performing arts (chairs); Association for
Retarded Citizens (van); Rescue Mission
(kitchen equipment, furniture); Housing
Authority (renovation); Childrens Home
(building funds); Trust for Historic
Preservation (building funds, renovation);
Soccer Association (building funds);
Hospice Foundation (equipment,
renovation); Library Board (books);
Children's Hospital (beds); American
Cancer Society (equipment); Women's
Center (building funds)

Typical grant range: $5,000 to $25,000

200
Rich Foundation, Inc.
10 Piedmont Center, Suite 802
Atlanta, GA 30305
(404) 262-2266

Building and equipment grants. Hospitals;
health organizations; social welfare; youth
organizations; cultural organizations

Grants awarded to organizations located
in the Atlanta vicinity.

201
Tull Charitable Foundation
50 Hurt Plaza, Suite 1245
Atlanta, GA 30303
(404) 659-7079

Building grants. Higher and secondary
education; health organizations; disabled;
child welfare; social welfare

Grants awarded to organizations located
in Georgia.

Typical grant range: $15,000 to $65,000

202
Joseph B. Whitehead Foundation
50 Hurt Plaza, Suite 1200
Atlanta, GA 30303
(404) 522-6755

Building and equipment grants. Social
welfare; health organizations; hospitals;
disabled; child welfare; renovation grants

Grants awarded to organizations located
in the Atlanta vicinity.

Typical grant range: $50,000 to $400,000

203
Frances Wood Wilson Foundation, Inc.
1501 Clairmont Road, Suite 104
Decatur, GA 30033
(404) 634-3363

Building and equipment grants. Child
welfare; health organizations

Most grants awarded to organizations
located in Georgia.

Typical grant range: $5,000 to $25,000

204
Robert W. Woodruff Foundation, Inc.
50 Hurt Plaza, Suite 1200
Atlanta, GA 30303
(404) 522-6755

Building and equipment grants. Higher
education; youth organizations; social
welfare; museums; performing arts;
historical societies; elderly; health
organizations; environment; AIDS;
renovation grants

Grants awarded to organizations located
in Atlanta.

Typical grant range: $50,000 to
$1,500,000

205
David, Helen and Marian Woodward Fund-Atlanta
Wachovia Bank of Georgia, N.A.
191 Peachtree Street
Atlanta, GA 30303
(404) 332-6677

Building grants. Social welfare; hospitals; health organizations; disabled; community development

Grants awarded to organizations located in the Atlanta vicinity.

Typical grant range: $5,000 to $40,000

206
Vasser Woolley Foundation, Inc.
c/o Alston & Bird, One Atlantic Center
1201 W. Peachtree Street, Suite 4200
Atlanta, GA 30309
(404) 881-7000

Building and equipment grants. Community development; youth organizations

Grants awarded to organizations located in the Atlanta vicinity.

HAWAII

207
Atherton Family Foundation
c/o Hawaii Community Foundation
222 Merchant Street
Honolulu, HI 96813
(808) 537-6333

Building and equipment grants. Health organizations; hospitals; performing arts; cultural organizations; alcohol abuse; social welfare; disabled; higher education; Churches; renovation grants

Grants awarded to organizations located in Hawaii.

Typical grant range: $2,000 to $20,000

208
Harold K.L. Castle Foundation
146 Hekili Street
Kailua, HI 96734
(808) 262-9413

Building and equipment grants. Cultural organizations; environment; hospitals; renovation grants

Grants awarded to organizations located in Hawaii.

Typical grant range: $20,000 to $175,000

209
Samuel N. and Mary Castle Foundation
222 Merchant Street
Honolulu, HI 96813
(808) 537-6333

Building and equipment grants. Higher and secondary education; hospitals; disabled; social welfare; cultural organizations; animal welfare; youth organizations; Hawaii Pacific University (renovation); Church (building funds); School for Girls (equipment)

Grants awarded to organizations located in Hawaii.

Typical grant range: $2,500 to $20,000

210
Jessie Ann Chalmers Charitable Trust
c/o Bishop Trust Co., Ltd.
P.O. Box 2390
Honolulu, HI 96804

Equipment grants. Episcopal Church (equipment); Salvation Army (kitchen equipment, recreation equipment)

Grants awarded to organizations located in Hawaii.

Typical grant range: $500 to $5,000

211
Cooke Foundation, Limited
c/o Hawaiian Trust Co., Ltd.
P.O. Box 3170
Honolulu, HI 96802
(808) 537-6333

Building and equipment grants. Social welfare; health organizations; cultural organizations; disabled; elderly; Food Bank (van); Honolulu Academy of Arts (renovation); YMCA (building funds)

Grants awarded to organizations located in Hawaii.

Typical grant range: $2,000 to $15,000

212
First Hawaiian Foundation
1132 Bishop Street
Honolulu, HI 96813
(808) 525-8144

Building grants. Higher education; cultural organizations; social welfare; renovation grants

Grants awarded to organizations located in Hawaii.

Typical grant range: $5,000 to $75,000

213
Mary D. and Walter F. Frear Eleemosynary Trust
c/o Bishop Trust Co., Ltd.
1000 Bishop Street
Honolulu, HI 96813
(808) 523-2234

Building and equipment grants. Hospitals; health organizations; disabled; community development; cultural organizations; Churches; Nature Center (renovation); YWCA (renovation); Oceanic Institute (renovation)

Grants awarded to organizations located in Hawaii.

Typical grant range: $1,000 to $8,000

214
Hawaii Community Foundation
222 Merchant Street
Honolulu, HI 96813
(808) 537-6333

Building and equipment grants. Cultural organizations; health organizations; social welfare; disabled; elderly; Alcoholic Rehabilitation Services (building funds); Aloha School Early Learning Center (fence); Planned Parenthood (building funds); Salvation Army (equipment, renovation)

Grants awarded to organizations located in Hawaii.

Typical grant range: $3,000 to $40,000

215
McInerny Foundation
c/o Bishop Trust Co., Ltd.
1000 Bishop Street
Honolulu, HI 96813
(808) 523-2234

Building and equipment grants. Hospitals; health organizations; social welfare; cultural organizations; disabled; animal welfare; AIDS (equipment); YMCA (building funds); Contemporary Museum (renovation); Honolulu Academy of Arts (renovation)

Grants awarded to organizations located in Hawaii.

Typical grant range: $5,000 to $20,000

216
Sophie Russell Testamentary Trust
c/o Bishop Trust Co., Ltd.
1000 Bishop Street
Honolulu, HI 96813
(808) 523-2233

Building and equipment grants. Disabled; animal welfare; renovation grants

Grants awarded to organizations located in Hawaii.

Typical grant range: $5,000 to $10,000

217
Albert T. and Wallace T. Teruya
Foundation
1276 Young Street
Honolulu, HI 96814
(808) 521-6946

Building grants. Japanese Cultural Center
(building funds)

Most grants awarded to organizations
located in Honolulu.

IDAHO

218
Leland D. Beckman Foundation
c/o Holden, Kidwell, Hahn & Crapo
P.O. Box 50130
Idaho Falls, ID 83405

Equipment grants. Social welfare; youth
organizations; Women Against Domestic
Violence (equipment); The Nature
Conservancy (purchase land); Workshop
for Disabled (equipment); Bonneville
Association of Retarded Citizens
(equipment)

Grants awarded to organizations located
in Idaho Falls.

Typical grant range: $1,000 to $8,000

219
Laura Moore Cunningham
Foundation, Inc.
510 Main
Boise, ID 83702
(208) 347-7852

Building and equipment grants. Hospitals;
child welfare; education

Grants awarded to organizations located
in Idaho.

Typical grant range: $2,000 to $15,000

220
Roger and Sybil Ferguson
Charitable Foundation
P.O. Box 519
Rexburg, ID 83440

Equipment grants. Elderly; elementary
and secondary education

Grants awarded to organizations located
in Idaho.

Typical grant range: $500 to $5,000

221
Idaho Community Foundation
205 N. 10th Street, Suite 625
Boise, ID 83702
(208) 342-3535

Building and equipment grants. Social
welfare; homeless; health organizations;
hospitals; elderly; Madison County Senior
Citizens (renovation); South Custer County
Historical Society (renovation)

Grants awarded to organizations located
in Idaho.

Typical grant range: $500 to $5,000

222
Harry W. Morrison Foundation, Inc.
3505 Crescent Rim Drive
Boise, ID 83706

Building and equipment grants. Hospital
(equipment); Center for the Arts and
Humanities (recording equipment); Rescue
Mission (refrigeration unit); Church (van)

Grants awarded to organizations located
in Boise.

Typical grant range: $500 to $10,000

223
Ray Foundation
P.O. Box 2156
Ketchum, ID 83340

Building and equipment grants. Performing
Arts (lighting system); Arizona Museum of
Science and Technology (audiovisual
equipment); Community Psychiatric Clinic
(equipment)

Typical grant range: $3,000 to $30,000

224

Claude and Ethel B. Whittenberger Foundation
P.O. Box 1073
Caldwell, ID 83606
(208) 459-0091

Equipment grants. Youth organizations; secondary education; cultural organizations

Grants awarded to organizations located in Idaho.

Typical grant range: $1,000 to $9,000

ILLINOIS

225

American National Bank and Trust Company of Chicago Foundation
33 N. LaSalle Street
Chicago, IL 60690
(312) 661-6115

Building grants. Hospitals; health organizations; youth organizations

Grants awarded to organizations located in areas of company operations, with an emphasis in the Chicago vicinity.

Typical grant range: $1,000 to $7,000

226

Amoco Foundation, Inc.
200 E. Randolph Drive
Chicago, IL 60601
(312) 856-6305

Building and equipment grants. Higher education; hospitals; DOHA Independent School (equipment)

Grants awarded to organizations located in areas of company operations.

Typical grant range: $4,000 to $60,000

227

Aurora Foundation
111 W. Downer Place, Suite 312
Aurora, IL 60506
(708) 896-7800

Building and equipment grants. Hospitals; health organizations; social welfare; higher education

Grants awarded to organizations located in the Aurora vicinity.

228

Blowitz-Ridgeway Foundation
2700 River Road, Suite 211
Des Plaines, IL 60018
(708) 298-2378

Building and equipment grants. Disabled; substance abuse; Mercy Boys Home (renovation); City of Des Plaines (child safety educational vehicle); Boys Hope (renovation); Foundation for Hearing and Speech Rehabilitation (equipment); Shelter, Inc. (van); Day Care Center (equipment)

Grants awarded to organizations located in Illinois.

Typical grant range: $2,000 to $25,000

229

Helen Brach Foundation
55 W. Wacker Drive, Suite 701
Chicago, IL 60601
(312) 372-4417

Building and equipment grants. Animal welfare; youth organizations; health organizations; environment; social welfare; disabled; renovation grants

Typical grant range: $1,000 to $65,000

230
Butz Foundation
c/o Northern Trust Co.
50 S. LaSalle Street
Chicago, IL 60675

Building and equipment grants. Hospitals; historical societies

Grants awarded to organizations located in Illinois.

231
Apollos Camp and Bennet Humiston Trust
300 W. Washington Street
Pontiac, IL 61764

Building and equipment grants. Youth organizations; recreation

Grants awarded to organizations located in Pontiac.

232
Chicago Community Trust
222 N. LaSalle Street, Suite 1400
Chicago, IL 60601
(312) 372-3356

Building and equipment grants. Hospitals; health organizations; social welfare; disabled; child welfare; women; elderly; community development; Robert Crown Center for Health Education (renovation); renovation grants

Grants awarded to organizations located in the Chicago vicinity.

Typical grant range: $15,000 to $70,000

233
Coleman Foundation, Inc.
575 W. Madison, Suite 4605-II
Chicago, IL 60661
(312) 902-7120

Building and equipment grants. Hospitals (equipment, building funds); Moody Bible Institute (building funds); Rehabilitation Institute of Chicago (furniture); Art Reach (equipment); Family Services and Mental Health Center (building funds)

Grants awarded to organizations located in the Chicago vicinity.

Typical grant range: $1,000 to $50,000

234
Henry P. Crowell and Susan C. Crowell Trust
Lock Box 442
Chicago, IL 60690
(312) 372-5202

Building and equipment grants. Christian related organizations

Typical grant range: $5,000 to $30,000

235
Arie and Ida Crown Memorial
222 N. LaSalle Street
Chicago, IL 60601
(312) 236-6300

Building and equipment grants. Health organizations; cultural organizations; youth organizations; Jewish organizations

Grants awarded to organizations located in the Chicago vicinity.

236
Cuneo Foundation
9101 Greenwood Avenue, Suite 210
Niles, IL 60648

Building and equipment grants. Social welfare; youth organizations; Roman Catholic organizations

Grants awarded to organizations located in the Chicago vicinity.

Typical grant range: $2,000 to $30,000

237
Doris and Victor Day Foundation, Inc.
1705 Second Avenue, Suite 424
Rock Island, IL 61201
(309) 788-2300

Building and equipment grants. Social
welfare; health organizations; youth
organizations; disabled; minorities; day
care; Christian Family Care Center
(renovation); Little League (equipment)

Grants awarded to organizations located
in the Illinois/Iowa Quad Cities.

Typical grant range: $1,000 to $15,000

238
John Deere Foundation
John Deere Road
Moline, IL 61265
(309) 765-4137

Building and equipment grants. Social
welfare; health organizations; youth
organizations; cultural organizations

Grants awarded to organizations located
in areas of company operations.

Typical grant range: $1,000 to $25,000

239
Dillon Foundation
P.O. Box 537
Sterling, IL 61081
(815) 626-9000

Building grants. Social welfare; youth
organizations; cultural organizations;
community development; hospitals

Grants awarded to organizations located
in the Sterling vicinity.

Typical grant range: $5,000 to $35,000

240
Duchossois Foundation
845 Larch Ave.
Elmhurst, IL 60126
(708) 279-3600

Building grants. Youth organizations;
social welfare; cultural organizations;
Aquarium; Girl Scouts

Most grants awarded to organizations
located in the Chicago vicinity.

241
Evanston Community Foundation
828 Davis Street, Suite 300
Evanston, IL 60201
(708) 475-2402

Equipment grants. Evanston Shelter for
Battered Women and Their Children
(furniture)

Grants awarded to organizations located
in Evanston.

Typical grant range: $1,000 to $12,000

242
Field Foundation of Illinois, Inc.
135 S. LaSalle Street
Chicago, IL 60603
(312) 263-3211

Building and equipment grants. Cultural
organizations; mental health; youth
organizations; health organizations;
hospitals; AIDS; higher education
(building funds, equipment); Lawndale
Christian Health Center (building funds);
renovation grants

Grants awarded to organizations located
in the Chicago vicinity.

Typical grant range: $5,000 to $45,000

243
First National Bank of Chicago Foundation
One First National Plaza
Chicago, IL 60670
(312) 732-6948

Building and equipment grants. Social welfare; community development; higher education (building funds)

Grants awarded to organizations located in the Chicago vicinity.

244
FMC Foundation
200 E. Randolph Drive
Chicago, IL 60601
(312) 861-6135

Building and equipment grants. Health organizations; higher education; youth organizations; community development

Grants awarded to organizations located in areas of company operations.

Typical grant range: $1,000 to $12,000

245
Lloyd A. Fry Foundation
135 S. LaSalle Street, Suite 1910
Chicago, IL 60603
(312) 580-0310

Equipment grants. Cultural organizations; social welfare; community development; youth organizations; health organizations; hospitals

Grants awarded to organizations located in the Chicago vicinity.

Typical grant range: $2,000 to $40,000

246
Hales Charitable Fund, Inc.
120 W. Madison Street, Suite 700-E
Chicago, IL 60602
(312) 641-7016

Building grants. Social welfare; health organizations; Protestant related organizations

Grants awarded to organizations located in Illinois.

247
Harris Bank Foundation
111 W. Monroe Street
Chicago, IL 60603
(312) 461-5834

Building and equipment grants. Social welfare; community development; cultural organizations; Counseling Center (building funds); YWCA (playground renovation)

Grants awarded to organizations located in the Chicago vicinity.

Typical grant range: $2,000 to $10,000

248
Grover Hermann Foundation
c/o Schiff, Hardin & Waite
7200 Sears Tower, 233 S. Wacker Drive
Chicago, IL 60606
(312) 876-1000

Building and equipment grants. Social welfare; health organizations; animal welfare; higher education; community development; Alliance on Aging, Inc. (equipment); Boy Scouts of America (truck); renovation grants

Typical grant range: $1,000 to $40,000

249
Illinois Tool Works Foundation
3600 W. Lake Avenue
Glenview, IL 60025
(708) 724-7500

Building grants. Social welfare; hospitals;
health organizations; disabled; community
development; culture; St. Thomas The
Apostle Church (building funds)

Grants awarded to organizations located
in areas of company operations, with an
emphasis in Chicago.

Typical grant range: $1,000 to $15,000

250
**Robert R. McCormick Tribune
Foundation**
435 N. Michigan Avenue, Suite 770
Chicago, IL 60611
(312) 222-3512

Building and equipment grants. Animal
welfare; higher education; disabled; social
welfare; health organizations; women;
cultural organizations; youth
organizations; renovation grants

Grants awarded to organizations located
in the Chicago vicinity.

Typical grant range: $5,000 to $75,000

251
McGraw Foundation
3436 N. Kennicott Drive
Arlington Heights, IL 60004
(708) 870-8014

Building and equipment grants. Social
welfare; hospitals; health organizations;
higher education; cultural organizations

Grants awarded to organizations located
in the Chicago vicinity.

Typical grant range: $2,000 to $30,000

252
Adah K. Millard Charitable Trust
c/o The Northern Trust Co.
50 S. LaSalle Street
Chicago, IL 60675
(312) 630-6000

Building and equipment grants. Social
welfare; youth organizations

253
Motorola Foundation
1303 E. Algonquin Road
Schaumburg, IL 60196
(708) 576-6200

Building grants. Social welfare; youth
organizations; hospitals; culture

Grants awarded to organizations located
in areas of company operations.

Typical grant range: $500 to $12,000

254
Nalco Foundation
One Nalco Center
Naperville, IL 60563
(708) 305-1556

Building and equipment grants. Social
welfare; disabled; minorities; health
organizations; hospitals; youth
organizations; elderly; higher education;
renovation grants

Grants awarded to organizations located
in areas of company operations.

Typical grant range: $1,000 to $12,000

255
**Frank E. Payne and Seba B. Payne
Foundation**
c/o Continental Bank, N.A.
30 N. LaSalle Street
Chicago, IL 60697
(312) 828-1785

Building and equipment grants. Social
welfare; hospitals; cultural organizations;
museums; animal welfare; disabled; youth
organizations; higher education (building
funds for a library)

Typical grant range: $10,000 to $95,000

256
Esper A. Petersen Foundation
1300 Skokie Highway
Gurnee, IL 60031

Building grants. Disabled; hospitals

257
Polk Bros. Foundation, Inc.
420 N. Wabash Avenue, Suite 204
Chicago, IL 60611
(312) 527-4684

Building and equipment grants. Social
welfare; hospitals; higher education
(building funds for a library); community
development; disabled; renovation grants

Grants awarded to organizations located
in the Chicago vicinity.

Typical grant range: $2,000 to $35,000

258
Quaker Oats Foundation
Quaker Tower
321 N. Clark Street
Chicago, IL 60610
(312) 222-7033

Building and equipment grants. Social
welfare; cultural organizations; youth
organizations; community development;
hospitals

Grants awarded to organizations located
in areas of company operations, with an
emphasis in Illinois.

Typical grant range: $1,500 to $25,000

259
Regenstein Foundation
8600 W. Bryn Mawr Ave., Suite 705N
Chicago, IL 60631
(312) 693-6464

Building and equipment grants. Cultural
organizations; disabled; colleges and
universities; social welfare; health
organizations; renovation grants

Grants awarded to organizations located
in the Chicago vicinity.

Typical grant range: $500 to $100,000

260
Rockford Community Trust
321 W. State Street, 13th Floor
Rockford, IL 61101
(815) 962-2110

Building and equipment grants. Social
welfare; child welfare; women; youth
organizations; cultural organizations;
disabled; renovation grants

Grants awarded to organizations located
in the Rockford vicinity.

Typical grant range: $1,000 to $5,000

261
Dr. Scholl Foundation
11 S. LaSalle Street, Suite 2100
Chicago, IL 60603
(312) 782-5210

Building and equipment grants. All levels
of education; social welfare; cultural
organizations; community development

Grants awarded to organizations located
in areas of company operations.

Typical grant range: $5,000 to $40,000

262
Square D Foundation
1415 S. Roselle Road
Palatine, IL 60067
(708) 397-2600

Building and equipment grants. Cultural
organizations; disabled; hospitals; health
organizations; youth organizations;
community development

Grants awarded to organizations located
in areas of company operations.

Typical grant range: $1,000 to $7,000

263
Irvin Stern Foundation
53 W. Jackson Blvd., Suite 838
Chicago, IL 60604
(312) 786-9355

Equipment grants. Social welfare;
homeless; elderly

Typical grant range: $4,000 to $20,000

264
Sunstrand Corporation Foundation
4949 Harrison Avenue
P.O. Box 7003
Rockford, IL 61125
(815) 226-6000

Building and equipment grants. Health
organizations; youth organizations; social
welfare; community development; elderly;
disabled

Grants awarded to organizations located
in areas of company operations.

Typical grant range: $1,000 to $15,000

265
A. Montgomery Ward Foundation
c/o Continental Bank
30 N. LaSalle Street
Chicago, IL 60697
(312) 828-1785

Building and equipment grants. Youth
organizations; hospitals; child welfare

Grants awarded to organizations located
in the Chicago vicinity.

266
Washington Square Health
Foundation, Inc.
875 N. Michigan Avenue, Suite 3516
Chicago, IL 60611
(312) 664-6488

Equipment grants. Hospitals; health
organizations

Grants awarded to organizations located
in the Chicago vicinity.

267
Woods Charitable Fund, Inc.
Three First National Plaza, Suite 2010
Chicago, IL 60602
(312) 782-2698

Building and equipment grants.
Social welfare; women; community
development; disabled; Food Bank

Typical grant range: $10,000 to $35,000

INDIANA

268
Arvin Foundation, Inc.
One Noblitt Plaza
Box 3000
Columbus, IN 47202
(812) 379-3285

Building and equipment grants. Health
organizations; youth organizations

Grants awarded to organizations located
in areas of company operations (Arvin
Industries).

Typical grant range: $100 to $4,000

269
Ball Brothers Foundation
222 S. Mulberry Street
P.O. Box 1408
Muncie, IN 47308

Building and equipment grants. Cultural
organizations; social welfare; youth
organizations; disabled; recreation;
Cultural Foundation (equipment);
University Foundation (building funds);
YMCA (renovation)

Grants awarded to organizations located
in Indiana.

Typical grant range: $1,500 to $30,000

270
George and Frances Ball Foundation
P.O. Box 1408
Muncie, IN 47308
(317) 741-5500

Building and equipment grants.
Higher education; health organizations;
community development; renovation
grants

Grants awarded to organizations located
in Muncie.

Typical grant range: $10,000 to $70,000

271
Brookville Foundation
814 Main Street
Brookville, IN 47012
(317) 647-4105

Building and equipment grants. Health
organizations; disabled; cultural
organizations

272
Clowes Fund, Inc.
250 E. 38th Street
Indianapolis, IN 46205
(317) 923-3264

Building and equipment grants. Hospitals;
museums; performing arts; social welfare;
higher education; disabled; libraries

Grants awarded to organizations located
in Indianapolis.

Typical grant range: $3,000 to $40,000

273
Olive B. Cole Foundation, Inc.
3242 Mallard Cove Lane
Fort Wayne, IN 46804
(219) 436-2182

Building and equipment grants. Youth
organizations; cultural organizations;
hospitals; higher education; Day Care
Center (equipment); Girl Scout Council
(renovation)

Typical grant range: $3,000 to $15,000

274
**Community Foundation of Muncie and
Delaware County, Inc.**
P.O. Box 807
Muncie, IN 47308
(317) 747-7181

Building and equipment grants. Social
welfare; community development; cultural
organizations; disabled; recreation; child
welfare; Salvation Army (van); renovation
grants

Grants awarded to organizations located
in Muncie and Delaware County.

Typical grant range: $2,000 to $12,000

275
**Elkhart County Community
Foundation, Inc.**
Ameritrust National Building
301 S. Main, P.O. Box 279
Elkhart, IN 46515
(219) 295-8761

Building and equipment grants. Social
welfare; community development; day
care; cultural organizations; performing
arts; literacy project; Habitat for Humanity
(furniture); renovation grants

Grants awarded to organizations located in
Elkhart County.

Typical grant range: $500 to $7,000

276
Foellinger Foundation
520 E. Berry Street
Ft. Wayne, IN 46802
(219) 422-2900

Building and equipment grants. Social
welfare; community development; women;
disabled; health organizations; recreation;
renovation grants

Grants awarded to organizations located in
the Ft. Wayne vicinity.

Typical grant range: $8,000 to $150,000

277
Froderman Foundation, Inc.
18 S. Ninth Street
Terre Haute, IN 47807

Building and equipment grants. Council
on Aging (equipment); Little League
(equipment); University Medical Center
(equipment); Rehabilitation Hospital of
Indiana (equipment); Volunteer Fire
Department (equipment); Christian
Athletes (equipment); Christian Services
(equipment); Jr. Achievement (equipment)

Grants awarded to organizations located
in Indiana.

Typical grant range: $2,000 to $15,000

278
W.C. Griffith Foundation
c/o National City Bank, Indiana
P.O. Box 5031
Indianapolis, IN 46255

Building grants. Health organizations;
hospitals

279
**Heritage Fund of Bartholomew
County, Inc.**
430 Second Street
P.O. Box 1547
Columbus, IN 47202
(812) 376-7772

Building and equipment grants. Health
organizations; social welfare; cultural
organizations; recreation; Foundation
for Youth (renovation)

Grants awarded to organizations located
in Bartholomew County.

280
Indianapolis Foundation
615 N. Alabama Street
Indianapolis, IN 46204
(317) 634-7497

Building and equipment grants. Social
welfare; community development; youth;
performing arts; public broadcasting;
disabled; health organizations; Lutheran
Child and Family Services (building funds);
renovation grants

Grants awarded to organizations located in
the Indianapolis vicinity.

Typical grant range: $5,000 to $75,000

281
Arthur Jordan Foundation
1230 N. Delaware Street
Indianapolis, IN 46202
(317) 635-1378

Building grants. Higher education;
museums; performing arts; youth
organizations; hospitals; social welfare;
disabled

Typical grant range: $3,000 to $15,000

282
Eli Lilly and Company Foundation
Lilly Corporate Center
Indianapolis, IN 46285
(317) 276-5342

Building grants. Cultural organizations;
health organizations; higher education;
social welfare

Grants awarded to organizations located
in areas of company operations, with an
emphasis in Indianapolis.

Typical grant range: $5,000 to $100,000

283
Lilly Endowment Inc.
2801 N. Meridian Street
P.O. Box 88068
Indianapolis, IN 46208
(317) 924-5471

Building and equipment grants. Cultural
organizations; youth organizations;
disabled

Grants awarded to organizations located
in Indiana, with an emphasis in
Indianapolis.

284
Martin Foundation, Inc.
500 Simpson Avenue
Elkhart, IN 46515
(219) 295-3343

Building and equipment grants.
Environment; cultural organizations;
social welfare; disabled; renovation grants

Grants awarded to organizations located
in Indiana.

Typical grant range: $1,000 to $20,000

285
Oliver Memorial Trust Foundation
112-114 W. Jefferson Blvd.
South Bend, IN 46601
(219) 237-3321

Building grants. Youth organizations;
community development; hospitals

Grants awarded to organizations located
in Indiana.

IOWA

286
**Marie H. Bechtel Charitable
Remainder Uni-Trust**
1000 Firstar Center
201 W. Second Street
Davenport, IA 52801
(319) 328-3333

Building grants. Social welfare; higher
education; libraries; renovation grants

287
Roy J. Carver Charitable Trust
P.O. Box 76
Muscatine, IA 52761
(319) 263-4010

Building and equipment grants. Youth
organizations; social welfare; secondary
and higher education; day care; women;
recreation; renovation grants

Grants awarded to organizations located
in Iowa.

Typical grant range: $25,000 to $200,000

288
**Gardner and Florence Call Cowles
Foundation, Inc.**
715 Locust Street
Des Moines, IA 50309
(515) 284-8116

Building and equipment grants. Cultural
organizations; child welfare; social
welfare; higher education

Grants awarded to organizations located
in Iowa, with an emphasis in Des Moines.

289
Greater Cedar Rapids Foundation
101 Second Street, S.E., Suite 306
Cedar Rapids, IA 52401
(319) 366-2862

Building and equipment grants. Cultural
organizations; disabled; renovation grants

Grants awarded to organizations located
in the Greater Cedar Rapids vicinity.

Typical grant range: $1,000 to $7,000

290
Hall Foundation, Inc.
115 Third Street, S.E., Suite 803
Cedar Rapids, IA 52401
(319) 362-9079

Building and equipment grants. Social
welfare; animal welfare; hospitals; health
organizations; disabled; community
development; youth organizations;
elderly; cultural organizations; renovation
grants

Grants awarded to organizations located
in the Cedar Rapids vicinity.

Typical grant range: $5,000 to $120,000

291
Hawley Foundation
1530 Financial Center
666 Walnut
Des Moines, IA 50309
(515) 280-7071

Building and equipment grants. Social
welfare; child welfare; women; homeless;
recreation; substance abuse; disabled;
renovation grants

292
Kinney-Lindstrom Foundation, Inc.
P.O. Box 520
Mason City, IA 50401
(515) 896-3888

Building and equipment grants. Libraries;
historical societies; museums; youth
organizations; disabled; social welfare;
substance abuse; child welfare; renovation
grants

Grants awarded to organizations located
in Iowa.

Typical grant range: $1,000 to $20,000

293
Lee Foundation
215 N. Main Street
Davenport, IA 52801

Building grants. Youth organizations;
cultural organizations; elderly; hospitals

Typical grant range: $1,000 to $8,000

294
Fred Maytag Family Foundation
200 First Street South
P.O. Box 426
Newton, IA 50208
(515) 792-1800

Building and equipment grants. Health
organizations; social welfare; child
welfare; performing arts; museums;
higher education; renovation grants

Most grants awarded to organizations
located in Newton and Des Moines.

Typical grant range: $2,000 to $30,000

295
R.J. McElroy Trust
KWWL Building
500 E. Fourth Street
Waterloo, IA 50703
(319) 291-1299

Building and equipment grants. Cultural
organizations; youth organizations;
community development; disabled;
hospitals; libraries; renovation grants

296
Mid-Iowa Health Foundation
550 39th Street, Suite 104
Des Moines, IA 50312
(515) 277-6411

Building and equipment grants. Child
welfare; disabled; elderly; health
organizations; social welfare; youth
organizations

297
**Harry and Virginia Murray
Foundation**
c/o Firstar Bank Burlington, N.A.
P.O. Box 1088
Burlington, IA 52601
(319) 752-2761

Building and equipment grants. Health
organizations; social welfare; Churches

298
Pella Rolscreen Foundation
c/o Rolscreen Corporation
102 Main Street
Pella, IA 50219
(515) 628-1000

Building grants. Cultural organizations;
higher education; social welfare; child
welfare; disabled; recreation

Grants awarded to organizations located
in areas of company operations.

Typical grant range: $300 to $8,000

299
**Principal Financial Group
Foundation, Inc.**
711 High Street
Des Moines, IA 50392
(515) 247-5209

Building grants. Social welfare; cultural
organizations; Animal Rescue League
(building funds)

Grants awarded to organizations located
in Iowa, with an emphasis in Des Moines.

300
Van Buren Foundation, Inc.
c/o Farmers State Bank
Keosauqua, IA 52565
(319) 293-3794

Building and equipment grants. Hospitals;
health organizations; elderly; community
development; Public Library; renovation
grants

301
Wahlert Foundation
c/o FDL Foods, Inc.
P.O. Box 898
Dubuque, IA 52001
(319) 588-5400

Building and equipment grants. Social
welfare; hospitals; health organizations;
disabled; cultural organizations

Grants awarded to organizations located
in the Dubuque vicinity.

Typical grant range: $500 to $10,000

302
Waterloo Civic Foundation
National Bank of Waterloo
P.O. Box 5300
Waterloo, IA 50704
(319) 233-8431

Equipment grants. Social welfare; cultural
organizations; youth organizations

Grants awarded to organizations located
in Waterloo.

303
John H. Witte, Jr. Foundation
Firstar Bank Burlington, N.A.
P.O. Box 1088, 201 Jefferson Street
Burlington, IA 52601
(319) 752-2761

Building and equipment grants.
Community development; cultural
organizations; youth organizations; Boy
Scouts (building funds); Catholic School
(bus); renovation grants

Grants awarded to organizations located
in Burlington.

KANSAS

304
Baughman Foundation
P.O. Box 1356
Liberal, KS 67901
(316) 624-1371

Building and equipment grants.
Abused women; community development;
elderly; animal welfare; hospitals; public
libraries; St. Anthony School (renovation,
equipment)

Grants awarded to organizations located
in the Liberal vicinity.

Typical grant range: $1,000 to $20,000

305
Beech Aircraft Foundation
9709 E. Central Avenue
Wichita, KS 67201
(316) 681-8177

Building grants. Hospitals; disabled;
elderly; youth organizations; renovation
grants

Grants awarded to organizations located
in areas of company operations, with an
emphasis in Kansas.

Typical grant range: $1,500 to $75,000

306
Cessna Foundation, Inc.
P.O. Box 7704
Wichita, KS 67277
(316) 941-6000

Building grants. Disabled; social welfare;
youth organizations; National Conference
of Christians and Jews (renovation)

Grants awarded to organizations located
in areas of company operations, with an
emphasis in Kansas.

Typical grant range: $1,000 to $15,000

307
DeVore Foundation, Inc.
P.O. Box 118
Wichita, KS 67201
(316) 267-3211

Building and equipment grants. Social
welfare; disabled; youth organizations;
health organizations; renovation grants

Grants awarded to organizations located
in the Wichita vicinity.

Typical grant range: $100 to $1,500

308
Garvey Foundation
300 W. Douglas Street
Wichita, KS 67202
(316) 261-5384

Building and equipment grants.
Community development; disabled

309
Dane G. Hansen Foundation
P.O. Box 187
Logan, KS 67646
(913) 689-4832

Building and equipment grants. Hospitals;
disabled; youth organizations; higher
education; Public Libraries

Typical grant range: $3,000 to $25,000

310
Marley Fund
1900 Shawnee Mission Parkway
Mission Woods, KS 66205
(913) 362-1818

Building and equipment grants. Hospitals;
health organizations; social welfare; youth
organizations

Grants awarded to organizations located
in areas of company operations.

311
Powell Family Foundation
10990 Roe Avenue
P.O. Box 7270
Shawnee Mission, KS 66207
(913) 345-3000

Building and equipment grants. Social
welfare; cultural organizations; youth
organizations; renovation grants

Grants awarded to organizations located
in the Kansas City vicinity.

Typical grant range: $1,000 to $25,000

312
Ethel & Raymond F. Rice Foundation
700 Massachusetts Street
Lawrence, KS 66044
(913) 843-0420

Building and equipment grants. Youth
organizations; social welfare; hospitals;
Churches

Grants awarded to organizations located
in the Lawrence vicinity.

Typical grant range: $1,000 to $8,000

KENTUCKY

313
James Graham Brown Foundation, Inc.
132 E. Gray Street
Louisville, KY 40202
(502) 583-4085

Building and equipment grants. Higher
education; museums; community
development; health organizations;
hospitals; social welfare; renovation
grants

Grants awarded to organizations located
in Kentucky.

Typical grant range: $10,000 to $200,000

314
V.V. Cooke Foundation Corp.
4350 Brownsboro Road, Suite 110
Louisville, KY 40207
(502) 893-4598

Building and equipment grants. Protestant
related organizations (higher education,
religious education); renovation grants

Grants awarded to organizations located
in Louisville.

Typical grant range: $500 to $12,000

315
**Foundation for the Tri-State
Community, Inc.**
P.O. Box 2096
Ashland, KY 41105
(606) 324-3888

Equipment grants. Child welfare

316
Gardner Foundation, Inc.
5330 S. Third Street, Suite 100
Louisville, KY 40214
(502) 363-2687

Building grants. Christian related
organizations; higher education

Most grants awarded to organizations
located in Louisville.

317
Gheens Foundation, Inc.
One Riverfront Plaza, Suite 705
Louisville, KY 40202
(502) 584-4650

Building and equipment grants. Social
welfare; health organizations; hospitals;
hospice; disabled; performing arts;
museums; youth organizations; elderly;
higher education; renovation grants

Most grants awarded to organizations
located in the Louisville vicinity.

Typical grant range: $5,000 to $60,000

318
Herman H. Nettleroth Fund
c/o PNC Bank, Kentucky
Citizens Plaza
Louisville, KY 40296

Equipment grants. Ministry (equipment);
Nature Center (equipment); Community
of Highland (equipment for youth
program)

Typical grant range: $4,000 to $15,000

319
Norton Foundation, Inc.
4350 Brownsboro Road, Suite 133
Louisville, KY 40207
(502) 893-9549

Equipment grants. Education; social
welfare

Grants awarded to organizations located
in the Louisville vicinity.

Typical grant range: $3,000 to $25,000

320
E.O. Robinson Mountain Fund
P.O. Box 54930
Lexington, KY 40555
(606) 233-0817

Building and equipment grants. Health
organizations; community development;
youth organizations; renovation grants

Typical grant range: $3,000 to $25,000

321
Thomas Foundation
4360 Brownsboro Road, Suite 300
Louisville, KY 40207

Building grants. Youth organizations;
social welfare; health organizations

Grants awarded to organizations located
in Kentucky.

LOUISIANA

322
Baton Rouge Area Foundation
One American Place, Suite 610
Baton Rouge, LA 70825
(504) 387-6126

Building and equipment grants. Social
welfare; youth organizations; disabled;
community development; Cancer Society
(renovation); Crisis Pregnancy Center
(building funds); renovation grants

Grants awarded to organizations located
in Baton Rouge.

323
**Joe and Dorothy Dorsett Brown
Foundation**
1801 Pere Marquette Building
New Orleans, LA 70112
(504) 522-4233

Building and equipment grants. Social
welfare; hospitals; disabled

Grants awarded to organizations located
in Louisiana.

Typical grant range: $1,000 to $9,000

324
Huie-Dellmon Trust
P.O. Box 330
Alexandria, LA 71301

Building and equipment grants. Hospital
(equipment); Episcopal School (building
funds)

325
Lupin Foundation
3715 Prytania Street, Suite 307
New Orleans, LA 70115
(504) 897-6125

Building and equipment grants. Health
organizations; hospitals; social welfare;
disabled; cultural organizations; Jewish
related organizations; renovation grants

Grants awarded to organizations located
in Louisiana.

326
J. Edgar Monroe Foundation
228 St. Charles Street, Suite 1402
New Orleans, LA 70130
(504) 529-3539

Building and equipment grants. Social
welfare; health organizations; hospitals

Grants awarded to organizations located
in Louisiana.

327
Salmen Family Foundation
431 Gravier Street, Suite 400
New Orleans, LA 70130
(504) 581-6084

Equipment grants. Secondary education;
Christian School (equipment)

Grants awarded to organizations located
in Louisiana.

328
**Edward G. Schlieder Educational
Foundation**
431 Gravier Street, Suite 400
New Orleans, LA 70130
(504) 581-6179

Building and equipment grants. Higher
education (building expansion and
equipment for the science department);
secondary education (building funds and
equipment for a science lab)

Grants awarded to organizations located
in Louisiana.

Typical grant range: $15,000 to $50,000

329
Fred B. and Ruth B. Zigler Foundation
P.O. Box 986
Jennings, LA 70546
(318) 824-2413

Building and equipment grants.
Hospitals; community development;
recreation; secondary education;
Baptist Church (building funds)

Typical grant range: $500 to $8,000

MAINE

330
George P. Davenport Trust Fund
55 Front Street
Bath, ME 04530
(207) 443-3431

Building and equipment grants.
Community development; hospitals;
health organizations; women; colleges
and universities

Grants awarded to organizations located
in Bath.

Typical grant range: $1,000 to $20,000

331
Maine Community Foundation, Inc.
210 Main Street
P.O. Box 148
Ellsworth, ME 04605
(207) 667-9735

Building and equipment grants. Homeless;
women; libraries; youth organizations;
community development; Churches;
renovation grants

Grants awarded to organizations located
in Maine.

Typical grant range: $250 to $7,500

332
Simmons Foundation, Inc.
One Canal Plaza
Portland, ME 04101
(207) 774-2635

Building and equipment grants. Mental
Health Services (equipment); Library
(equipment); Historical Museum
(equipment); Church (renovation);
Salvation Army (equipment)

Grants awarded to organizations located
in Portland.

333
Warren Memorial Foundation
29 Hillview Road
Gorham, ME 04038
(207) 839-8744

Building and equipment grants. Children's
Museum (build an exhibit); Public Library
(equipment)

Grants awarded to organizations located
in Maine.

Typical grant range: $500 to $2,000

MARYLAND

334
Charles S. Abell Foundation, Inc.
8401 Connecticut Avenue
Chevy Chase, MD 20815
(301) 652-2224

Building and equipment grants. Homeless;
women; disabled; Church (building and
equipment grants for a homeless shelter);
Food Bank (equipment)

Typical grant range: $5,000 to $30,000

335
Abell Foundation, Inc.
1116 Fidelity Building
210 N. Charles Street
Baltimore, MD 21201
(301) 547-1300

Building and equipment grants. Child
welfare; homeless; health organizations;
community development; youth
organizations; Meals on Wheels (building
funds); Adult Literacy Center (equipment,
renovation)

Grants awarded to organizations located
in Maryland, with an emphasis in
Baltimore.

Typical grant range: $3,000 to $50,000

336
William G. Baker, Jr. Memorial Fund
Two E. Read Street, 9th Floor
Baltimore, MD 21202
(301) 332-4171

Building and equipment grants.
Education; cultural organizations

Grants awarded to organizations located
in the Baltimore vicinity.

337
Campbell Foundation, Inc.
100 W. Pennsylvania Avenue
Baltimore, MD 21204

Building grants. Social welfare; child
welfare; health organizations; cultural
organizations

Grants awarded to organizations located
in the Baltimore vicinity.

Typical grant range: $1,500 to $7,000

338
Eugene B. Casey Foundation
800 S. Frederick Avenue, Suite 100
Gaithersburg, MD 20877

Building and equipment grants. Higher
education; hospitals; health organizations;
social welfare; community development

Typical grant range: $15,000 to $120,000

339
Clark-Winchcole Foundation
4550 Montgomery Ave., Suite 345N
Bethesda, MD 20814
(301) 654-3607

Building grants. Social welfare; disabled;
health organizations; Protestant related
organizations

Grants awarded to organizations located
in Howard County.

Typical grant range: $2,000 to $25,000

340
Emmert Hobbs Foundation, Inc.
c/o Friedman & Friedman
409 Washington Ave., Suite 900
Towson, MD 21204

Building and equipment grants. Women;
homeless; youth organizations; higher
education; Meals on Wheels (building
funds); St. Vincent de Paul (building
funds); Salvation Army (building funds);
Mental Health Center (equipment)

Grants awarded to organizations located
in the Baltimore vicinity.

Typical grant range: $2,000 to $10,000

341
Hoffberger Foundation
800 Garrett Building
233 E. Redwood Street
Baltimore, MD 21202
(301) 576-4258

Building and equipment grants. Social
welfare; colleges and universities; Jewish
organizations; disabled; child welfare

Grants awarded to organizations located
in the Baltimore vicinity.

Typical grant range: $500 to $20,000

342
**Marion I. and Henry J. Knott
Foundation, Inc.**
3904 Hickory Avenue
Baltimore, MD 21211
(410) 235-7068

Building and equipment grants.
Community development; secondary
education; higher education; disabled;
Queen of Peace School (building funds);
Children's Guild (building funds)

Typical grant range: $1,000 to $25,000

343
Morton and Sophia Macht Foundation
II E. Fayette Street
Baltimore, MD 21202
(301) 539-2370

Building and equipment grants. Social
welfare; disabled; Jewish organizations

Grants awarded to organizations located
in Maryland.

Typical grant range: $100 to $1,500

344
Middendorf Foundation, Inc.
803 Cathedral Street
Baltimore, MD 21201
(410) 752-7088

Building and equipment grants. Disabled
(equipment); St. Peter's School (building,
equipment); Historical Society
(renovation, furnishings); Church
(building funds); Diocese of Maryland
(equipment, furnishings)

Grants awarded to organizations located
in Maryland.

Typical grant range: $1,000 to $25,000

345
USF&G Foundation, Inc.
100 Light Street
Baltimore, MD 21202
(410) 547-3752

Building grants. Disabled; health organizations; child welfare; cultural organizations; community development; social welfare; colleges and universities; youth organizations

Grants awarded to organizations located in areas of company operations, with an emphasis in Baltimore.

Typical grant range: $1,000 to $25,000

MASSACHUSETTS

346
George I. Alden Trust
370 Main Street, Suite 1250
Worcester, MA 01608
(508) 798-8621

Building and equipment grants. Cultural organizations; higher education; disabled; youth; Public Radio (equipment); YMCA (renovation); Audubon Society (building funds); renovation grants

Most grants awarded to organizations located in the Worcester vicinity.

Typical grant range: $2,000 to $45,000

347
Bank of Boston Corporation
Charitable Foundation
c/o Bank of Boston
100 Federal Street
Boston, MA 02110
(617) 434-2171

Building and equipment grants. Health organizations; social welfare; youth organizations; cultural organizations; colleges and universities; renovation grants

Grants awarded to organizations located in areas of company operations.

348
Boston Edison Foundation
800 Boylston Street
Boston, MA 02199
(617) 424-2235

Building and equipment grants. Cultural organizations; youth organizations; hospitals; higher education

Grants awarded to organizations located in areas of company operations, with an emphasis in Boston.

Typical grant range: $1,000 to $15,000

349
Boston Foundation, Inc.
One Boston Place, 24th Floor
Boston, MA 02108
(617) 723-7415

Building grants. Disabled; homeless; child welfare; cultural organizations; community development; social welfare; health organizations; renovation grants

Grants awarded to organizations located in the Boston vicinity.

Typical grant range: $10,000 to $55,000

350
Cabot Corporation Foundation, Inc.
75 State Street
Boston, MA 02109
(617) 345-0100

Building and equipment grants. Community development; cultural organizations; higher education; health organizations

Grants awarded to organizations located in areas of company operations.

351
Cabot Family Charitable Trust
c/o Cabot Corp.
75 State Street
Boston, MA 02109
(617) 345-0100

Building grants. Cultural organizations; environment; family planning; youth organizations; colleges and universities; renovation grants

Typical grant range: $3,000 to $25,000

352
Bushrod H. Campbell and Adah F. Hall Charity Fund
c/o Palmer & Dodge
One Beacon Street
Boston, MA 02108
(617) 573-0328

Building and equipment grants. Health organizations; homeless; elderly; hospice; hospitals; disabled; renovation grants

Grants awarded to organizations located in the Boston vicinity.

Typical grant range: $2,000 to $10,000

353
Alice P. Chase Trust
Boston Safe Deposit & Trust Co.
One Boston Place
Boston, MA 02108
(617) 722-7340

Building and equipment grants. Environment; youth organizations; elderly; disabled; homeless; higher education; renovation grants

354
Clipper Ship Foundation, Inc.
c/o Hill & Barlow, 100 Oliver Street
One International Plaza, 20th Floor
Boston, MA 02110
(617) 439-3555

Building and equipment grants. Disabled; homeless; women; youth organizations; elderly; child welfare; renovation grants

Grants awarded to organizations located in the Boston vicinity.

Typical grant range: $2,000 to $15,000

355
Eugene A. Dexter Charitable Fund
Community Foundation of Western Massachusetts
BayBank Valley Tower
1500 Main Street, P.O. Box 15769
Springfield, MA 01115

Building and equipment grants. Health organizations; social welfare; youth organizations; disabled; renovation grants

Typical grant range: $3,000 to $30,000

356
Fidelity Foundation
82 Devonshire Street
Boston, MA 02109
(617) 570-6806

Building grants. Disabled; cultural organizations; health organizations; social welfare; elderly; community development

Grants awarded to organizations located in areas of company operations, with an emphasis in Massachusetts.

357
George F. and Sybil H. Fuller Foundation
P.O. Box 252
Boylston, MA 01505

Building grants. Higher education; social welfare; cultural organizations; hospitals; community development

358
Grass Foundation
77 Reservoir Road
Quincy, MA 02170
(617) 773-0002

Equipment grants. Higher education

359
Greater Worcester Community Foundation, Inc.
44 Front Street, Suite 530
Worcester, MA 01608
(508) 755-0980

Building grants. Youth organizations; higher education; health organizations; cultural organizations; renovation grants

Grants awarded to organizations located in the Worcester vicinity.

Typical grant range: $2,000 to $30,000

360
Nan and Matilda Heydt Fund
c/o BayBank Valley Trust Company
P.O. Box 3422
Burlington, MA 01803
(617) 273-1700

Building and equipment grants. Community development; disabled; health organizations; child welfare; renovation grants

361
Hyams Foundation
One Boston Place, 32nd Floor
Boston, MA 02108
(617) 720-2238

Building grants. Youth organizations; community development; cultural organizations; health organizations; renovation grants

Typical grant range: $5,000 to $30,000

362
Island Foundation, Inc.
589 Mill Street
Marion, MA 02738
(508) 748-2809

Building grants. Environment; social welfare; youth organizations; community development; renovation grants

Typical grant range: $2,000 to $15,000

363
Edward Bangs Kelley and Elza Kelley Foundation, Inc.
243 South Street
P.O. Drawer M
Hyannis, MA 02601
(508) 775-3117

Building and equipment grants. Elderly; environment; hospitals; community development; health organizations; child welfare; disabled; youth organizations

Grants awarded to organizations located in Barnstable County.

Typical grant range: $1,000 to $9,000

364
Arthur D. Little Foundation
25 Acorn Park
Cambridge, MA 02140
(617) 498-5524

Building and equipment grants. Higher education; social welfare; Museum of Science (renovation grant)

Grants awarded to organizations located in areas of company operations (Arthur D. Little, Inc.), with an emphasis in Cambridge.

Typical grant range: $1,500 to $5,000

365
Morgan-Worcester, Inc.
15 Belmont Street
Worcester, MA 01605
(508) 755-6111

Building and equipment grants. Cultural organizations; community development

Grants awarded to organizations located in the Worcester vicinity.

366
Thomas Anthony Pappas Charitable Foundation, Inc.
P.O. Box 463
Belmont, MA 02178
(617) 862-2802

Building grants. Higher education; cultural organizations; social welfare; youth organizations; Greek Orthodox Church

Grants awarded to organizations located in Massachusetts.

367
Theodore Edson Parker Foundation
Grants Management Associates, Inc.
230 Congress Street
Boston, MA 02110
(617) 426-7172

Building and equipment grants. Youth organizations; cultural organizations; minorities; social welfare; community development; renovation grants

368
Ellis L. Phillips Foundation
29 Commonwealth Avenue
Boston, MA 02116
(617) 424-7607

Building and equipment grants. Cultural organizations; higher education; social welfare; Whaling Museum (building funds); renovation grants

Typical grant range: $2,000 to $10,000

369
Polaroid Foundation, Inc.
750 Main Street, 2M
Cambridge, MA 02139
(617) 577-4035

Building and equipment grants. Community development; child welfare; disabled; higher education; cultural organizations; youth organizations; hospice; renovation grants

Grants awarded to organizations located in Massachusetts.

Typical grant range: $1,000 to $12,000

370
A.C. Ratshesky Foundation
38 Concord Avenue
Cambridge, MA 02138
(617) 547-4590

Building and equipment grants. Child welfare; disabled; cultural organizations; women; youth organizations; social welfare; renovation grants

371
Mabel Louise Riley Foundation
Grants Management Assocs.
230 Congress St., 3rd Floor
Boston, MA 02110
(617) 426-7172

Building and equipment grants. Social welfare; cultural organizations; women; health organizations; youth organizations; disabled; renovation grants

Most grants awarded to organizations located in the Boston vicinity.

Typical grant range: $10,000 to $90,000

372
State Street Foundation
c/o State Street Bank and Trust Co.
P.O. Box 351
Boston, MA 02101
(617) 654-3381

Building and equipment grants. Youth
organizations; culture; social welfare;
hospitals; community development;
health organizations; higher education

Grants awarded to organizations located
in Massachusetts.

Typical grant range: $5,000 to $75,000

373
Albert Steiger Memorial Fund, Inc.
1477 Main Street
Springfield, MA 01101

Building grants. Health organizations;
culture; higher education; community
development; youth organizations

374
Abbot and Dorothy Stevens Foundation
P.O. Box 111
N. Andover, MA 01845
(508) 688-7211

Building and equipment grants. Social
welfare; cultural organizations; disabled;
youth organizations; health organizations

Grants awarded to organizations located
in Massachusetts.

Typical grant range: $2,000 to $10,000

375
**Nathaniel and Elizabeth P. Stevens
Foundation**
P.O. Box 111
N. Andover, MA 01845
(508) 688-7211

Building and equipment grants. Social
welfare; cultural organizations; health
organizations; renovation grants

Grants awarded to organizations located
in Massachusetts.

Typical grant range: $1,000 to $11,000

376
Stoddard Charitable Trust
370 Main Street
Worcester, MA 01608
(617) 798-8621

Building and equipment grants. Social
welfare; community development; cultural
organizations; youth organizations; higher
education; renovation grants

Grants awarded to organizations located
in the Worcester vicinity.

377
Stone Charitable Foundation, Inc.
P.O. Box 728
Wareham, MA 02571

Building and equipment grants. Cultural
organizations; hospitals; higher education;
health organizations

Grants awarded to organizations located
in Massachusetts.

378
Totsy Foundation
P.O. Box 509
Holyoke, MA 01041

Building grants. Youth organizations;
Jewish related organizations

379
Blanche M. Walsh Charity Trust
174 Central Street, Suite 329
Lowell, MA 01852
(508) 454-5654

Building and equipment grants. Elderly;
youth organizations; Catholic
organizations

Typical grant range: $500 to $3,000

380
Edwin S. Webster Foundation
Grants Management Associates, Inc.
230 Congress Street, 3rd Floor
Boston, MA 02110
(617) 426-7172

Building and equipment grants. Social
welfare; youth organizations; child
welfare; community development;
cultural organizations; hospitals; health
organizations

Most grants awarded to organizations
located in the Boston vicinity.

381
Wyman-Gordon Foundation
244 Worcester Street
P.O. Box 8001
North Grafton, MA 01536
(508) 756-5111

Building grants. Higher education;
cultural organizations; hospitals; social
welfare

Grants awarded to organizations located
in areas of company operations.

MICHIGAN

382
Battle Creek Community Foundation
One Riverwalk Center
34 W. Jackson Street
Battle Creek, MI 49017
(616) 962-2181

Building and equipment grants. Youth
organizations; disabled; recreation;
cultural organizations; community
development; social welfare; minorities;
health organizations; Salvation Army
(equipment); renovation grants

Grants awarded to organizations located
in the Battle Creek vicinity.

Typical grant range: $1,000 to $20,000

383
Bauervic-Paisley Foundation
2855 Coolidge Highway, Suite 100
Troy, MI 48084

Building and equipment grants. Health
organizations; higher education; hospitals;
culture; youth; renovation grants

Typical grant range: $1,000 to $15,000

384
Besser Foundation
123 N. Second Avenue, Suite 4
Alpena, MI 49707
(517) 354-4722

Building and equipment grants. Higher
education; culture; child welfare; social
welfare; health organizations

Most grants awarded to organizations
located in Alpena.

Typical grant range: $4,000 to $50,000

385
Chrysler Corporation Fund
12000 Chrysler Drive
Highland Park, MI 48288
(313) 956-5194

Building grants. Higher education;
cultural organizations; health
organizations; community development

Grants awarded to organizations located
in areas of company operations.

386
**Community Foundation for
Southeastern Michigan**
333 W. Fort Street, Suite 2010
Detroit, MI 48226
(313) 961-6675

Building and equipment grants. Cultural
organizations; hospitals; social welfare;
child welfare; health organizations;
elderly; disabled; Churches

Grants awarded in the following Counties:
Wayne, Oakland, Macomb, Washtenaw,
St. Clair, Monroe, Livingston.

Typical grant range: $1,000 to $25,000

387

Dorothy U. Dalton Foundation, Inc.
c/o Arcadia Bank
P.O. Box 50566
Kalamazoo, MI 49003

Building and equipment grants. Health
organizations; homeless; community
development; cultural organizations;
youth organizations; higher education;
social welfare; disabled; libraries;
renovation grants

Grants awarded to organizations located in
Kalamazoo County.

Typical grant range: $5,000 to $30,000

388

Detroit Edison Foundation
2000 Second Avenue, #642 WCB
Detroit, MI 48226
(313) 237-9271

Building grants. Higher education; child
welfare; youth organizations; cultural
organizations; social welfare

Grants awarded to organizations located in
areas of company operations.

Typical grant range: $3,000 to $20,000

389

Domino's Foundation
30 Frank Lloyd Wright Dr.
P.O. Box 997
Ann Arbor, MI 48106

Building grants. Youth organizations;
higher education; community
development; Churches; renovation grants

Typical grant range: $25,000 to $120,000

390

Eleanor and Edsel Ford Fund
100 Renaissance Center, 34th Floor
Detroit, MI 48243

Building grants. Higher education;
community development; cultural
organizations; animal welfare

Grants awarded to organizations located
in Detroit.

391

Ford Motor Company Fund
The American Road
Dearborn, MI 48121
(313) 845-8711

Building and equipment grants. Social
welfare; higher education; hospitals;
community development; cultural
organizations

Grants awarded to organizations located
in areas of company operations, with an
emphasis in Detroit.

Typical grant range: $1,500 to $30,000

392

Fremont Area Foundation
108 South Stewart
Fremont, MI 49412
(616) 924-5350

Building and equipment grants. Child
welfare; health organizations; cultural
organizations; community development;
youth organizations; renovation grants

Typical grant range: $2,000 to $20,000

393

Frey Foundation
48 Fountain Street, N.W.
Grand Rapids, MI 49503
(616) 451-0303

Building and equipment grants.
Child welfare; youth organizations;
environment; higher education; social
welfare; women; elderly; cultural
organizations; hospitals; health
organizations; disabled; community
development; renovation grants

394
General Motors Foundation, Inc.
13-145 General Motors Building
3044 W. Grand Blvd.
Detroit, MI 48202
(313) 556-4260

Building and equipment grants. Health organizations; higher education; social welfare; disabled; youth organizations; cultural organizations; community development; hospitals; renovation grants

Grants awarded to organizations located in areas of company operations.

Typical grant range: $2,000 to $125,000

395
Rollin M. Gerstacker Foundation
P.O. Box 1945
Midland, MI 48640
(517) 631-6097

Building and equipment grants. Health organizations; community development; disabled; cultural organizations; elderly; youth organizations; higher education

Typical grant range: $5,000 to $50,000

396
Irving S. Gilmore Foundation
136 E. Michigan Avenue, Suite 615
Kalamazoo, MI 49007
(616) 342-6411

Building and equipment grants. Social welfare; cultural organizations; child welfare; youth organizations; elderly; health organizations; higher education; community development; Churches; Crisis Pregnancy Center (renovation); Child Care Center (equipment); Senior Services (equipment); renovation grants

Grants awarded to organizations located in the Kalamazoo vicinity.

Typical grant range: $20,000 to $150,000

397
Grand Haven Area Community Foundation, Inc.
One South Harbor
Grand Haven, MI 49417
(616) 842-6378

Building and equipment grants. Environment; social welfare; youth organizations; women; community development; American Red Cross (mannequins for CPR and First Aid courses); Center for Women in Transition (renovation)

Typical grant range: $1,000 to $12,000

398
Grand Rapids Foundation
209-C Waters Building
161 Ottawa, N.W.
Grand Rapids, MI 49503
(616) 454-1751

Building and equipment grants. Animal welfare; child welfare; youth organizations; environment; health organizations; community development; cultural organizations; higher education; renovation grants

Grants awarded to organizations located in the Grand Rapids vicinity.

Typical grant range: $5,000 to $75,000

399
Herrick Foundation
150 W. Jefferson, Suite 2500
Detroit, MI 48226
(313) 496-7656

Building and equipment grants. Cultural organizations; health organizations; hospitals; community development; higher education; youth organizations; child welfare; Protestant organizations; renovation grants

Grants awarded to organizations located in Michigan.

Typical grant range: $5,000 to $75,000

400
James and Lynelle Holden Fund
802 E. Big Beaver
Troy, MI 48083

Building and equipment grants. Elderly;
health organizations; child welfare;
cultural organizations; hospitals; youth
organizations; higher education

Grants awarded to organizations located
in Michigan.

Typical grant range: $4,000 to $30,000

401
Hudson-Webber Foundation
333 W. Fort Street, Suite 1310
Detroit, MI 48226
(313) 963-7777

Building and equipment grants. Museums;
performing arts; child welfare; hospitals;
higher education; social welfare; health
organizations; community development;
renovation grants

Grants awarded to organizations located
in the Detroit vicinity.

Typical grant range: $15,000 to $50,000

402
Jackson Community Foundation
230 W. Michigan Avenue
Jackson, MI 49201
(517) 787-1321

Building and equipment grants. Higher
education; social welfare; child welfare;
cultural organizations; disabled; youth
organizations; Girl Scouts (building
funds)

Grants awarded to organizations located
in Jackson County.

Typical grant range: $1,500 to $25,000

403
Kalamazoo Foundation
151 S. Rose St., Suite 332
Kalamazoo, MI 49007
(616) 381-4416

Building and equipment grants. Youth
organizations; child welfare; social
welfare; community development; higher
education; health organizations; hospitals;
cultural organizations; recreation;
Goodwill Industries (renovation); United
Way (building funds); Boys & Girls Club
(building funds); renovation grants

Grants awarded to organizations located
in Kalamazoo County.

404
Kantzler Foundation
900 Center Avenue
Bay City, MI 48708
(517) 892-0591

Building and equipment grants.
Community development; recreation;
health organizations; women; youth
organizations; social welfare; disabled;
higher education

Grants awarded to organizations located
in the Bay City vicinity.

Typical grant range: $5,000 to $50,000

405
Louis G. Kaufman Endowment Fund
MFC First National Bank
P.O. Box 580
Marquette, MI 49855
(906) 228-1244

Building grants. Community
development; youth organizations;
secondary education; renovation grants

Grants awarded to organizations located
in Marquette.

Typical grant range: $1,000 to $9,000

406
Kresge Foundation
P.O. Box 3151
3215 W. Big Beaver Road
Troy, MI 48007
(313) 643-9630

Building and equipment grants. Social welfare; performing arts; museums; higher education; youth organizations; disabled; child welfare; hospitals; health organizations; community development; environment; animal welfare; Nature Conservancy (building funds); Catholic Charities (building funds); renovation grants

Typical grant range: $125,000 to $600,000

407
McGregor Fund
333 West Fort Street, Suite 1380
Detroit, MI 48226
(313) 963-3495

Building and equipment grants. Higher education; social welfare; child welfare; cultural organizations; women; health organizations; hospitals; disabled; elderly; homeless; renovation grants

Grants awarded to organizations located in Detroit.

Typical grant range: $20,000 to $60,000

408
Midland Foundation
812 W. Main Street
P.O. Box 289
Midland, MI 48640
(517) 839-9661

Building and equipment grants. Social welfare; education; culture; community development; elderly; youth; City of Midland (building funds); West Midland Family Center (van); Community Center (equipment); Habitat for Humanity (building funds)

Grants awarded to organizations located in Midland County.

409
Frances Goll Mills Fund
Second National Bank of Saginaw
101 N. Washington Avenue
Saginaw, MI 48607
(517) 776-7582

Building and equipment grants. Health organizations; higher education; hospitals; social welfare; Churches

Grants awarded to organizations located in Saginaw County.

Typical grant range: $1,000 to $9,000

410
Morley Brothers Foundation
One Tuscola Street
P.O. Box 2485
Saginaw, MI 48605
(517) 753-3438

Building and equipment grants. Health organizations; hospitals; community development; cultural organizations; secondary education; higher education; youth organizations

Grants awarded to organizations located in the Saginaw vicinity.

411
Charles Stewart Mott Foundation
1200 Mott Foundation Building
Flint, MI 48502
(313) 238-5651

Building grants. Community development; higher education; minorities; renovation grants

Typical grant range: $15,000 to $150,000

412
Muskegon County Community Foundation, Inc.
Community Foundation Building
425 W. Western Avenue
Muskegon, MI 49440
(616) 722-4538

Building and equipment grants. Cultural organizations; social welfare; health organizations; disabled; renovation grants

Grants awarded to organizations located in Muskegon County.

Typical grant range: $2,000 to $25,000

413
May Mitchell Royal Foundation
c/o Comerica Bank-Midland
201 McDonald Street
Midland, MI 48640

Building and equipment grants. Hospitals; health organizations; child welfare; social welfare; disabled

Typical grant range: $2,000 to $15,000

414
Saginaw Community Foundation
118 E. Genesee
Saginaw, MI 48607
(517) 755-0545

Building and equipment grants. Community development; child welfare; women; recreation; culture; youth

Grants awarded to organizations located in Saginaw County.

415
Skillman Foundation
333 West Fort St., Suite 1350
Detroit, MI 48226
(313) 961-8850

Building and equipment grants. Child welfare; health organizations; disabled; culture; elderly; social welfare; homeless; community development; minorities; higher education; youth organizations; hospitals; recreation; renovation grants

Typical grant range: $25,000 to $150,000

416
Steelcase Foundation
P.O. Box 1967
Grand Rapids, MI 49507
(616) 246-4695

Building grants. Social welfare; higher education; disabled; cultural organizations

Grants awarded to organizations located in areas of company operations.

417
Charles J. Strosacker Foundation
P.O. Box 471
Midland, MI 48640

Building and equipment grants. Cultural organizations; child welfare; higher education; disabled; elderly; social welfare; recreation

Grants awarded to organizations located in Michigan.

Typical grant range: $3,000 to $45,000

418
Harry A. and Margaret D. Towsley Foundation
Plymouth Orchard Building, Suite 200
3055 Plymouth Road
Ann Arbor, MI 48105
(313) 662-6777

Building grants. Health organizations; social welfare; child welfare; elderly; higher education

Typical grant range: $5,000 to $75,000

419
Whirlpool Foundation
400 Riverview Drive, Suite 410
Benton Harbor, MI 49022
(616) 923-5112

Building and equipment grants. Social welfare; culture; disabled; higher education; community development

Grants awarded to organizations located in areas of company operations.

Typical grant range: $1,000 to $20,000

420
Whiting Foundation
901 Citizens Bank Building
328 South Saginaw Street
Flint, MI 48502
(313) 767-3600

Building and equipment grants.
Education; youth organizations; social
welfare; community development; cultural
organizations; Planned Parenthood
(renovation); Home for Boys (vehicle);
Board of Education (equipment for an
auditorium); renovation grants

Grants awarded to organizations located
in the Flint vicinity.

Typical grant range: $250 to $20,000

421
Harvey Randall Wickes Foundation
Plaza North, Suite 472
4800 Fashion Square Blvd.
Saginaw, MI 48604
(517) 799-1850

Building and equipment grants. Youth
organizations; cultural organizations;
community organizations; hospitals;
health organizations; homeless; child
welfare; recreation; social welfare; higher
education; Public Library (building
funds); Salvation Army (equipment);
Catholic Family Services (equipment);
renovation grants

Grants awarded to organizations located
in the Saginaw vicinity.

Typical grant range: $5,000 to $40,000

MINNESOTA

422
AHS Foundation
c/o First Trust, N.A.
P.O. Box 64704
St. Paul, MN 55164
(612) 291-5128

Building grants. Higher education;
disabled; child welfare; social welfare;
community development; youth
organizations

Typical grant range: $2,000 to $8,000

423
Hugh J. Andersen Foundation
287 Central Avenue
Bayport, MN 55003
(612) 439-1557

Equipment grants. Social welfare; health
organizations; cultural organizations;
disabled; hospitals

Typical grant range: $2,000 to $25,000

424
Athwin Foundation
4900 IDS Tower
80 South 8th Street
Minneapolis, MN 55402
(612) 340-3616

Building grants. Youth organizations;
community development; cultural
organizations; homeless; disabled; health
organizations; higher education; Churches

Grants awarded to organizations located
in the Minneapolis-St. Paul vicinity.

Typical grant range: $2,000 to $25,000

425
Bemis Company Foundation
222 S. Ninth Street, Suite 2300
Minneapolis, MN 55402
(612) 340-6198

Building grants. Cultural organizations;
community development; disabled; social
welfare; higher education; hospitals

Grants awarded to organizations located
in areas of company operations.

426
F.R. Bigelow Foundation
600 Norwest Center
St. Paul, MN 55101
(612) 224-5463

Building grants. Higher education;
cultural organizations; minorities; social
welfare; hospitals; elderly; renovation
grants

Grants awarded to organizations located
in the St. Paul vicinity.

Typical grant range: $5,000 to $50,000

427
Blandin Foundation
100 Pokegama Avenue North
Grand Rapids, MN 55744
(218) 326-0523

Building and equipment grants. Health
organizations; community development;
cultural organizations; recreation;
Churches

Grants awarded to organizations located
in Minnesota.

Typical grant range: $5,000 to $75,000

428
Otto Bremer Foundation
445 Minnesota Street, Suite 2000
St. Paul, MN 55101
(612) 227-8036

Building and equipment grants.
Community development; minorities;
youth organizations; health organizations;
recreation; higher education; disabled;
social welfare; child welfare; Public
Library (building funds); Domestic
Violence Crisis Center (van); Boys and
Girls Clubs (building funds); renovation
grants

Grants awarded to organizations located
in areas of company operations (Bremer
Bank).

Typical grant range: $2,000 to $20,000

429
Bush Foundation
E. 900 First National Bank Bldg.
332 Minnesota Street
St. Paul, MN 55101
(612) 227-0891

Building and equipment grants. Social
welfare; women; youth organizations;
minorities; higher education; renovation
grants

Typical grant range: $30,000 to $100,000

430
**Patrick and Aimee Butler Family
Foundation**
First National Bank Bldg.
332 Minnesota St., E-1420
St. Paul, MN 55101
(612) 222-2565

Building grants. Cultural organizations;
higher education; social welfare; women;
elderly

Grants awarded to organizations located
in the Minneapolis-St. Paul vicinity.

431
Cargill Foundation
P.O. Box 5690
Minneapolis, MN 55440
(612) 472-6209

Building grants. Social welfare; youth
organizations; higher education; cultural
organizations; disabled; environment

Grants awarded to organizations located
in the Minneapolis-St. Paul vicinity.

Typical grant range: $5,000 to $35,000

432
Carolyn Foundation
4800 First Bank Place
Minneapolis, MN 55402
(612) 339-7101

Building and equipment grants. Youth
organizations; cultural organizations;
social welfare; disabled; community
development; environment; renovation
grants

Typical grant range: $5,000 to $30,000

433
Albert W. Cherne Foundation
P.O. Box 975
Minneapolis, MN 55440
(612) 944-4378

Building grants. Higher education;
cultural organizations; social welfare;
disabled

Grants awarded to organizations located
in the Minneapolis-St. Paul vicinity.

434
Cowles Media Foundation
329 Portland Avenue
Minneapolis, MN 55415
(612) 673-7051

Building and equipment grants. Social
welfare; cultural organizations; disabled;
child welfare; youth organizations;
minorities; renovation grants

Grants awarded to organizations located
in Minneapolis.

Typical grant range: $2,000 to $20,000

435
Dayton Hudson Foundation
777 Nicollet Mall
Minneapolis, MN 55402
(612) 370-6555

Building and equipment grants. Cultural
organizations; minorities; child welfare;
youth organizations; social welfare;
community development; Bridge for
Runaway Youth (renovation); Zoological
Garden (building funds); renovation
grants

Grants awarded to organizations located
in areas of company operations.

Typical grant range: $5,000 to $80,000

436
Deluxe Corporation Foundation
P.O. Box 64399
St. Paul, MN 55164
(612) 483-7842

Building and equipment grants. Cultural
organizations; disabled; hospitals; higher
education; youth organizations; homeless;
elderly; women; animal welfare; child
welfare; social welfare; renovation grants

Grants awarded to organizations located
in areas of company operations.

Typical grant range: $1,000 to $14,000

437
**Duluth-Superior Area Community
Foundation**
618 Missabe Building
227 W. First Street
Duluth, MN 55802
(218) 726-0232

Building and equipment grants. Animal
welfare; disabled; social welfare; child
welfare

Typical grant range: $1,000 to $9,000

438

Edwards Memorial Trust
c/o First Trust, N.A.
P.O. Box 64704
St. Paul, MN 55164
(612) 291-6043

Building and equipment grants. Hospitals; health organizations; disabled; social welfare; renovation grants

Grants awarded to organizations located in the Minneapolis-St. Paul vicinity.

Typical grant range: $3,000 to $15,000

439

First Bank System Foundation
P.O. Box 522
Minneapolis, MN 55480

Building and equipment grants. Social welfare; cultural organizations; youth organizations; community development; disabled; Public Library; renovation grants

Grants awarded to organizations located in areas of company operations.

Typical grant range: $1,000 to $8,000

440

General Mills Foundation
P.O. Box 1113
Minneapolis, MN 55440
(612) 540-7891

Building and equipment grants. Cultural organizations; community development; youth organizations; higher education; hospitals; homeless; disabled; renovation grants

Grants awarded to organizations located in areas of company operations, with an emphasis in Minneapolis.

Typical grant range: $3,000 to $25,000

441

Graco Foundation
P.O. Box 1441
Minneapolis, MN 55440
(612) 623-6684

Building grants. Community development; social welfare; higher education; secondary education; elderly; hospitals; youth organizations; animal welfare

Grants awarded to organizations located in areas of company operations.

Typical grant range: $1,000 to $5,000

442

Grand Metropolitan Food Sector Foundation
Mail Station 37X5
200 S. Sixth Street
Minneapolis, MN 55402
(612) 330-5434

Building and equipment grants. Community development; health organizations; disabled; social welfare; recreation; youth organizations; all levels of education

Grants awarded to organizations located in areas of company operations (Pillsbury Company).

Typical grant range: $1,000 to $20,000

443

Honeywell Foundation
Honeywell Plaza
P.O. Box 524
Minneapolis, MN 55440
(612) 951-2368

Building grants. Disabled; community development; women; higher education; cultural organizations; elderly; health organizations; social welfare; youth organizations; renovation grants

Grants awarded to organizations located in areas of company operations, with an emphasis in Minneapolis.

Typical grant range: $1,000 to $25,000

444
Emma B. Howe Memorial Foundation
A200 Foshay Tower
821 Marquette Avenue
Minneapolis, MN 55402
(612) 339-7343

Building grants. Youth organizations;
disabled; health organizations; hospitals;
renovation grants

Grants awarded to organizations located
in Minnesota.

Typical grant range: $5,000 to $30,000

445
MAHADH Foundation
287 Central Avenue
Bayport, MN 55003
(612) 439-1557

Building grants. Cultural organizations;
homeless; disabled; social welfare;
environment; higher education

446
Marbrook Foundation
400 Baker Building
Minneapolis, MN 55402
(612) 332-2454

Building and equipment grants. Social
welfare; disabled; higher education;
culture; youth organizations; renovation
grants

Typical grant range: $1,000 to $15,000

447
Mardag Foundation
600 Norwest Center
St. Paul, MN 55101
(612) 224-5463

Building and equipment grants. Higher
education; minorities; child welfare;
elderly; environment; youth organizations;
social welfare; cultural organizations;
renovation grants

Grants awarded to organizations located
in Minnesota.

Typical grant range: $5,000 to $50,000

448
McKnight Foundation
600 TCF Tower
121 S. Eighth Street
Minneapolis, MN 55402
(612) 333-4220

Building and equipment grants. Social
welfare; cultural organizations; youth
organizations; child welfare; community
development; homeless; environment;
minorities; AIDS; Churches; renovation
grants

Grants awarded to organizations located
in Minnesota.

Typical grant range: $20,000 to $200,000

449
Minneapolis Foundation
A200 Foshay Tower
821 Marquette Avenue South
Minneapolis, MN 55402
(612) 339-7343

Building and equipment grants.
Community development; child welfare;
minorities; disabled; health organizations;
youth organizations; social welfare;
renovation grants

Grants awarded to organizations located
in the Minneapolis-St. Paul vicinity.

Typical grant range: $1,000 to $25,000

450
**Minnesota Mining and Manufacturing
Foundation, Inc.**
3 M Center Building 591-30-02
St. Paul, MN 55144

Building and equipment grants. Cultural
organizations; youth organizations; higher
education; community development;
disabled; elderly; women; minorities;
environment; social welfare

Grants awarded to organizations located
in areas of company operations.

451
Alice M. O'Brien Foundation
324 Forest
Mahtomedi, MN 55115
(612) 426-2143

Building and equipment grants. Higher education; disabled; social welfare

Grants awarded to organizations located in Minnesota.

Typical grant range: $1,000 to $8,000

452
Casey Albert T. O'Neil Foundation
c/o First Trust, N.A.
P.O. Box 64704
St. Paul, MN 55164
(612) 291-5139

Building and equipment grants. Youth organizations; disabled; child welfare; health organizations

Grants awarded to organizations located in the St. Paul vicinity.

Typical grant range: $1,500 to $15,000

453
I.A. O'Shaughnessy Foundation, Inc.
c/o First Trust, N.A.
P.O. Box 64704
St. Paul, MN 55164
(612) 222-2323

Building and equipment grants. Higher education; cultural organizations; youth organizations; health organizations; Catholic organizations; renovation grants

Typical grant range: $5,000 to $65,000

454
Ordean Foundation
501 Ordean Building
424 W. Superior Street
Duluth, MN 55802
(218) 726-4785

Building and equipment grants. Homeless; health organizations; disabled; community development; youth organizations; women; elderly; minorities; Churches

Typical grant range: $500 to $25,000

455
Jay and Rose Phillips Family Foundation
2345 N.E. Kennedy Street
Minneapolis, MN 55413
(612) 623-1654

Building and equipment grants. Social welfare; hospitals; health organizations; disabled; higher education

Grants awarded to organizations located in Minnesota.

Typical grant range: $1,000 to $15,000

456
Elizabeth C. Quinlan Foundation, Inc.
5217 Wayzata Blvd., Suite 200
St. Louis Park, MN 55416
(612) 544-6956

Building and equipment grants. Social welfare; higher education; cultural organizations; Roman Catholic organizations

457
Red Wing Shoe Company Foundation
314 Main Street
Red Wing, MN 55066
(612) 388-8211

Building grants. Environment; health organizations; disabled; cultural organizations; community development

458
Rochester Area Foundation
220 S. Broadway, Suite 112
Rochester, MN 55904
(507) 282-0203

Building and equipment grants. Youth organizations; community development; cultural organizations; disabled; child welfare; health organizations; hospitals; elderly; social welfare; environment; Christian Ranch (renovation)

Grants awarded to organizations located in Olmstead County.

Typical grant range: $1,000 to $11,000

459
Saint Paul Foundation, Inc.
600 Norwest Center
St. Paul, MN 55101
(612) 224-5464

Building and equipment grants. Disabled;
higher education; youth organizations;
cultural organizations; social welfare;
health organizations; community
development; Catholic Charities Day Care
Center (building funds); renovation grants

Grants awarded to organizations located
in the St. Paul vicinity.

Typical grant range: $1,000 to $30,000

460
Wasie Foundation
Foshay Tower
Minneapolis, MN 55402
(612) 332-3883

Building grants. Disabled; higher
education

Grants awarded to organizations located
in the Minneapolis-St. Paul vicinity.

MISSISSIPPI

461
**First Mississippi Corporation
Foundation, Inc.**
700 North Street
P.O. Box 1249
Jackson, MS 39215
(601) 948-7550

Building and equipment grants.
Community development; youth
organizations; higher education

Grants awarded to organizations located
in areas of company operations.

462
Phil Hardin Foundation
c/o Citizens National Bank
P.O. Box 911
Meridian, MS 39302
(601) 483-4282

Building and equipment grants. All levels
of education; disabled; child welfare;
cultural organizations

Grants awarded to organizations located
in Mississippi.

Typical grant range: $5,000 to $40,000

MISSOURI

463
H & R Block Foundation
4410 Main Street
Kansas City, MO 64111
(816) 753-6900

Building and equipment grants. Higher
education; cultural organizations;
community development; youth
organizations; social welfare; health
organizations; disabled

Grants awarded to organizations located
in the Kansas City vicinity.

464
Brown Group, Inc. Charitable Trust
8400 Maryland Avenue
Clayton, MO 63105
(314) 854-4093

Building and equipment grants. Cultural
organizations; community development;
health organizations; hospitals; higher
education; youth organizations;
renovation grants

Grants awarded to organizations located
in areas of company operations, with an
emphasis in the St. Louis vicinity.

Typical grant range: $100 to $12,000

465
Community Foundation, Inc.
901 St. Louis Street, Suite 303
Springfield, MO 65806
(417) 864-6199

Building and equipment grants. Cultural organizations; disabled; social welfare; child welfare; homeless; community development; youth organizations; elderly; Autism (equipment); Regional Girls' Shelter (furniture); renovation grants

Grants awarded to organizations located in the City of Springfield and Greene County.

466
Louetta M. Cowden Foundation
Boatmen's First National Bank of Kansas City
14 W. Tenth Street
Kansas City, MO 64183
(816) 691-7481

Building and equipment grants. Hospitals; child welfare; cultural organizations

Grants awarded to organizations located in the Kansas City vicinity.

467
Harry Edison Foundation
501 North Broadway
St. Louis, MO 63102
(314) 331-6540

Building grants. Social welfare; disabled; cultural organizations; higher education; hospitals; youth organizations; health organizations; Jewish organizations

Grants awarded to organizations located in the St. Louis vicinity.

468
Enterprise Leasing Foundation
35 Hunter Avenue
St. Louis, MO 63124
(314) 863-7000

Building grants. Cultural organizations; community development; disabled; youth organizations; child welfare

Typical grant range: $1,000 to $15,000

469
Milton W. Feld Charitable Trust
2345 Grand Avenue, Suite 2800
Kansas City, MO 64108
(816) 292-2124

Building grants. Disabled; social welfare; cultural organizations; Jewish related organizations; renovation grants

Most grants awarded to organizations located in Kansas City and St. Louis.

Typical grant range: $1,000 to $11,000

470
Forster-Powers Charitable Trust
4635 Wyandotte, Suite 206
Kansas City, MO 64112

Building grants. Higher education; social welfare; disabled; Churches; renovation grants

471
Catherine Manley Gaylord Foundation
314 N. Broadway, Room 1230
St. Louis, MO 63102
(314) 421-0181

Building and equipment grants. Higher education; social welfare; cultural organizations; youth organizations; child welfare; health organizations; Churches

Grants awarded to organizations located in the St. Louis vicinity.

Typical grant range: $300 to $3,500

472
Allen P. and Josephine B. Green
Foundation
P.O. Box 523
Mexico, MO 65265
(314) 581-5568

Building and equipment grants. Youth
organizations; child welfare; cultural
organizations; higher education; women;
elderly; recreation; community
development; animal welfare; renovation
grants

Grants awarded to organizations located
in the Mexico, Missouri vicinity.

Typical grant range: $3,000 to $20,000

473
Hall Family Foundations
Charitable & Crown Investment - 323
P.O. Box 419580
Kansas City, MO 64141
(816) 274-8516

Building and equipment grants. Child
welfare; minorities; social welfare;
cultural organizations; disabled; health
organizations; homeless; elderly; higher
education; community development;
youth organizations; renovation grants

Typical grant range: $15,000 to $200,000

474
Hallmark Corporate Foundation
P.O. Box 419580, Mail Drop 323
Kansas City, MO 64141

Building grants. Cultural organizations;
community development; hospitals; health
organizations; renovation grants

Typical grant range: $2,000 to $25,000

475
Mary Ranken Jordan and Ettie A.
Jordan Charitable Foundation
c/o Mercantile Bank, N.A.
P.O. Box 387
St. Louis, MO 63166
(314) 231-7626

Building grants. Higher education; social
welfare; cultural organizations; health
organizations

Grants awarded to organizations located
in Missouri.

Typical grant range: $5,000 to $50,000

476
Laclede Gas Charitable Trust
720 Olive Street, Room 1525
St. Louis, MO 63101
(314) 342-0859

Building and equipment grants. Cultural
organizations; disabled; social welfare;
higher education; secondary education;
elderly; women; child welfare; hospitals

Grants awarded to organizations located
in areas of company operations.

477
McDonnell Douglas Foundation
P.O. Box 516, Mail Code 1001510
St. Louis, MO 63166
(314) 232-8464

Building and equipment grants. All
levels of education; social welfare;
health organizations; environment;
youth organizations; homeless; cultural
organizations

Grants awarded to organizations located
in areas of company operations.

Typical grant range: $5,000 to $12,000

478
Monsanto Fund
800 North Lindbergh Blvd.
St. Louis, MO 63167

Building and equipment grants. Social
welfare; disabled; elderly; hospitals;
recreation; community development;
higher education; cultural organizations;
homeless

Grants awarded to organizations located
in areas of company operations.

Typical grant range: $500 to $11,000

479
Oppenstein Brothers Foundation
911 Main Street, Suite 100
P.O. Box 13095
Kansas City, MO 64199
(816) 234-8671

Equipment grants. Community
development; social welfare; health
organizations; cultural organizations;
child welfare; secondary education;
homeless; women; renovation grants

Grants awarded to organizations located
in the Kansas City vicinity.

480
**PET Incorporated Community
Support Foundation**
400 South Fourth St.
St. Louis, MO 63102
(314) 621-5400

Building and equipment grants. Youth
organizations; cultural organizations

Grants awarded to organizations
located in Missouri, with an emphasis
in St. Louis.

Typical grant range: $2,000 to $15,000

481
**Pulitzer Publishing Company
Foundation**
900 N. Tucker Blvd.
St. Louis, MO 63101
(314) 622-7000

Building and equipment grants. Cultural
organizations; social welfare; higher
education

Most grants awarded to organizations
located in the St. Louis vicinity.

482
J.B. Reynolds Foundation
3520 Broadway
P.O. Box 139
Kansas City, MO 64111
(816) 753-7000

Building and equipment grants.
Community development; social welfare;
cultural organizations; recreation; higher
education

Grants awarded to organizations located
in the Kansas City vicinity.

Typical grant range: $500 to $15,000

483
**John W. and Effie E. Speas
Memorial Trust**
c/o Boatmen's First National Bank of
Kansas City
14 W. Tenth Street
Kansas City, MO 64183
(816) 691-7481

Building and equipment grants. Health
organizations; child welfare; elderly;
disabled; higher education; renovation
grants

Most grants awarded to organizations
located in the Kansas City vicinity.

Typical grant range: $5,000 to $80,000

484
Victor E. Speas Foundation
Boatmen's First National Bank of
Kansas City
14 W. Tenth Street
Kansas City, MO 64183
(816) 691-7481

Building and equipment grants. Disabled;
elderly; youth organizations; higher
education; health organizations; women;
child welfare; Churches; renovation grants

Grants awarded to organizations located
in the Kansas City vicinity.

485
St. Louis Community Foundation
818 Olive Street, Suite 935
St. Louis, MO 63101
(314) 241-2703

Equipment grants. Cultural organizations;
minorities; disabled; child welfare; youth
organizations; homeless; social welfare;
health organizations; environment

Grants awarded to organizations located
in the St. Louis vicinity.

Typical grant range: $500 to $9,000

486
Lester T. Sunderland Foundation
8080 Ward Parkway, Suite 155
Kansas City, MO 64114
(913) 451-8900

Building and equipment grants. Hospitals;
youth organizations; higher education;
community development

487
Sunnen Foundation
7910 Manchester Avenue
St. Louis, MO 63143
(314) 781-2100

Building and equipment grants. Disabled;
youth organizations; renovation grants

488
Courtney S. Turner Charitable Trust
c/o Boatmen's First National Bank of
Kansas City
P.O. Box 419038
Kansas City, MO 64183
(816) 691-7481

Building grants. Higher education;
hospitals; cultural organizations; youth
organizations; community development;
renovation grants

Typical grant range: $3,000 to $80,000

489
**Union Electric Company
Charitable Trust**
1901 Chouteau Street
P.O. Box 149
St. Louis, MO 63166
(314) 621-3222

Building and equipment grants. Cultural
organizations; social welfare; community
development; higher education; hospitals;
youth organizations; elderly; renovation
grants

Grants awarded to organizations located
in areas of company operations.

Typical grant range: $5,000 to $35,000

490
Dennis R. Washington Foundation, Inc.
P.O. Box 7067
Missoula, MO 59807
(406) 523-1300

Building and equipment grants. Hospitals;
youth organizations; elderly; recreation;
cultural organizations

491
Lyndon C. Whitaker Charitable Foundation
120 S. Central Street, Suite 1122
St. Louis, MO 63105
(314) 726-5734

Building and equipment grants. Elderly; higher education; disabled; health organizations; child welfare; renovation grants

Grants awarded to organizations located in St. Louis.

MONTANA

492
MPCo/Entech Foundation, Inc.
40 E. Broadway
Butte, MT 59701
(406) 723-5454

Building and equipment grants. Health organizations; higher education; youth organizations; cultural organizations

Typical grant range: $500 to $25,000

NEBRASKA

493
Cooper Foundation
304 Cooper Plaza
211 N. Twelfth Street
Lincoln, NE 68508
(402) 476-7571

Building and equipment grants. Cultural organizations; women; child welfare; social welfare; youth organizations; community development; disabled; health organizations

Grants awarded to organizations located in Nebraska.

Typical grant range: $1,000 to $7,000

494
Hamilton Community Foundation, Inc.
1108 L Street
P.O. Box 283
Aurora, NE 68818
(402) 694-3200

Equipment grants. Youth organizations; recreation; Christian related organizations

Grants awarded to organizations located in Hamilton County.

495
Gilbert M. and Martha H. Hitchcock Foundation
Kennedy Holland Building
10306 Regency Parkway Drive
Omaha, NE 68114
(402) 397-0203

Building and equipment grants. Youth organizations; secondary education; higher education; disabled; cultural organizations; community development; social welfare; renovation grants

Most grants awarded to organizations located in the Omaha vicinity.

Typical grant range: $1,000 to $20,000

496
Kaufmann-Cummings Trust
c/o FirsTier Bank, N.A.
P.O. Box 2006
Grand Island, NE 68802

Building and equipment grants. Animal welfare; youth organizations; recreation; higher education; hospitals; community development; child welfare; health organizations

Grants awarded to organizations located in Nebraska.

Typical grant range: $500 to $20,000

497
Kiewit Companies Foundation
1000 Kiewit Plaza
Omaha, NE 68131
(402) 342-2052

Building and equipment grants. Higher education; community development; health organizations; youth organizations; elderly; cultural organizations; social welfare; child welfare; renovation grants

Most grants awarded to organizations located in Nebraska.

Typical grant range: $1,000 to $15,000

498
Peter Kiewit Foundation
900 Woodmen Tower
Seventeenth at Farnam Street
Omaha, NE 68102
(402) 344-7890

Building and equipment grants. Disabled; elderly; youth organizations; recreation; social welfare; cultural organizations; health organizations; higher education; community development; hospitals; renovation grants

499
Lied Foundation Trust
10050 Regency Circle, Suite 200
Omaha, NE 68114

Building grants. Youth organizations; higher education; cultural organizations; community development; disabled; homeless; social welfare

500
Lincoln Foundation, Inc.
215 Centennial Mall South, Suite 200
Lincoln, NE 68508
(402) 474-2345

Building and equipment grants. Higher education; cultural organizations; health organizations; social welfare; elderly; environment; child welfare

501
Milton S. and Corinne N. Livingston Foundation, Inc.
1125 S. 103rd Street, Suite 600
Omaha, NE 68124
(402) 390-1112

Building grants. Health organizations; cultural organizations; higher education; Jewish organizations

Grants awarded to organizations located in Nebraska.

502
Mid-Nebraska Community Foundation, Inc.
410 Rodeo Road
P.O. Box 1321
North Platte, NE 69103
(308) 534-3315

Building and equipment grants. Social welfare; child welfare; community development; hospitals; renovation grants

503
Omaha Community Foundation
Two Central Park Plaza
222 S. 15th Street
Omaha, NE 68102
(402) 342-3458

Building and equipment grants. Disabled; elderly; homeless; child welfare; cultural organizations; community development; hospitals; renovation grants

Grants awarded to organizations located in the Omaha vicinity.

Typical grant range: $500 to $15,000

504
Omaha World-Herald Foundation
c/o Omaha World-Herald Company
14th and Dodge Streets
Omaha, NE 68102
(402) 444-1000

Building grants. Youth organizations;
minorities; cultural organizations; social
welfare; community development;
disabled

Grants awarded to organizations located
in the Omaha vicinity.

505
Pamida Foundation
P.O. Box 3856
Omaha, NE 68103
(402) 339-2400

Building and equipment grants. Youth
organizations; recreation; hospitals;
health organizations; higher education;
secondary education; disabled; Public
Libraries; renovation grants

Grants awarded to organizations located
in areas of company operations.

506
Edgar Reynolds Foundation, Inc.
204 N. Walnut Street
Grand Island, NE 68801
(308) 384-0957

Building and equipment grants. Higher
education; community development;
youth organizations; social welfare

Grants awarded to organizations located
in Nebraska.

Typical grant range: $2,000 to $20,000

507
Robert D. Wilson Foundation
Guarantee Center, Suite 280
8805 Indian Hills Drive
Omaha, NE 68114
(402) 390-0390

Building and equipment grants. Disabled;
social welfare; health organizations; youth
organizations

Grants awarded to organizations located
in Nebraska.

NEVADA

508
Cord Foundation
200 Court Street
Reno, NV 89501
(702) 323-0373

Building and equipment grants. Higher
education; secondary education; youth
organizations; disabled; social welfare;
cultural organizations; Episcopal Church
(furniture)

Typical grant range: $5,000 to $50,000

509
**First Interstate Bank of Nevada
Foundation**
P.O. Box 98588
Las Vegas, NV 89193
(702) 791-6462

Building and equipment grants. Youth
organizations; community development;
disabled; higher education; social welfare;
elderly

Grants awarded to organizations located
in Nevada.

Typical grant range: $5,000 to $12,000

510
Gabelli Foundation, Inc.
c/o Avansino, Melarkey & Knobel
165 W. Liberty Street
Reno, NV 89501

Building grants. Secondary education;
higher education

Typical grant range: $1,000 to $20,000

511
Conrad N. Hilton Foundation
100 W. Liberty Street, Suite 840
Reno, NV 89501
(702) 323-4221

Building and equipment grants. Higher
education; disabled; youth organizations;
renovation grants

Typical grant range: $5,000 to $75,000

512
Nell J. Redfield Foundation
1755 E. Plumb Lane, Suite 212
Reno, NV 89504
(702) 323-1373

Building and equipment grants. Disabled;
elderly; child welfare; social welfare;
health organizations; youth organizations;
cultural organizations

Most grants awarded to organizations
located in Reno.

Typical grant range: $2,000 to $25,000

513
E.L. Wiegand Foundation
Wiegand Center
165 Liberty Street
Reno, NV 89501
(702) 333-0310

Building and equipment grants. Disabled;
community development; women;
recreation; all levels of education; elderly;
hospitals; health organizations; cultural
organizations; child welfare; Roman
Catholic organizations; renovation grants

Typical grant range: $5,000 to $75,000

NEW HAMPSHIRE

514
**Norwin S. and Elizabeth N. Bean
Foundation**
c/o N.H. Charitable Foundation
37 Pleasant Street, P.O. Box 1335
Concord, NH 03302
(603) 225-6641

Building and equipment grants. Higher
education; youth organizations; child
welfare; health organizations; community
development; recreation; disabled;
cultural development; social welfare;
Churches; renovation grants

Typical grant range: $3,000 to $15,000

515
Chatam, Inc.
Liberty Lane
Hampton, NH 03842
(603) 926-5911

Building grants. Higher education;
disabled; youth organizations; cultural
organizations; health organizations

Typical grant range: $2,000 to $35,000

516
Foundation for Seacoast Health
P.O. Box 4606
Portsmouth, NH 03801
(603) 433-4001

Equipment grants. Health organizations;
disabled; youth organizations; child
welfare; elderly; community development;
AIDS

Typical grant range: $2,000 to $20,000

517
Samuel P. Hunt Foundation
First NH Investment Services Corporation
P.O. Box 150
Manchester, NH 03105
(603) 634-6783

Building and equipment grants. Health
organizations; higher education; elderly;
cultural organizations; renovation grants

Grants awarded to organizations located
in New Hampshire.

518
Agnes M. Lindsay Trust
95 Market Street
Manchester, NH 03101
(603) 669-4140

Building and equipment grants. Youth
organizations; cultural organizations;
child welfare; health organizations;
hospitals; community development;
higher education; homeless; disabled;
elderly; social welfare; renovation grants

Typical grant range: $1,500 to $7,500

519
Mascoma Savings Bank Foundation
c/o Mascoma Savings Bank
67 North Park Street
Lebanon, NH 03766
(603) 448-3650

Building and equipment grants. Health
organizations; hospitals; animal welfare;
community development; Alliance for the
Mentally Ill (supplies); Historical Society
(renovation of stage set); Volunteer Fire
Department (rescue equipment); City of
Lebanon (renovation of historical house);
Church (building funds); renovation
grants

Typical grant range: $1,000 to $5,000

520
New Hampshire Charitable Foundation
37 Pleasant Street
P.O. Box 1335
Concord, NH 03302
(603) 225-6641

Building and equipment grants. Homeless;
social welfare; community development;
women; elderly; health organizations;
child welfare; youth organizations;
cultural organizations; higher education

Grants awarded to organizations located
in New Hampshire.

Typical grant range: $2,000 to $8,000

521
**Lou and Lutza Smith Charitable
Foundation**
c/o New Hampshire Charitable Fdn.
37 Pleasant Street, P.O. Box 1335
Concord, NH 03302
(603) 225-6641

Building grants. Social welfare; health
organizations; community development;
cultural organizations

Grants awarded to organizations located
in New Hampshire.

522
Walker Foundation
P.O. Box 614
Hollis, NH 03049

Equipment grants. Elementary and
secondary schools (equipment for the
science and mathematics departments)

Grants awarded to organizations located
in New Hampshire.

Typical grant range: $1,000 to $12,000

NEW JERSEY

523
Allied-Signal Foundation
P.O. Box 2245
Morristown, NJ 07962
(201) 455-5877

Building and equipment grants. Social welfare; community development; elderly; cultural organizations; youth organizations; higher education; health organizations; disabled; American Heart Association (building funds); Boy Scouts (renovation)

Grants awarded to organizations located in areas of company operations.

Typical grant range: $1,000 to $12,000

524
Mary Owen Borden Memorial Foundation
160 Hodge Road
Princeton, NJ 08540
(609) 924-3637

Building grants. Social welfare; women; youth organizations

Typical grant range: $1,000 to $10,000

525
Emil Buehler Perpetual Trust
305 Route 17
Paramus, NJ 07652
(201) 262-6292

Building grants. Higher education; cultural organizations; community development; renovation grants

526
Campbell Soup Foundation
Campbell Place
Camden, NJ 08103
(609) 342-6431

Building grants. Social welfare; minorities; community development; cultural organizations; hospitals; higher education; recreation; women; renovation grants

Grants awarded to organizations located in areas of company operations, with an emphasis in Camden.

Typical grant range: $3,000 to $20,000

527
Community Foundation of New Jersey
P.O. Box 317
Knox Hill Road
Morristown, NJ 07963
(201) 267-5533

Building and equipment grants. Health organizations; hospitals; community development; youth organizations; child welfare; recreation; women; disabled; Haitian Dance Group (equipment)

Grants awarded to organizations located in New Jersey.

Typical grant range: $500 to $10,000

528
E.J. Grassman Trust
P.O. Box 4470
Warren, NJ 07059
(908) 753-2440

Building and equipment grants. Health organizations; hospitals; higher education; disabled; child welfare; environment

Typical grant range: $5,000 to $25,000

529
Hyde and Watson Foundation
437 Southern Blvd.
Chatham, NJ 07928
(201) 966-6024

Building and equipment grants. Youth organizations; social welfare; child welfare; disabled; health organizations; hospitals; renovation grants

Typical grant range: $5,000 to $25,000

530
F.M. Kirby Foundation, Inc.
17 DeHart Street
P.O. Box 151
Morristown, NJ 07963
(201) 538-4800

Building and equipment grants. Health organizations; hospitals; disabled; youth organizations; culture; social welfare; recreation; higher education

Typical grant range: $10,000 to $25,000

531
Merck Company Foundation
One Merck Drive
P.O. Box 100
Whitehouse Station, NJ 08889
(908) 423-2042

Building and equipment grants. Health organizations; hospitals; social welfare; cultural organizations; higher education; community development; renovation grants

Grants awarded to organizations located in areas of company operations.

Typical grant range: $5,000 to $45,000

532
Nabisco Foundation
Nabisco Brands Plaza
Parsippany, NJ 07054
(201) 682-7098

Building grants. Higher education; community development; cultural organizations; youth organizations; mentally disabled

Grants awarded to organizations located in areas of company operations.

Typical grant range: $5,000 to $50,000

533
Theresa and Edward O'Toole Foundation
12 Sullivan Street
Westwood, NJ 07675

Building grants. Hospitals; Catholic related organizations

534
Prudential Foundation
Prudential Plaza
751 Broad Street
Newark, NJ 07102
(201) 802-7354

Building and equipment grants. Cultural organizations; all levels of education; community development; child welfare; elderly; disabled; health organizations; hospitals; recreation; youth organizations; minorities

Grants awarded to organizations located in areas of company operations, with an emphasis in Newark.

535
Fannie E. Rippel Foundation
P.O. Box 569
Annandale, NJ 08801
(908) 735-0990

Building and equipment grants. Health organizations; disabled; child welfare; elderly; hospitals; higher education; women; renovation grants

Typical grant range: $75,000 to $200,000

536
Schering-Plough Foundation, Inc.
One Giralda Farms
P.O. Box 1000
Madison, NJ 07940
(201) 822-7412

Building and equipment grants. Social welfare; cultural organizations; higher education; environment; hospitals; health organizations

Grants awarded to organizations located in areas of company operations.

Typical grant range: $10,000 to $25,000

537
Florence and John Schumann Foundation
33 Park Street
Montclair, NJ 07042
(201) 783-6660

Building and equipment grants. Community development; disabled; elderly; youth organizations; social welfare; public libraries; cultural organizations; environment; animal welfare; higher education; renovation grants

Typical grant range: $15,000 to $50,000

538
Standish Foundation
P.O. Box 4470
Warren, NJ 07059
(908) 753-2440

Building and equipment grants. Social welfare; hospitals

Typical grant range: $500 to $4,500

539
Turrell Fund
111 Northfield Avenue
West Orange, NJ 07052
(201) 325-5108

Building and equipment grants. Community development; child welfare; social welfare; youth organizations; disabled; recreation; health organizations; Catholic Youth Organization (renovation); YWCA (renovation)

Grants awarded to organizations located in New Jersey.

Typical grant range: $5,000 to $35,000

540
Union Camp Charitable Trust
c/o Union Camp Corporation
1600 Valley Road
Wayne, NJ 07470
(201) 628-2248

Building and equipment grants. Youth organizations; social welfare; community development; cultural organizations; higher education; elementary education; disabled; women; hospitals; environment

Grants awarded to organizations located in areas of company operations.

Typical grant range: $500 to $10,000

541
Union Foundation
31C Mountain Blvd.
P.O. Box 4470
Warren, NJ 07060
(908) 753-2440

Building and equipment grants. Social welfare; higher education; secondary education; cultural organizations; youth organizations; environment; hospitals; health organizations

Grants awarded to organizations located in Union County.

542
Warner-Lambert Charitable Foundation
201 Tabor Road
Morris Plains, NJ 07950
(201) 540-3652

Building and equipment grants. Social welfare; hospitals; health organizations; community development; minorities; disabled; higher education; youth organizations

Grants awarded to organizations located in areas of company operations.

Typical grant range: $5,000 to $30,000

543
Westfield Foundation
301 North Ave. West
P.O. Box 2295
Westfield, NJ 07091
(908) 233-9787

Building and equipment grants. Disabled; health organizations; renovation grants

Grants awarded to organizations located in Westfield.

NEW MEXICO

544
Albuquerque Community Foundation
P.O. Box 36960
Albuquerque, NM 87176
(505) 883-6240

Building grants. Social welfare; youth organizations; child welfare; homeless; community development; hospitals; health organizations; disabled

Grants awarded to organizations located in the Albuquerque vicinity.

545
Dale J. Bellamah Foundation
P.O. Box 36600, Station D
Albuquerque, NM 87176
(505) 293-1098

Equipment grants. Health organizations; hospitals; higher education; disabled; youth organizations; recreation; social welfare

Typical grant range: $5,000 to $80,000

546
R.D. and Joan Dale Hubbard Foundation
P.O. Box 1679
Ruidoso Downs, NM 88346
(505) 378-4142

Building grants. Disabled; cultural organizations; International Space Hall of Fame (building funds)

547
J.F. Maddox Foundation
P.O. Box 5410
Hobbs, NM 88241
(505) 393-6338

Building and equipment grants. Youth organizations; child welfare; social welfare; homeless; disabled; higher education; elderly; cultural organizations; Churches; renovation grants

Most grants awarded to organizations located in New Mexico.

Typical grant range: $5,000 to $75,000

NEW YORK

548
Achelis Foundation
c/o Morris & McVeigh
767 Third Avenue
New York, NY 10017
(212) 418-0588

Building and equipment grants. Disabled;
youth organizations; health organizations;
child welfare; cultural organizations;
women; community development;
minorities; environment; homeless;
renovation grants

Grants awarded to organizations located
in New York City.

Typical grant range: $10,000 to $25,000

549
Joseph Alexander Foundation
400 Madison Avenue, Suite 906
New York, NY 10017
(212) 355-3688

Building and equipment grants. Jewish
organizations; elderly; hospitals; health
organizations; higher education; disabled;
women; cultural organizations; renovation
grants

Most grants awarded to organizations
located in New York City.

Typical grant range: $3,000 to $30,000

550
Altman Foundation
220 East 42nd Street, Suite 411
New York, NY 10017
(212) 682-0970

Building and equipment grants. Child
welfare; elderly; youth organizations;
health organizations; hospitals; women;
cultural organizations; renovation grants

Grants awarded to organizations located
in the New York City vicinity.

Typical grant range: $5,000 to $100,000

551
Amax Foundation, Inc.
200 Park Avenue
New York, NY 10166
(212) 856-4250

Building and equipment grants. Social
welfare; health organizations; higher
education; minorities; cultural programs;
community development; elderly;
recreation; disabled

Typical grant range: $500 to $11,000

552
American Express Foundation
American Express Tower
World Financial Center
New York, NY 10285
(212) 640-5661

Building and equipment grants. Cultural
organizations; youth organizations;
recreation; disabled; social welfare; all
levels of education; minorities

Grants awarded to organizations located
in areas of company operations.

Typical grant range: $2,000 to $30,000

553
The Area Fund
Nine Vassar Street
Poughkeepsie, NY 12601
(914) 452-3077

Building and equipment grants. Disabled;
community development; social welfare;
youth organizations; recreation; health
organizations; cultural organizations;
YMCA (equipment)

Grants awarded to organizations located
in Dutchess County.

Typical grant range: $300 to $4,000

554
Arkell Hall Foundation, Inc.
66 Montgomery Street
Canajoharie, NY 13317
(518) 673-5417

Building and equipment grants. Hospitals;
social welfare; higher education; elderly;
women; disabled; youth organizations

Grants awarded to organizations located
in the Canajoharie vicinity.

555
Vincent Astor Foundation
405 Park Avenue
New York, NY 10022
(212) 758-4110

Building and equipment grants. Homeless;
disabled; community development;
cultural organizations; recreation; youth
organizations; elderly; animal welfare;
Churches; renovation grants

Grants awarded to organizations located
in the New York City vicinity.

Typical grant range: $3,000 to $35,000

556
AT&T Foundation
1301 Avenue of the Americas, Suite 3100
New York, NY 10019
(212) 841-4747

Building and equipment grants. Cultural
organizations; higher education; child
welfare; youth organizations; minorities;
community development; health
organizations; hospitals; disabled

Grants awarded to organizations located
in areas of company operations.

Typical grant range: $5,000 to $40,000

557
Barker Welfare Foundation
P.O. Box 2
Glen Head, NY 11545
(516) 759-5592

Building and equipment grants. Social
welfare; child welfare; elderly; youth
organizations; recreation; environment;
culture; disabled; Churches; renovation
grants

Typical grant range: $2,000 to $10,000

558
Bodman Foundation
c/o Morris & McVeigh
767 Third Avenue, 22nd Floor
New York, NY 10017
(212) 418-0500

Building and equipment grants. Child
welfare; youth organizations; hospitals;
health organizations; women; disabled;
higher education; minorities; elderly;
community development; renovation
grants

Grants awarded to organizations located
in the New York City vicinity.

Typical grant range: $15,000 to $50,000

559
Booth Ferris Foundation
Morgan Guaranty Trust Co. of New York
60 Wall Street
New York, NY 10260
(212) 809-1630

Building and equipment grants. Higher
education; secondary education; disabled;
social welfare; youth organizations;
recreation; hospitals; health organizations;
elderly; child welfare; culture; community
development; Churches; renovation grants

Grants awarded to organizations located
in the New York City vicinity.

Typical grant range: $20,000 to $100,000

560
Albert C. Bostwick Foundation
Hillside Avenue and Bacon Road
P.O. Box A
Old Westbury, NY 11568
(516) 334-5566

Building grants. Disabled; community
development; social welfare; hospitals;
health organizations; Police Department
(building funds); Recording for the Blind
(building funds)

561
Gladys Brooks Foundation
90 Broad Street
New York, NY 10004
(212) 943-3217

Building and equipment grants. Hospitals;
health organizations; higher education;
public libraries; disabled

Typical grant range: $10,000 to $75,000

562
BT Foundation
280 Park Ave.
New York, NY 10017
(212) 454-3086

Building and equipment grants. Culture;
disabled; community development libraries;
homeless; higher education; child welfare

Typical grant range: $10,000 to $20,000

563
Buffalo Foundation
1601 Main-Seneca Building
237 Main Street
Buffalo, NY 14203
(716) 852-2857

Building and equipment grants. Disabled;
community development; child welfare;
health organizations; hospitals; animal
welfare; zoos; culture; higher education;
recreation; elderly; youth; Hispanic's United
(equipment); Buffalo Hearing and Speech
Center (building funds)

Grants awarded to organizations located
in Erie County.

Typical grant range: $1,000 to $15,000

564
Louis Calder Foundation
Contact: The Trustees
230 Park Avenue, Suite 1530
New York, NY 10169
(212) 687-1680

Building and equipment grants. Disabled;
hospitals; social welfare; minorities;
health organizations; youth organizations;
child welfare; higher education; secondary
education

Grants awarded to organizations located
in New York City.

Typical grant range: $10,000 to $75,000

565
**Ed Lee and Jean Campe
Foundation, Inc.**
U.S. Trust Co. of New York
114 W. 47th Street
New York, NY 10036

Building grants. Social welfare; youth
organizations

Typical grant range: $300 to $5,000

566
**Central New York Community
Foundation, Inc.**
500 S. Salina Street, Suite 428
Syracuse, NY 13202
(315) 422-9538

Building and equipment grants. Hospitals;
health organizations; child welfare; youth
organizations; disabled; recreation;
elderly; women; homeless; cultural
organizations; Child and Family Services
(equipment); Food Bank (building funds);
renovation grants

Grants awarded to organizations located
in Onondaga and Madison Counties.

111

567
Chase Manhattan Foundation
The Chase Manhattan Bank, N.A.
Two Chase Manhattan Plaza
New York, NY 10081
(212) 552-8205

Building grants. Higher education; child
welfare; youth organizations; community
development

Typical grant range: $2,000 to $8,000

568
**Chautauqua Region Community
Foundation, Inc.**
104 Hotel Jamestown Mezzanine
Jamestown, NY 14701
(716) 661-3390

Building and equipment grants. Elderly;
cultural organizations; social welfare;
youth organizations; public libraries;
disabled; community development

Grants awarded to organizations located
in Chautauqua County.

Typical grant range: $1,000 to $9,000

569
Clark Foundation
30 Wall Street
New York, NY 10005
(212) 269-1833

Building and equipment grants. Higher
education; community development;
cultural organizations; recreation; youth
organizations; disabled; hospitals; health
organizations; child welfare; minorities;
homeless; environment

Typical grant range: $15,000 to $80,000

570
**Community Foundation for the Capital
Region, N.Y.**
P.O. Box 3198
Albany, NY 12203
(518) 273-8596

Building and equipment grants. Social
welfare; disabled; cultural organizations;
homeless; child welfare; renovation grants

Typical grant range: $500 to $2,500

571
**Community Foundation of the Elmira-
Corning Area**
168 N. Main Street, Box 714
Elmira, NY 14902
(607) 734-6412

Building and equipment grants. Social
welfare; youth organizations; disabled;
elderly

572
Peter C. Cornell Trust
c/o Fiduciary Services, Inc.
120 Delaware Avenue, Suite 430
Buffalo, NY 14202
(716) 854-1244

Building and equipment grants. Social
welfare; disabled; elderly; hospitals;
health organizations

Typical grant range: $2,000 to $9,000

573
Corning Incorporated Foundation
MP-LB-02-1
Corning, NY 14831
(607) 974-8746

Building and equipment grants. Cultural
organizations; hospitals; public libraries;
community development; social welfare;
higher education; secondary education;
youth organizations; Civic Theatre
(renovation); Salvation Army (building
funds); renovation grants

Grants awarded to organizations located
in areas of company operations.

Typical grant range: $500 to $2,000

574
Cowles Charitable Trust
630 Fifth Avenue, Suite 1612
New York, NY 10111
(212) 765-6262

Building and equipment grants. Social
welfare; cultural organizations; higher
education; community development;
hospitals; renovation grants

575
James H. Cummings Foundation, Inc.
1807 Elmwood Avenue, Suite 112
Buffalo, NY 14207
(716) 874-0040

Building and equipment grants. Child
welfare; community development;
hospitals; health organizations; youth
organizations; women; higher education;
social welfare; disabled; elderly;
renovation grants

Typical grant range: $2,000 to $50,000

576
Davenport-Hatch Foundation, Inc.
c/o Fleet Bank, N.A.
One East Avenue
Rochester, NY 14638
(716) 546-9121

Building and equipment grants. Social
welfare; disabled; higher education;
community development; cultural
organizations; elderly; hospitals; health
organizations; Baptist Home (van);
Visiting Nurses (equipment); American
Red Cross (building funds); renovation
grants

Grants awarded to organizations located
in the Rochester vicinity.

Typical grant range: $3,000 to $15,000

577
Ira W. DeCamp Foundation
Mudge Rose Guthrie Alexander & Ferdon
630 Fifth Avenue, Suite 1650
New York, NY 10011
(212) 332-1612

Building and equipment grants. Hospitals;
health organizations; elderly; disabled;
child welfare; higher education;
renovation grants

Typical grant range: $15,000 to $85,000

578
Dewar Foundation, Inc.
16 Dietz Street
Oneonta, NY 13820
(607) 432-3530

Building grants. Higher education; child
welfare; youth organizations; cultural
organizations; renovation grants

Grants awarded to organizations located
in the Oneonta vicinity.

579
Dillon Fund
1270 Ave. of the Americas, Room 2300
New York, NY 10020
(212) 315-8343

Building grants. Cultural organizations;
public libraries; higher education;
community development; renovation
grants

Typical grant range: $1,500 to $30,000

580
Cleveland H. Dodge Foundation, Inc.
670 West 247th Street
Bronx, NY 10471
(718) 543-1220

Building and equipment grants. Youth
organizations; community development;
social welfare; child welfare; higher
education; secondary education; cultural
organizations

Typical grant range: $500 to $5,000

581
Dolan Family Foundation
One Media Crossways
Woodbury, NY 11797
(516) 496-1136

Building grants. Higher education;
disabled; health organizations; hospitals;
social welfare

Typical grant range: $10,000 to $100,000

582
William H. Donner Foundation, Inc.
500 Fifth Avenue, Suite 1230
New York, NY 10110
(212) 719-9290

Building grants. Youth organizations;
recreation; disabled; higher education;
health organizations

Typical grant range: $20,000 to $85,000

583
Fred L. Emerson Foundation, Inc.
63 Genesee Street
P.O. Box 276
Auburn, NY 13021
(315) 253-9621

Building and equipment grants. Social
welfare; community development; cultural
organizations; disabled; public libraries;
recreation; youth organizations; higher
education; Churches; renovation grants

584
Eugene and Estelle Ferkauf Foundation
67 Allenwood Road
Great Neck, NY 11023
(516) 773-3269

Building grants. Cultural organizations;
health organizations; hospitals; higher
education; disabled

Grants awarded to organizations located
in New York State.

585
Gebbie Foundation, Inc.
Hotel Jamestown Building, Suite 308
P.O. Box 1277
Jamestown, NY 14702
(716) 487-1062

Building and equipment grants. Social
welfare; hospitals; higher education;
youth organizations; recreation;
environment; public libraries; child
welfare; women; cultural organizations;
renovation grants

Most grants awarded to organizations
located in Chautauqua County.

Typical grant range: $2,000 to $35,000

586
**Rosamond Gifford Charitable
Corporation**
731 James Street, Room 404
Syracuse, NY 13203
(315) 474-2489

Building and equipment grants.
Community development; higher
education; cultural organizations;
hospitals; elderly; youth organizations;
social welfare; recreation; disabled;
renovation grants

Grants awarded to organizations located
in the Syracuse vicinity.

587
Glens Falls Foundation
237 Glen Street
Glens Falls, NY 12801
(518) 792-1151

Building and equipment grants. Health
organizations; community development;
cultural organizations; disabled; youth
organizations; renovation grants

588
Herman Goldman Foundation
61 Broadway, 18th Floor
New York, NY 10006
(212) 797-9090

Building grants. Higher education;
recreation; disabled; social welfare;
hospitals; health organizations

Grants awarded to organizations located
in the New York City vicinity.

Typical grant range: $5,000 to $40,000

589
Josephine Goodyear Foundation
1920 Liberty Building
Buffalo, NY 14202
(716) 856-2112

Building and equipment grants. Child
welfare; women; youth organizations;
community development; hospitals

Grants awarded to organizations located
in the Buffalo vicinity.

590
Hagedorn Fund
c/o Chemical Bank
270 Park Avenue
New York, NY 10017

Building grants. Higher education; youth
organizations; child welfare; minorities;
public libraries; elderly; community
development; disabled; Churches

Typical grant range: $3,000 to $20,000

591
Hasbro Children's Foundation
32 W. 23rd Street
New York, NY 10010
(212) 645-2400

Equipment grants. Disabled; health
organizations; hospitals; all levels of
education; youth organizations; social
welfare

Typical grant range: $5,000 to $60,000

592
Charles Hayden Foundation
One Bankers Trust Plaza
130 Liberty Street
New York, NY 10006
(212) 938-0790

Building and equipment grants. Youth
organizations; cultural organizations;
recreation; disabled; social welfare; health
organizations; child welfare; secondary
education; elementary education;
community development; minorities;
renovation grants

Typical grant range: $15,000 to $125,000

593
Hearst Foundation, Inc.
888 Seventh Avenue, 45th Floor
New York, NY 10106
(212) 586-5404

Building and equipment grants. Hospitals;
health organizations; minorities; disabled;
higher education; cultural organizations;
child welfare; youth organizations;
recreation; renovation grants

Typical grant range: $10,000 to $40,000

594
William Randolph Hearst Foundation
888 Seventh Avenue
New York, NY 10106
(212) 586-5404

Building and equipment grants. Cultural
organizations; disabled; minorities;
hospitals; social welfare; child welfare;
youth organizations; homeless; elderly;
higher education; elementary education;
recreation; renovation grants

Typical grant range: $15,000 to $70,000

595
Heckscher Foundation for Children
17 East 47th Street
New York, NY 10017
(212) 371-7775

Building and equipment grants. Child
welfare; youth organizations; community
development; environment; recreation;
social welfare; homeless; hospitals;
disabled; health organizations; cultural
organizations; renovation grants

Most grants awarded to organizations
located in the New York City vicinity.

Typical grant range: $500 to $10,000

596
Howard and Bush Foundation, Inc.
Two Belle Avenue
Troy, NY 12180
(518) 273-6005

Building and equipment grants. Social
welfare; disabled; child welfare; youth
organizations; health organizations;
cultural organizations; recreation

Grants awarded to organizations located
in Rensselaer County.

Typical grant range: $6,500 to $20,000

597
**Stewart W. & Willma C. Hoyt
Foundation**
105-107 Court Street, Suite 400
Binghamton, NY 13901
(607) 722-6706

Building and equipment grants. Health
organizations; recreation; public libraries;
animal welfare; youth organizations;
social welfare; disabled; culture; United
Methodist Homes (renovation); American
Red Cross (renovation)

Grants awarded to organizations located
in Broome County.

Typical grant range: $5,000 to $25,000

598
Hugoton Foundation
900 Park Avenue
New York, NY 10021
(212) 734-5447

Building and equipment grants. Hospitals;
health organizations; higher education

Most grants awarded to organizations
located in New York City.

Typical grant range: $5,000 to $35,000

599
**Christian A. Johnson Endeavor
Foundation**
1060 Park Avenue
New York, NY 10128
(212) 534-6620

Building and equipment grants. Higher
education; cultural organizations; youth
organizations; disabled

600
Daisy Marquis Jones Foundation
620 Granite Building
130 E. Main Street
Rochester, NY 14604
(716) 263-3331

Building and equipment grants. Child
welfare; youth organizations; disabled;
elderly; health organizations; hospitals;
women; recreation; social welfare;
community development

Grants awarded to organizations located
in Monroe and Yates Counties.

Typical grant range: $3,000 to $20,000

601
Julia R. and Estelle L. Foundation, Inc.
817 Washington Street
Buffalo, NY 14203
(716) 857-3325

Building grants. Social welfare; youth
organizations; higher education; elderly;
disabled; hospitals; health organizations

Grants awarded to organizations located
in the Buffalo vicinity.

Typical grant range: $3,000 to $30,000

602
David and Sadie Klau Foundation
c/o Rochlin, Lipsky, Goodkin, Stoler &
Company, P.C.
125 W. 45th Street
New York, NY 10036
(212) 840-6444

Building grants. Cultural organizations;
health organizations; social welfare; child
welfare; youth organizations; disabled;
higher education; Jewish organizations

Grants awarded to organizations located
in New York City.

Typical grant range: $500 to $10,000

603
**Jay E. Klock and Lucia L. Klock
Kingston Foundation**
267 Wall Street
Kingston, NY 12401

Building grants. Youth organizations;
disabled; hospitals; health organizations

Typical grant range: $2,000 to $12,000

604
George Link, Jr. Foundation, Inc.
c/o Emmet, Marvin and Martin
48 Wall Street
New York, NY 10005
(212) 238-3000

Building grants. Youth organizations;
elderly; higher education; secondary
education; social welfare; child welfare;
hospitals; health organizations; cultural
organizations

Typical grant range: $7,500 to $20,000

605
**James J. McCann Charitable Trust and
McCann Foundation, Inc.**
35 Market Street
Poughkeepsie, NY 12601
(914) 452-3085

Building and equipment grants. Higher
education; secondary education;
recreation; homeless; women; child
welfare; youth organizations; cultural
organizations; community development;
social welfare; hospitals; health
organizations; Churches

Grants awarded to organizations located
in the Poughkeepsie vicinity.

Typical grant range: $1,000 to $45,000

606
J.M. McDonald Foundation, Inc.
P.O. Box 470
Cortland, NY 13045
(607) 756-9283

Building and equipment grants. Disabled;
elderly; child welfare; higher education;
youth organizations; health organizations;
hospitals; renovation grants

607
**Merrill Lynch & Company
Foundation, Inc.**
South Tower, 6th Floor
World Financial Center
New York, NY 10080
(212) 236-4319

Building grants. Higher education;
community development; cultural
organizations; disabled; hospitals;
renovation grants

Grants awarded to organizations located
in areas of company operations.

Typical grant range: $3,000 to $40,000

608
Stanley W. Metcalf Foundation, Inc.
120 Genesee St., Suite 503
Auburn, NY 13021
(315) 253-9321

Building grants. Health organizations;
hospitals; community development; public
libraries; cultural organizations; youth
organizations; Churches; Girl Scout
Council (building funds)

Grants awarded to organizations located
in Cayuga County.

609
Edward S. Moore Foundation, Inc.
c/o Walter, Conston, Alexander and Green
90 Park Avenue
New York, NY 10016
(212) 210-9400

Building and equipment grants. Cultural
organizations; youth organizations; child
welfare; recreation; hospitals

Typical grant range: $3,000 to $25,000

610
J. P. Morgan Charitable Trust
60 Wall Street, 46th Floor
New York, NY 10260
(212) 648-9673

Building and equipment grants. Elderly;
youth organizations; higher education;
elementary education; community
development; minorities; environment;
health organizations; disabled; cultural
organizations

Grants awarded to organizations located
in the New York City vicinity.

Typical grant range: $5,000 to $30,000

611
Henry and Lucy Moses Fund, Inc.
c/o Moses & Singer
1301 Avenue of the Americas
New York, NY 10019
(212) 554-7800

Building grants. Cultural organizations;
disabled; elderly; higher education;
minorities; child welfare; youth
organizations; environment; health
organizations; hospitals; Jewish
organizations

Grants awarded to organizations located
in the New York City vicinity.

Typical grant range: $3,000 to $12,000

612
New York Community Trust
Two Park Avenue, 24th Floor
New York, NY 10016
(212) 686-0010

Building and equipment grants. Cultural
organizations; youth organizations; child
welfare; disabled; women; elderly;
community development; homeless;
environment; health organizations

Grants awarded to organizations located
in New York City, Long Island and
Westchester County.

Typical grant range: $5,000 to $45,000

613
New York Life Foundation
51 Madison Avenue
New York, NY 10010
(212) 576-7341

Building grants. Social welfare; health
organizations; community development;
disabled; cultural organizations; hospitals;
youth organizations; minorities; higher
education

Typical grant range: $1,000 to $20,000

614
Nichols Foundation, Inc.
630 Fifth Ave., Room 1964
New York, NY 10111
(212) 581-1160

Building and equipment grants. Social
welfare; environment; hospitals; youth
organizations; disabled

Typical grant range: $1,000 to $25,000

615
**Northern Chautauqua Community
Foundation**
212 Lake Shore Drive West
Dunkirk, NY 14048
(716) 366-4892

Building and equipment grants. Cultural
organizations; social welfare; community
development; environment; hospitals;
elderly; American Red Cross (equipment);
Historical Society (renovation)

Grants awarded to organizations located
in Northern Chautauqua County.

616
**Northern New York Community
Foundation, Inc.**
120 Washington Street
Watertown, NY 13601
(315) 782-7110

Building and equipment grants. Child
welfare; recreation; cultural organizations;
hospitals; health organizations; elderly;
disabled; community development; youth
organizations; higher education;
renovation grants

617
**A. Lindsay and Olive B. O'Connor
Foundation**
P.O. Box D
Hobart, NY 13788
(607) 538-9248

Building and equipment grants. Youth
organizations; community development;
public libraries; higher education; health
organizations; child welfare; cultural
organizations; environment

618
F.W. Olin Foundation, Inc.
780 Third Avenue
New York, NY 10017
(212) 832-0508

Building and equipment grants. Higher
education

Few grants awarded.

619
Pfizer Foundation, Inc.
235 East 42nd Street
New York, NY 10017
(212) 573-3351

Building and equipment grants. Health
organizations; hospitals; community
development; social welfare; youth
organizations; minorities; recreation;
cultural organizations; higher education;
disabled; elderly

Grants awarded to organizations located
in areas of company operations, with an
emphasis in the New York City vicinity.

Typical grant range: $1,000 to $25,000

620
Primerica Foundation
65 E. 55th Street
New York, NY 10022
(212) 891-8884

Building and equipment grants. Social
welfare; youth organizations; elderly;
public libraries; all levels of education;
minorities; cultural organizations;
disabled

Grants awarded to organizations located
in areas of company operations.

Typical grant range: $5,000 to $15,000

621
Prospect Hill Foundation, Inc.
420 Lexington Avenue, Suite 3020
New York, NY 10170
(212) 370-1144

Building and equipment grants. Cultural
organizations; higher education; social
welfare; recreation; environment;
hospitals; community development

Typical grant range: $3,000 to $30,000

622
**Gerald & May Ellen Ritter
Memorial Fund**
c/o Proskauer Rose Goetz & Mendelsohn
1585 Broadway, 25th Floor
New York, NY 10036

Building and equipment grants. Social
welfare; higher education; cultural
organizations; youth organizations;
Jewish organizations

Grants awarded to organizations located
in the New York City vicinity.

Typical grant range: $1,000 to $35,000

623
Dorothea Haus Ross Foundation
1036 Monroe Avenue
Rochester, NY 14620
(716) 473-6006

Building and equipment grants. Youth
organizations; health organizations;
hospitals; all levels of education; child
welfare; recreation; homeless; disabled;
Churches; Help the Children (equipment);
Food for the Poor (equipment); renovation
grants

Typical grant range: $1,000 to $8,000

624
**Fan Fox and Leslie R. Samuels
Foundation, Inc.**
630 Fifth Avenue, Suite 2255
New York, NY 10111
(212) 315-2940

Building and equipment grants. Elderly;
social welfare; cultural organizations;
youth organizations; hospitals; health
organizations; renovation grants

Most grants awarded to organizations
located in New York City.

Typical grant range: $5,000 to $100,000

625
Ralph C. Sheldon Foundation, Inc.
P.O. Box 417
Jamestown, NY 14702
(716) 664-9890

Building and equipment grants. Social
welfare; disabled; health organizations;
community development; environment

Grants awarded to organizations located
in Chautauqua County.

Typical grant range: $10,000 to $65,000

626
John Ben Snow Memorial Trust
P.O. Box 378
Pulaski, NY 13142
(315) 298-6401

Building and equipment grants. Child welfare; minorities; community development; health organizations; cultural organizations; disabled; higher education; recreation; elderly; youth organizations; renovation grants

Most grants awarded to organizations located in Oswego County.

Typical grant range: $10,000 to $35,000

627
St. Giles Foundation
420 Lexington Avenue, Suite 1641
New York, NY 10170
(212) 338-9001

Building and equipment grants. Hospitals; health organizations; disabled; child welfare; youth organizations

Typical grant range: $30,000 to $125,000

628
Starr Foundation
70 Pine Street
New York, NY 10270
(212) 770-6882

Building and equipment grants. Social welfare; hospitals; health organizations; recreation; cultural organizations; disabled; higher education; minorities

629
Tripp Foundation, Inc.
c/o Mrs. S. Roberts Rose
855 Euclid Avenue
Elmira, NY 14901

Building and equipment grants. Hospitals; performing arts; museums; youth organizations

Typical grant range: $1,000 to $5,000

630
Uris Brothers Foundation, Inc.
300 Park Avenue
New York, NY 10022
(212) 355-7080

Building grants. Health organizations; hospitals; higher education; disabled; social welfare; cultural organizations; elderly; homeless; youth organizations; public libraries; renovation grants

Grants awarded to organizations located in the New York City vicinity.

Typical grant range: $10,000 to $27,000

631
Utica Foundation, Inc.
270 Genesee Street
Utica, NY 13502
(315) 735-8212

Building and equipment grants. Health organizations; hospitals; higher education; cultural organizations; elderly; youth organizations; public libraries; disabled; animal welfare; renovation grants

Grants awarded to organizations located in Oneida and Herkimer Counties.

Typical grant range: $5,000 to $25,000

632
Margaret L. Wendt Foundation
40 Fountain Plaza, Suite 277
Buffalo, NY 14202
(716) 855-2146

Building and equipment grants. Health organizations; hospitals; disabled; cultural organizations; youth organizations; social welfare; Churches

Grants awarded to organizations located in the Buffalo vicinity.

Typical grant range: $3,000 to $30,000

633
Western New York Foundation
Main Seneca Building, Suite 1402
237 Main Street
Buffalo, NY 14203
(716) 847-6440

Building and equipment grants. Cultural
organizations; community development;
youth organizations; public libraries;
social welfare; health organizations;
disabled; higher education; renovation
grants

Typical grant range: $2,500 to $20,000

634
Ralph Wilkens Foundation
222 Groton Avenue
Cortland, NY 13045
(607) 756-7548

Building and equipment grants. Health
organizations; culture; disabled; youth
organizations; recreation; Practical Bible
Training School (equipment); YMCA
(building funds); renovation grants

Grants awarded to organizations located
in Cortland County.

Typical grant range: $500 to $7,000

635
**Marie C. and Joseph C. Wilson
Foundation**
160 Allens Creek Road
Rochester, NY 14618
(716) 461-4699

Building grants. Youth organizations;
social welfare; cultural organizations;
health organizations

Grants awarded to organizations located
in Rochester.

Typical grant range: $3,000 to $20,000

636
Robert W. Wilson Foundation
990 Sixth Avenue, Suite 19G
New York, NY 10018

Building and equipment grants. Social
welfare; cultural organizations

Grants awarded to organizations located
in New York City.

NORTH CAROLINA

637
Belk Foundation
2801 W. Tyvola Road
Charlotte, NC 28217
(704) 357-1000

Building grants. Higher education; youth
organizations; hospitals; social welfare;
cultural organizations

Typical grant range: $2,000 to $20,000

638
**Kathleen Price and Joseph M. Bryan
Family Foundation**
One N. Pointe, Suite 170
3101 N. Elm Street
Greensboro, NC 27408
(919) 288-5455

Building and equipment grants. Cultural
organizations; higher education; animal
welfare; child welfare; elderly; minorities;
disabled; renovation grants

Grants awarded to organizations located
in North Carolina.

Typical grant range: $5,000 to $35,000

639
Burlington Industries Foundation
P.O. Box 21207
3330 W. Friendly Avenue
Greensboro, NC 27420
(919) 379-2515

Building grants. Higher education; community development; health organizations; hospitals; cultural organizations

Grants awarded to organizations located in areas of company operations.

640
Cannon Foundation, Inc.
P.O. Box 548
Concord, NC 28026
(704) 786-8216

Building and equipment grants. Social welfare; community development; youth organizations; higher education; hospitals; disabled; renovation grants

Grants awarded to organizations located in areas of company operations, with an emphasis in Cabarrus County.

Typical grant range: $15,000 to $65,000

641
Cumberland Community Foundation
P.O. Box 2171
Fayetteville, NC 28302
(919) 483-4449

Building and equipment grants. Cultural organizations; social welfare; community development; renovation grants

Grants awarded to organizations located in Cumberland County.

642
Duke Endowment
100 N. Tryon Street, Suite 3500
Charlotte, NC 28202
(704) 376-0291

Building and equipment grants. Higher education; hospitals; women; disabled; child welfare; Churches; renovation grants

643
Fieldcrest Cannon Foundation
326 E. Stadium
Eden, NC 27288
(919) 665-4346

Building grants. Higher education; community development; youth organizations

Grants awarded to organizations located in areas of company operations.

644
Foundation of Greater Greensboro, Inc.
P.O. Box 1207
Greensboro, NC 27402
(919) 379-9100

Building and equipment grants. Community development; cultural organizations; social welfare; disabled; Industries of the Blind (equipment)

Most grants awarded to organizations located in the Greensboro vicinity.

645
John W. and Anna H. Hanes Foundation
Wachovia Bank of North Carolina, N.A.
P.O. Box 3099, MC 31022
Winston-Salem, NC 27150
(919) 770-5274

Building and equipment grants. Child welfare; disabled; cultural organizations; health organizations; social welfare; youth organizations; elderly; community development; Rescue Squad (equipment); YMCA (building funds); Senior Services, Inc. (equipment); renovation grants

Grants awarded to organizations located in North Carolina.

Typical grant range: $2,000 to $22,000

646
Outer Banks Community Foundation, Inc.
P.O. Box 1100
Kill Devil Hills, NC 27948

Building and equipment grants. Rescue organizations (equipment); Veterans Committee of American Legion (building funds)

Grants awarded to organizations located in the Outer Banks vicinity.

647
Kate B. Reynolds Charitable Trust
2422 Reynolda Road
Winston-Salem, NC 27106
(919) 723-1456

Building and equipment grants. Social welfare; hospitals; health organizations; child welfare; disabled; renovation grants

Grants awarded to organizations located in North Carolina.

Typical grant range: $25,000 to $75,000

648
Z. Smith Reynolds Foundation, Inc.
101 Reynolda Village
Winston-Salem, NC 27106
(919) 725-7541

Building and equipment grants. Cultural organizations; community development; disabled; youth organizations; women; renovation grants

Grants awarded to organizations located in North Carolina.

Typical grant range: $15,000 to $30,000

649
Wachovia Foundation Inc.
Wachovia Bank & Trust Co., N.A.
P.O. Box 3099
Winston-Salem, NC 27150

Building grants. Social welfare; higher education; community development; renovation grants

Grants awarded to organizations located in North Carolina, with an emphasis in communities with a Wachovia Bank branch.

650
Winston-Salem Foundation
310 W. Fourth Street, Suite 229
Winston-Salem, NC 27101
(919) 725-2382

Building and equipment grants. Social welfare; abused women; homeless; disabled; elderly; health organizations; community development; cultural organizations; renovation grants

Grants awarded to organizations located in Forsyth County.

NORTH DAKOTA

651
Fargo-Moorhead Area Foundation
609-1/2 First Avenue North
Fargo, ND 58102
(701) 234-0756

Building and equipment grants. Health organizations; youth organizations; social welfare; hospice; public radio; Camp Fire Council (capital improvements); Bethel Orthodox Presbyterian Church (capital improvements); renovation grants

652
**Tom and Frances Leach
Foundation, Inc.**
P.O. Box 1136
Bismarck, ND 58502
(701) 255-0479

Building grants. Elderly; social services;
youth organizations; higher education;
disabled

Grants awarded to organizations located
in North Dakota.

Typical grant range: $1,500 to $9,000

653
Myra Foundation
P.O. Box 1536
Grand Forks, ND 58206
(701) 775-9420

Building and equipment grants. Youth
organizations; cultural organizations;
homeless; recreation; disabled; elderly;
renovation grants

Grants awarded to organizations located
in Grand Forks County.

654
North Dakota Community Foundation
P.O. Box 387
Bismarck, ND 58502
(701) 222-8349

Building and equipment grants. Health
organizations; recreation; social welfare;
cultural organizations; elderly; youth
organizations; community development

Grants awarded to organizations located
in North Dakota.

655
Alex Stern Family Foundation
Bill Stern Building, Suite 205
609-1/2 First Avenue North
Fargo, ND 58102

Building and equipment grants.
Community development; recreation;
health organizations; youth organizations;
disabled; elderly; child welfare;
renovation grants

OHIO

656
Akron Community Foundation
Society Building, Suite 900
159 S. Main Street
Akron, OH 44308
(216) 376-8522

Building and equipment grants. Cultural
organizations; social welfare; higher
education; women; youth organizations;
disabled; St. John School (renovation);
Good Shepherd Boxing Club (equipment);
renovation grants

Grants awarded to organizations located
in the Akron vicinity.

Typical grant range: $1,000 to $20,000

657
Akron Jaycee Foundation
1745 W. Market Street
Akron, OH 44313
(216) 867-8055

Building and equipment grants. Youth
organizations; elderly; abused women;
recreation; disabled; Catholic Youth
Organization (equipment, renovation);
Haven Ministries (tables and chairs);
Keep Akron Beautiful (van)

Grants awarded to organizations located
in Akron.

Typical grant range: $1,000 to $4,000

658
**American Financial Corporation
Foundation**
One E. Fourth Street
Cincinnati, OH 45202
(513) 579-2400

Building grants. Higher education; social
welfare; hospitals; minorities; cultural
organizations; disabled

Grants awarded to organizations located
in areas of company operations, with an
emphasis in Cincinnati.

125

659
Anderson Foundation
P.O. Box 119
Maumee, OH 43537
(419) 891-6404

Building and equipment grants. Cultural organizations; community development; higher education; youth organizations; social welfare

Grants awarded to organizations located in the Toledo vicinity.

660
Elsie and Harry Baumker Charitable Foundation, Inc.
2828 Barrington Drive
Toledo, OH 43606
(419) 535-6969

Building and equipment grants. Higher education; Maternal Health League (renovation)

Grants awarded to organizations located in Ohio, with an emphasis in Toledo.

661
William Bingham Foundation
1250 Leader Building
Cleveland, OH 44114
(216) 781-3275

Building and equipment grants. Environment; cultural organizations; disabled; all levels of education; National Public Radio (building funds); Natural Resources Defense Council (building funds)

Typical grant range: $5,000 to $40,000

662
Borden Foundation, Inc.
180 East Broad St., 34th Floor
Columbus, OH 43215
(614) 225-4340

Equipment grants. Disabled; social welfare; elderly; youth organizations; community development; higher education; minorities; cultural organizations

Grants awarded to organizations located in areas of company operations.

Typical grant range: $3,000 to $20,000

663
Eva L. and Joseph M. Bruening Foundation
1422 Euclid Avenue, Suite 627
Cleveland, OH 44115
(216) 621-2632

Building and equipment grants. Elderly; disabled; cultural organizations; health organizations; higher education; Churches; renovation grants

Grants awarded to organizations located in the Cleveland vicinity.

Typical grant range: $5,000 to $75,000

664
Centerior Energy Foundation
6200 Oaktree Blvd.
Independence, OH 44131
(216) 479-4907

Building and equipment grants. Social welfare; hospitals; youth organizations; cultural organizations; higher education; community development; renovation grants

665
Cleveland Foundation
1422 Euclid Avenue, Suite 1400
Cleveland, OH 44115
(216) 861-3810

Building and equipment grants.
Community development; hospitals;
health organizations; child welfare;
cultural organizations; minorities;
disabled; all levels of education; elderly;
Community Center (renovation); Child
Guidance Center (renovation)

Grants awarded to organizations located
in the Cleveland vicinity.

Typical grant range: $1,000 to $75,000

666
Columbus Foundation
1234 E. Broad Street
Columbus, OH 43205
(614) 251-4000

Building and equipment grants. Cultural
organizations; disabled; homeless; child
welfare; women; recreation; youth
organizations; animal welfare; elderly;
environment; minorities; Diocesan Child
Guidance Center (building funds);
renovation grants

Grants awarded to organizations located
in Central Ohio.

667
Coshocton Foundation
P.O. Box 15
Coshocton, OH 43812
(614) 622-0010

Building and equipment grants. Social
welfare; health organizations; recreation;
community development; cultural
organizations; disabled; renovation grants

Grants awarded to organizations located
in Coshocton County.

668
Dana Corporation Foundation
P.O. Box 1000
Toledo, OH 43697
(419) 535-4601

Building and equipment grants. Social
welfare; community development;
elderly; cultural organizations; youth
organizations; higher education

Grants awarded to organizations located
in areas of company operations.

669
Charles H. Dater Foundation, Inc.
508 Atlas Bank Building
Cincinnati, OH 45202
(513) 241-1234

Building and equipment grants. Social
welfare; disabled; child welfare; cultural
organizations; recreation; community
development; Zoo and Botanical Gardens
(van); READ to Succeed (audiovisual aids
and equipment); St. Joseph's Home
(therapeutic equipment); Junior League
(renovation); Care Center (equipment for
playground); Museum Foundation
(renovation); Big Brothers/Big Sisters
(renovation); Salvation Army
(equipment); renovation grants

Grants awarded to organizations located
in the Cincinnati vicinity.

Typical grant range: $1,000 to $11,000

670
Dayton Foundation
2100 Kettering Tower
Dayton, OH 45423
(513) 222-0410

Building and equipment grants. Cultural
organizations; homeless; minorities;
women; health organizations; hospice;
child welfare; recreation; disabled; youth
organizations; higher education;
renovation grants

Many grants awarded to organizations
located in the Dayton vicinity.

671
Eaton Charitable Fund
Eaton Corporation
Eaton Center
Cleveland, OH 44114
(216) 523-4822

Building grants. Youth organizations;
hospitals; community development;
cultural organizations; higher education;
health organizations

Grants awarded to organizations located
in areas of company operations.

Typical grant range: $1,000 to $8,000

672
1525 Foundation
1525 National City Bank Building
Cleveland, OH 44114
(216) 696-4200

Building and equipment grants. Higher
education; recreation; social welfare;
disabled; environment; youth
organizations

Grants awarded to organizations located
in Ohio.

Typical grant range: $10,000 to $100,000

673
GAR Foundation
50 South Main Street
P.O. Box 1500
Akron, OH 44309
(216) 376-5300

Building and equipment grants. Youth
organizations; higher education; elderly;
disabled; recreation; social welfare;
cultural organizations; Churches;
Cleveland Clinic Foundation (building
funds); Museum of National History
(building funds); renovation grants

Grants awarded to organizations located
in the Akron vicinity.

Typical grant range: $10,000 to $75,000

674
Greater Cincinnati Foundation
425 Walnut Street, Suite 1110
Cincinnati, OH 45202
(513) 241-2880

Building and equipment grants. Social
welfare; community development; child
welfare; health organizations; cultural
organizations; elderly; environment;
youth organizations; higher education;
renovation grants

Grants awarded to organizations located
in the Cincinnati vicinity.

675
H.C.S. Foundation
1801 E. 9th Street, Suite 1035
Cleveland, OH 44114
(216) 781-3502

Building grants. Hospitals; health
organizations; higher education;
community development; disabled

Grants awarded to organizations located
in Ohio.

676
Hoover Foundation
101 E. Maple Street
North Canton, OH 44720
(216) 499-9200

Building grants. Health organizations;
hospitals; community development;
higher education; youth organizations;
social welfare; disabled; Child and
Adolescent Center (renovation); Family
Services (equipment for day care center);
YMCA (renovation); Juvenile Detention
Center (equipment); Career Services
(renovation); Stark County Courthouse
(building funds); Junior Achievement
(renovation); renovation grants

Grants awarded to organizations located
in areas of company operations, with an
emphasis in Stark County.

Typical grant range: $10,000 to $80,000

OHIO

677
George M. and Pamela S. Humphrey Fund
Advisory Services, Inc.
1010 Hanna Building, 1422 Euclid Ave.
Cleveland, OH 44115
(216) 363-6483

Building and equipment grants. Disabled; community development; health organizations; cultural organizations

Grants awarded to organizations located in Ohio.

Typical grant range: $2,000 to $12,000

678
Iddings Foundation
Kettering Tower, Suite 1620
Dayton, OH 45423
(513) 224-1773

Building and equipment grants. Community development; education; cultural organizations; disabled; elderly; social welfare; environment; renovation grants

Grants awarded to organizations located in Ohio, with an emphasis in Dayton.

Typical grant range: $2,000 to $15,000

679
Kulas Foundation
Tower City Center
610 Terminal Tower
Cleveland, OH 44113
(216) 623-4770

Building and equipment grants. Cultural organizations; social welfare; disabled; higher education

Grants awarded to organizations located in the Cleveland vicinity.

Typical grant range: $5,000 to $35,000

680
Lubrizol Foundation
29400 Lakeland Blvd.
Wickliffe, OH 44092
(216) 943-4200

Building and equipment grants. Health organizations; hospitals; community development; elderly; social welfare; disabled; culture; higher education

Grants awarded to organizations located in areas of company operations.

Typical grant range: $1,000 to $11,000

681
Elizabeth Ring Mather and William Gwinn Mather Fund
650 Citizens Building
850 Euclid Avenue
Cleveland, OH 44114
(216) 861-5341

Building and equipment grants. Social welfare; higher education; cultural organizations; hospitals

Grants awarded to organizations located in Ohio.

682
S. Livingston Mather Charitable Trust
803 Tower East
20600 Chagrin Blvd.
Shaker Heights, OH 44122
(216) 942-6484

Building and equipment grants. Child welfare; youth organizations; culture; disabled; environment; social welfare

683
Mead Corporation Foundation
Courthouse Plaza Northeast
Dayton, OH 45463
(513) 495-3428

Building and equipment grants. Disabled; social welfare; community development; recreation; youth organizations; minorities

Grants awarded to organizations located in areas of company operations.

Typical grant range: $1,000 to $20,000

129

684
Charles Moerlein Foundation
c/o Fifth Third Bank
Dept. 00864
Cincinnati, OH 45263
(513) 579-6034

Building and equipment grants. Social welfare; performing arts; community development; Center for Alcoholism Treatment (equipment); St. Francis School (equipment); Outdoor Education Center (building funds); Family and Child Care Center (renovation); renovation grants

Grants awarded to organizations located in the Cincinnati vicinity.

685
John P. Murphy Foundation
Tower City Center
Suite 610 Terminal Tower
50 Public Square
Cleveland, OH 44113
(216) 623-4770

Building and equipment grants. Social welfare; cultural organizations; higher education; community development; child welfare; disabled; renovation grants

Grants awarded to organizations located in the Cleveland vicinity.

Typical grant range: $2,000 to $50,000

686
NCR Foundation
1700 S. Patterson Blvd.
Dayton, OH 45479
(513) 445-2577

Building and equipment grants. Social welfare; community development; higher education; minorities; cultural organizations; disabled

Grants awarded to organizations located in areas of company operations, with an emphasis in Dayton.

Typical grant range: $5,000 to $50,000

687
Nord Family Foundation
347 Midway Blvd.
Elyria, OH 44035
(216) 324-2822

Building grants. Child welfare; homeless; disabled; health organizations; cultural organizations; minorities; renovation grants

Grants awarded to organizations located in Cuyahoga and Lorain Counties.

688
Piqua-Miami County Foundation
618 N. Wayne Street
Piqua, OH 45356

Building and equipment grants. Social welfare; libraries; cultural organizations; education

Grants awarded to organizations located in Miami County.

689
**Elisabeth Severance Prentiss
Foundation**
c/o National City Bank
P.O. Box 5756
Cleveland, OH 44101
(216) 575-2760

Building and equipment grants. Hospitals; health organizations; elderly; disabled; youth organizations; higher education; Alzheimer's Association (building funds); Center for Women (purchase building); Child Guidance Center (renovation); renovation grants

Grants awarded to organizations located in the Cleveland vicinity.

690
Procter & Gamble Fund
P.O. Box 599
Cincinnati, OH 45201

Building and equipment grants.
Community development; minorities;
higher education; health organizations;
disabled; youth organizations

Grants awarded to organizations located
in areas of company operations.

691
Reeves Foundation
232-4 West Third Street
P.O. Box 441
Dover, OH 44622
(216) 364-4660

Building and equipment grants. Hospitals;
community development; recreation;
cultural organizations; disabled; youth
organizations; higher education; County
Health Department (car seats); Big
Brothers/Big Sisters (video equipment);
Police Department/Fire Department
(telephone equipment, radio for truck);
Self-Help, Inc. (equipment); Quaker Club
(all-weather track); Medical Foundation
(building and medical equipment);
Salvation Army (wheelchair lift)

Grants awarded to organizations located
in Ohio, with an emphasis in Dover.

692
Reinberger Foundation
27600 Chagrin Blvd.
Cleveland, OH 44122
(216) 292-2790

Building and equipment grants. Disabled;
higher education; social welfare; cultural
organizations; youth organizations;
Churches; Museum of Natural History
(building funds); Arboretum (building
funds); Museum of Art (renovate garden);
Public Television (equipment); Historical
Society (building funds); Salvation Army
(renovation); Music School (renovation);
renovation grants

Typical grant range: $10,000 to $80,000

693
**Richland County Foundation of
Mansfield, Ohio**
24 W. Third Street, Suite 100
Mansfield, OH 44902
(419) 525-3020

Building and equipment grants. Health
organizations; hospitals; community
development; elderly; disabled; youth
organizations; cultural organizations;
animal welfare; higher education;
renovation grants

Grants awarded to organizations located
in Richland County.

694
Fran and Warren Rupp Foundation
40 Sturges Avenue
Mansfield, OH 44902
(419) 522-2345

Building grants. Youth organizations;
environment; social welfare; hospitals

Typical grant range: $2,000 to $25,000

695
Josephine S. Russell Charitable Trust
PNC Bank, Ohio, N.A.
P.O. Box 1198
Cincinnati, OH 45201
(513) 651-8377

Building and equipment grants. Disabled;
cultural organizations; social welfare;
health organizations; renovation grants

Grants awarded to organizations located
in the Cincinnati vicinity.

Typical grant range: $3,000 to $12,000

696
Jacob G. Schmidlapp Trust No. 1
c/o The Fifth Third Bank
Dept. 00864, Foundation Office
Cincinnati, OH 45263
(513) 579-6034

Building and equipment grants. Child
welfare; hospitals; health organizations;
disabled; cultural organizations; social
welfare; Mental Health Association
(equipment); Dominican Sisters (window
replacement); Catholic High School
(equipment); Restoration, Inc. (roof
repairs); Counseling Center (van);
Community Center (building repairs);
Franciscan Home Development
(renovation); Home for Adults
(equipment); Jewish Early Learning
Cooperative (renovation); Habitat for
Humanity (housing renovation); New Life
Youth Services (equipment); Sr. Citizens
Services (equipment); renovation grants

Grants awarded to organizations located
in the Cincinnati vicinity.

Typical grant range: $5,000 to $60,000

697
Jacob G. Schmidlapp Trust No. 2
c/o The Fifth Third Bank
Dept. 00864
Cincinnati, OH 45263
(513) 579-6034

Building and equipment grants. Disabled;
elderly; cultural organizations; higher
education; youth organizations; hospitals;
renovation grants

Grants awarded to organizations located
in the Cincinnati vicinity.

Typical grant range: $5,000 to $25,000

698
Scioto County Area Foundation
BancOhio Building, Suite 801
Portsmouth, OH 45662
(614) 354-4612

Building and equipment grants. Cultural
organizations; child welfare; disabled;
higher education; social welfare; youth
organizations; community development

Grants awarded to organizations located
in Scioto County.

Typical grant range: $1,000 to $15,000

699
Sears-Swetland Foundation
907 Park Building
Cleveland, OH 44114
(216) 241-6434

Building and equipment grants. Cultural
organizations; hospitals; environment

Grants awarded to organizations located
in the Cleveland vicinity.

Typical grant range: $500 to $3,000

700
Louise Taft Semple Foundation
1800 Star Bank Center
Cincinnati, OH 45202
(513) 381-2838

Building grants. All levels of education;
community development; social welfare;
cultural organizations

701
Sherwick Fund
c/o The Cleveland Foundation
1422 Euclid Avenue, Suite 1400
Cleveland, OH 44115
(216) 861-3810

Building and equipment grants. Health
organizations; community development;
public libraries; youth organizations;
disabled; cultural organizations

Typical grant range: $5,000 to $50,000

702
Sherwin-Williams Foundation
101 Prospect Ave., NW, 12th Floor
Cleveland, OH 44115
(216) 566-2511

Building and equipment grants. Social
welfare; minorities; higher education;
community development; disabled; health
organizations; cultural organizations

Grants awarded to organizations located
in areas of company operations, with an
emphasis in Cleveland.

703
Kelvin and Eleanor Smith Foundation
1100 National City Bank Bldg.
Cleveland, OH 44114
(216) 566-5500

Building and equipment grants. Hospitals;
cultural organizations; higher education;
social welfare; disabled

Grants awarded to organizations located
in the Cleveland vicinity.

Typical grant range: $5,000 to $40,000

704
Stark County Foundation
United Bank Building, Suite 350
220 Market Avenue South
Canton, OH 44702
(216) 454-3426

Building and equipment grants. Social
welfare; disabled; hospitals; health
organizations; community development;
recreation; higher education; cultural
organizations; youth organizations;
elderly; American Red Cross (equipment);
Planned Parenthood (building and
equipment grants); renovation grants

Grants awarded to organizations located
in Stark County.

Typical grant range: $3,000 to $20,000

705
Stocker Foundation
209 Sixth Street, Suite 25
Lorain, OH 44052
(216)246-5719

Building and equipment grants.
Community development; cultural
organizations; youth organizations;
all levels of education; social welfare;
disabled

Typical grant range: $2,000 to $12,000

706
Stranahan Foundation
4149 Holland-Sylvania Road
Toledo, OH 43623
(419) 882-6575

Building and equipment grants. Higher
education; cultural organizations; social
welfare; youth organizations; community
development; disabled; renovation grants

Grants awarded to organizations located
in the Toledo vicinity.

Typical grant range: $10,000 to $125,000

707
Frank M. Tait Foundation
Courthouse Plaza, S.W., 10th Floor
Dayton, OH 45402
(513) 222-2401

Building and equipment grants. Cultural
organizations; higher education; youth
organizations; recreation; disabled; child
welfare; health organizations; renovation
grants

Grants awarded to organizations located
in Montgomery County.

Typical grant range: $1,000 to $15,000

708
Timken Foundation of Canton
236 Third Street, S.W.
Canton, OH 44702
(216) 455-5281

Building and equipment grants. Higher
education; community development;
cultural organizations; public libraries;
recreation; youth organizations; health
organizations; disabled; renovation grants

Grants awarded to organizations located
in areas of company operations.

Typical grant range: $15,000 to $200,000

709
Troy Foundation
c/o Star Bank, N.A., Troy
910 W. Main Street
Troy, OH 45373
(513) 335-8351

Building and equipment grants. Health
organizations; recreation; community
development; cultural organizations;
disabled; elderly; renovation grants

Grants awarded to organizations located
in the Troy vicinity.

710
TRW Foundation
1900 Richmond Road
Cleveland, OH 44124
(216) 291-7166

Building and equipment grants.
Minorities; community development; all
levels of education; hospitals; health
organizations; social welfare; cultural
organizations

Grants awarded to organizations located
in areas of company operations, with an
emphasis in Cleveland.

Typical grant range: $5,000 to $35,000

711
Vernay Foundation
P.O. Box 184
Yellow Springs, OH 45387

Building and equipment grants. Social
welfare; youth organizations; recreation;
renovation grants

712
Evelyn E. Walter Foundation
116 S. Main Street
Marion, OH 43302

Building and equipment grants. Social
welfare; cultural organizations

Grants awarded to organizations located
in Marion.

Typical grant range: $1,500 to $7,000

713
Charles Westheimer Family Fund
1126 Fort View Place
Cincinnati, OH 45202
(513) 421-3030

Building grants. Cultural organizations;
youth organizations

Grants awarded to organizations located
in Cincinnati.

Typical grant range: $100 to $2,000

714
**White Consolidated Industries
Foundation, Inc.**
c/o White Consolidated Industries, Inc.
11770 Berea Road
Cleveland, OH 44111
(216) 252-3700

Building and equipment grants. Higher
education; community development;
cultural organizations; hospitals;
minorities

Grants awarded to organizations located
in areas of company operations.

Typical grant range: $2,000 to $75,000

715
Thomas H. White Foundation
627 Hanna Building
1422 Euclid Avenue
Cleveland, OH 44115
(216) 696-7273

Building and equipment grants. All levels
of education; recreation; disabled; elderly;
child welfare; youth organizations

Grants awarded to organizations located
in Cleveland.

Typical grant range: $1,000 to $35,000

716
Wolfe Associates Inc.
34 S. Third Street
Columbus, OH 43215
(614) 461-5220

Building and equipment grants. All levels
of education; cultural organizations; social
welfare; community development; youth
organizations; hospitals; disabled;
renovation grants

Typical grant range: $2,000 to $20,000

717
Leo Yassenoff Foundation
16 E. Broad Street, Suite 403
Columbus, OH 43215
(614) 221-4315

Building and equipment grants. Child
welfare; elderly; hospitals; health
organizations; minorities; youth
organizations; disabled; cultural
organizations; renovation grants

Grants awarded to organizations located
in Franklin County.

718
Youngstown Foundation
P.O. Box 1162
Youngstown, OH 44501
(216) 744-0320

Building and equipment grants. Disabled;
cultural organizations; hospitals; health
organizations; community development;
youth organizations; renovation grants

Grants awarded to organizations located
in the Youngstown vicinity.

OKLAHOMA

719
**Mary K. Ashbrook Foundation for
El Reno, Oklahoma**
P.O. Box 627
El Reno, OK 73036

Building and equipment grants. Hospitals;
social welfare; community development;
college (upgrade sound and lighting
system); El Reno Public Schools
(equipment); Mobile Wheels of Reno
(equipment); Fire Department
(equipment)

Grants awarded to organizations located
in El Reno.

Typical grant range: $1,000 to $15,000

720
Broadhurst Foundation
401 S. Boston, Suite 100
Tulsa, OK 74103
(918) 584-0661

Building and equipment grants. Cultural
organizations; community development;
hospitals; health organizations; elderly;
child welfare; disabled; Methodist Church
(books for library); renovation grants

Most grants awarded to organizations
located in Oklahoma.

721
Cuesta Foundation, Inc.
One Williams Center, Suite 4400
Tulsa, OK 74172
(918) 584-7266

Building grants. Cultural organizations;
social welfare; higher education

Grants awarded to organizations located
in Oklahoma.

Typical grant range: $1,000 to $5,000

722
Harris Foundation, Inc.
6403 N.W. Grand Blvd., Suite 211
Oklahoma City, OK 73116
(405) 848-3371

Building and equipment grants. Health
organizations; higher education; social
welfare; disabled; youth organizations;
Habitat for Humanity (equipment);
Infant Crisis Center (equipment)

Grants awarded to organizations located
in Oklahoma.

Typical grant range: $1,000 to $20,000

723
Helmerich Foundation
1579 East 21st St.
Tulsa, OK 74114
(918) 742-5531

Building and equipment grants. Cultural
organizations; community development;
higher education; health organizations;
hospitals; women

Grants awarded to organizations located
in the Tulsa vicinity.

Typical grant range: $30,000 to $100,000

724
**Robert S. and Grayce B. Kerr
Foundation, Inc.**
6301 N. Western, Suite 220
Oklahoma City, OK 73118
(405) 848-0975

Building and equipment grants. Cultural
organizations; environment; social welfare

Grants awarded to organizations located
in Oklahoma.

725
J.E. and L.E. Mabee Foundation, Inc.
3000 Mid-Continent Tower
401 South Boston
Tulsa, OK 74103
(918) 584-4286

Building and equipment grants. Elderly;
hospitals; health organizations; disabled;
youth organizations; higher education;
renovation grants

Typical grant range: $50,000 to $450,000

726
McCasland Foundation
P.O. Box 400
McCasland Building
Duncan, OK 73534
(405) 252-5580

Building grants. Higher education; child
welfare; cultural organizations; youth
organizations; community development;
health organizations

Typical grant range: $2,000 to $65,000

727
McMahon Foundation
714-716 C Avenue
P.O. Box 2156
Lawton, OK 73502

Building and equipment grants. Cultural
organizations; social welfare; higher
education; youth; Department of Public
Safety (renovation); Salvation Army
(renovation); YMCA (building funds)

Grants awarded to organizations located
in Oklahoma.

Typical grant range: $1,000 to $50,000

728
Samuel Roberts Noble Foundation, Inc.
P.O. Box 2180
2510 State Highway 199 East
Ardmore, OK 73402
(405) 223-5810

Building and equipment grants. Cultural
organizations; environment; disabled;
higher education; health organizations;
community development; recreation;
youth organizations

Grants awarded to organizations located
in Oklahoma.

Typical grant range: $10,000 to $125,000

729
**Oklahoma City Community
Foundation, Inc.**
115 Park Avenue
Oklahoma City, OK 73103
(405) 235-5603

Building and equipment grants. Child
welfare; community development; youth
organizations; higher education; health
organizations; elderly; recreation; cultural
organizations; disabled

Grants awarded to organizations located
in the Oklahoma City vicinity.

Typical grant range: $2,000 to $15,000

730
**Oklahoma Gas and Electric Company
Foundation, Inc.**
101 North Robinson
P.O. Box 321
Oklahoma City, OK 73101
(405) 272-3196

Building and equipment grants. Higher
education; social welfare; cultural
organizations; youth organizations; health
organizations; disabled; community
development

Grants awarded to organizations located
in Oklahoma.

731
Phillips Petroleum Foundation, Inc.
Phillips Building
Bartlesville, OK 74001
(918) 661-6248

Building and equipment grants.
Community development; higher
education; cultural organizations; social
welfare; elderly; disabled; health
organizations; renovation grants

Grants awarded to organizations located
in areas of company operations.

Typical grant range: $1,000 to $20,000

732
Sarkeys Foundation
116 S. Peters, Suite 219
Norman, OK 73069
(405) 364-3703

Building and equipment grants. Social
welfare; homeless; elderly; disabled;
hospitals; health organizations; youth
organizations; higher education; culture;
Oklahoma Medical Research Foundation
(building funds); American Diabetes
Association (equipment); Billy Graham
Evangelistic Association (equipment);
Public Library (purchase books); Mental
Health Association (renovation);
renovation grants

Grants awarded to organizations located
in Oklahoma.

Typical grant range: $5,000 to $80,000

733
**Herman P. and Sophia Taubman
Foundation**
Attention: Mrs. Billie Coffee
P.O. Box 2300
Tulsa, OK 74192
(918) 588-6423

Building grants. Higher education;
disabled; community development;
minorities; child welfare

Typical grant range: $1,000 to $25,000

734
Williams Companies Foundation, Inc.
P.O. Box 2400
Tulsa, OK 74102
(918) 588-2106

Building and equipment grants. Disabled; social welfare; environment; hospitals; health organizations; higher education; community development; cultural organizations

Grants awarded to organizations located in areas of company operations with an emphasis in Tulsa.

OREGON

735
Carpenter Foundation
711 E. Main Street, Suite 10
P.O. Box 816
Medford, OR 97501
(503) 772-5851

Building and equipment grants. Health organizations; social welfare; cultural organizations; community development; higher education

Grants awarded to organizations located in Jackson and Josephine Counties.

Typical grant range: $2,000 to $15,000

736
Chiles Foundation
111 S.W. Fifth Ave., Suite 4050
Portland, OR 97204
(503) 222-2143

Building and equipment grants. Higher education; cultural organizations; youth organizations; health organizations

Most grants awarded to organizations located in Oregon.

Typical grant range: $5,000 to $50,000

737
Collins Foundation
1618 S.W. First Avenue, Suite 305
Portland, OR 97201
(503) 227-7171

Building and equipment grants. Youth organizations; cultural organizations; hospitals; health organizations; disabled; homeless; community development; renovation grants

Grants awarded to organizations located in Oregon.

Typical grant range: $5,000 to $100,000

738
Jeld-Wen Foundation
P.O. Box 1329
Klamath Falls, OR 97601
(503) 882-3451

Building and equipment grants. Higher education; community development; youth organizations; social welfare; libraries

Typical grant range: $1,000 to $40,000

739
Meyer Memorial Trust
1515 S.W. Fifth Ave., Suite 500
Portland, OR 97201
(503) 228-5512

Building and equipment grants. Youth organizations; disabled; social welfare; environment; health organizations; elderly; child welfare; all levels of education; cultural organizations; homeless; renovation grants

Most grants awarded to organizations located in Oregon.

740
Oregon Community Foundation
621 S.W. Morrison, Suite 725
Portland, OR 97205
(503) 227-6846

Building and equipment grants.
Community development; cultural
organizations; social welfare; disabled;
elderly; hospitals; youth organizations;
renovation grants

Grants awarded to organizations located
in Oregon.

Typical grant range: $1,000 to $20,000

741
Tektronix Foundation
P.O. Box 1000
Wilsonville, OR 97077
(503) 627-7084

Building and equipment grants. Social
welfare; cultural organizations; health
organizations; disabled; community
development; higher education;
renovation grants

Grants awarded to organizations located
in Oregon.

Typical grant range: $12,000 to $25,000

742
Rose E. Tucker Charitable Trust
900 S.W. Fifth Avenue
Portland, OR 97204
(503) 224-3380

Building and equipment grants. Cultural
organizations; social welfare; disabled;
community development; hospitals; health
organizations; youth organizations;
renovation grants

Grants awarded to organizations located
in the Portland vicinity.

Typical grant range: $2,000 to $11,000

PENNSYLVANIA

743
Air Products Foundation
7201 Hamilton Blvd.
Allentown, PA 18195
(215) 481-8079

Building and equipment grants. Higher
education; community development;
disabled; hospitals; social welfare;
museums; cultural organizations; youth
organizations; renovation grants

Grants awarded to organizations located
in areas of company operations.

Typical grant range: $500 to $9,000

744
Alcoa Foundation
2202 Alcoa Building
425 Sixth Avenue
Pittsburgh, PA 15219
(412) 553-2343

Building and equipment grants. Child
welfare; community development; higher
education; health organizations; hospitals;
social welfare; elderly; disabled;
renovation grants

Grants awarded to organizations located
in areas of company operations.

Typical grant range: $1,000 to $15,000

745
Arcadia Foundation
105 East Logan Street
Norristown, PA 19401
(215) 275-8460

Building and equipment grants. Hospitals;
health organizations; social welfare;
higher education; disabled; environment;
youth organizations; renovation grants

Grants awarded to organizations located
in Pennsylvania.

Typical grant range: $1,000 to $25,000

746
**Claude Worthington Benedum
Foundation**
1400 Benedum-Trees Building
Pittsburgh, PA 15222
(412) 288-0360

Building and equipment grants. Health
organizations; community development;
homeless; elderly; all levels of education;
social welfare; youth organizations; child
welfare; environment; public libraries;
recreation; renovation grants

Typical grant range: $25,000 to $50,000

747
**Allen H. & Selma W. Berkman
Charitable Trust**
5000 Fifth Avenue
Pittsburgh, PA 15232
(412) 355-8640

Building grants. Social welfare; health
organizations; hospitals; community
development; cultural organizations;
higher education; disabled

Grants awarded to organizations located
in the Pittsburgh vicinity.

748
**E. Rhodes and Leona B. Carpenter
Foundation**
c/o Joseph A. O'Connor, Jr., Morgan,
Lewis & Bockius
2000 One Logan Square
Philadelphia, PA 19103
(215) 963-5212

Building grants. Higher education;
cultural organizations; environment;
hospitals; health organizations; hospice;
youth organizations; renovation grants

Typical grant range: $10,000 to $85,000

749
Eden Foundation
4915 Monument Road
Philadelphia, PA 19131

Building and equipment grants.
Organizations helping military
personnel; cultural organizations;
Churches; renovation grants

Grants awarded to organizations located
in the Philadelphia vicinity.

Typical grant range: $500 to $7,000

750
Eden Hall Foundation
Pittsburgh Office and Research Park
5500 Corporate Dr., Suite 210
Pittsburgh, PA 15237
(412) 364-6670

Building and equipment grants. Elderly;
disabled; higher education; hospitals;
health organizations; recreation; child
welfare; youth organizations; renovation
grants

Typical grant range: $15,000 to $125,000

751
Erie Community Foundation
127 W. Sixth Street
Erie, PA 16501
(814) 454-0843

Building and equipment grants. Animal
welfare; youth organizations; culture;
social welfare; disabled; elderly; health
organizations; community development;
recreation; higher education; renovation
grants

Grants awarded to organizations located
in Erie County.

Typical grant range: $2,000 to $15,000

752
Graham Foundation Trust
P.O. Box 1104
York, PA 17405
(717) 848-3755

Building grants. Higher education;
disabled; health organizations; cultural
organizations; youth organizations

Grants awarded to organizations located
in York, Pennsylvania.

Typical grant range: $2,000 to $50,000

753
Grundy Foundation
680 Radcliffe Street
P.O. Box 701
Bristol, PA 19007
(215) 788-5460

Building and equipment grants. Elderly;
disabled; child welfare; community
development; health organizations;
hospitals; public libraries; youth
organizations; higher education;
renovation grants

Grants awarded to organizations located
in Bucks County.

754
H.J. Heinz Company Foundation
P.O. Box 57
Pittsburgh, PA 15230
(412) 456-5772

Building and equipment grants. Social
welfare; health organizations; hospitals;
higher education; cultural organizations;
recreation; community development;
disabled; renovation grants

Grants awarded to organizations located
in areas of company operations.

755
Howard Heinz Endowment
30 CNG Tower
625 Liberty Avenue
Pittsburgh, PA 15222-2494
(412) 281-5777

Building and equipment grants. Youth
organizations; disabled; minorities; health
organizations; higher education; elderly;
community development; recreation;
cultural organizations; renovation grants

Grants awarded to organizations located
in Pennsylvania.

Typical grant range: $50,000 to $300,000

756
Vira I. Heinz Endowment
30 CNG Tower
625 Liberty Avenue
Pittsburgh, PA 15222
(412) 391-5122

Building and equipment grants. All levels
of education; elderly; homeless; cultural
organizations; child welfare; women;
recreation; renovation grants

Most grants awarded to organizations
located in the Pittsburgh vicinity.

757
Hershey Foods Corporation Fund
100 Crystal Drive
Hershey, PA 17033
(717) 534-7574

Building and equipment grants.
Community development; higher
education; hospitals; youth organizations;
child welfare; disabled; environment

Grants awarded to organizations located
in Pennsylvania.

Typical grant range: $500 to $15,000

758
Hillman Foundation, Inc.
2000 Grant Building
Pittsburgh, PA 15219
(412) 338-3466

Building and equipment grants. Higher
education; youth organizations; health
organizations; community development;
disabled; cultural organizations; social
welfare; renovation grants

Grants awarded to organizations located
in the Pittsburgh vicinity.

Typical grant range: $5,000 to $75,000

759
T. James Kavanagh Foundation
57 Northwood Road
Newton Square, PA 19073
(215) 356-0743

Building and equipment grants. Hospice;
community development; child welfare;
elderly; recreation; youth organizations;
disabled; Catholic organizations

Grants awarded to organizations located
in Pennsylvania.

Typical grant range: $500 to $3,000

760
**Josiah W. and Bessie H. Kline
Foundation, Inc.**
42 Kline Village
Harrisburg, PA 17104
(717) 232-0266

Building and equipment grants. Social
welfare; community development; higher
education; hospitals; youth organizations;
disabled; cultural organizations; child
welfare; renovation grants

Typical grant range: $2,000 to $25,000

761
Laurel Foundation
6th Floor North
Three Gateway Center
Pittsburgh, PA 15222
(412) 765-2400

Building and equipment grants. Cultural
organizations; higher education; hospice;
youth organizations; environment; health
organizations; social welfare

762
McCune Foundation
1104 Commonwealth Building
316 Fourth Avenue
Pittsburgh, PA 15222
(412) 644-8779

Building and equipment grants. Elderly;
disabled; higher education; hospitals;
health organizations; youth organizations;
cultural organizations; public libraries;
renovation grants

Typical grant range: $50,000 to $400,000

763
**Katherine Mabis McKenna
Foundation, Inc.**
P.O. Box 186
Latrobe, PA 15650
(412) 537-6900

Building and equipment grants. Higher
education; disabled; cultural organizations

764
Philip M. McKenna Foundation, Inc.
P.O. Box 186
Latrobe, PA 15650
(412) 537-6900

Building and equipment grants. Disabled;
higher education; social welfare; hospitals

Typical grant range: $3,000 to $65,000

765
McLean Contributionship
945 Haverford Road
Bryn Mawr, PA 19010
(215) 527-6330

Building and equipment grants. Social welfare; hospitals; youth organizations; environment; disabled; renovation grants

766
Mellon Bank Foundation
c/o Mellon Bank Corp.
One Mellon Bank Center, Suite 1830
Pittsburgh, PA 15258
(412) 234-2732

Building grants. Social welfare; community development; cultural organizations; hospitals; youth organizations; disabled

Grants awarded to organizations located in areas of company operations.

767
R.K. Mellon Family Foundation
P.O. Box 2930
Pittsburgh, PA 15230
(412) 392-2800

Building and equipment grants. Higher education; disabled; social welfare; cultural organizations; hospitals; health organizations; Churches; renovation grants

Typical grant range: $5,000 to $35,000

768
Richard King Mellon Foundation
P.O. Box 2930
Pittsburgh, PA 15230
(412) 392-2800

Building and equipment grants. Social welfare; community development; environment; child welfare; disabled; higher education; youth organizations; cultural organizations; renovation grants

Most grants awarded to organizations located in Pittsburgh.

Typical grant range: $40,000 to $250,000

769
Grace S. and W. Linton Nelson Foundation
West Valley Business Center
940 W. Valley Road, Suite 1601
Wayne, PA 19087
(215) 975-9169

Equipment grants. Women; youth organizations; disabled; child welfare

Grants awarded to organizations located in Pennsylvania.

Typical grant range: $5,000 to $35,000

770
W.I. Patterson Charitable Fund
407 Oliver Building
Pittsburgh, PA 15222
(412) 281-5580

Building and equipment grants. Health organizations; hospitals; social welfare; elderly; disabled; child welfare

Grants awarded to organizations located in Allegheny County.

Typical grant range: $1,000 to $7,500

771
William Penn Foundation
1630 Locust Street
Philadelphia, PA 19103
(215) 732-5114

Building and equipment grants. Women; environment; homeless; all levels of education; youth organizations; cultural organizations; disabled; social welfare; community development; elderly; renovation grants

Typical grant range: $5,000 to $125,000

772
Pew Charitable Trusts
One Commerce Square
2005 Market Street, Suite 1700
Philadelphia, PA 19103
(215) 575-9050

Building and equipment grants. Cultural organizations; all levels of education; community development; women; youth organizations; elderly; minorities; child welfare; disabled; hospitals; health organizations; environment; renovation grants

773
Dr. & Mrs. Arthur William Phillips
Charitable Trust
229 Elm St.
P.O. Box 316
Oil City, PA 16301
(215) 676-2736

Building and equipment grants. Cultural organizations; animal welfare; community development; higher education; health organizations; hospitals; public libraries; youth organizations; renovation grants

Most grants awarded to organizations located in Northwestern Pennsylvania.

774
Pittsburgh Foundation
One PPG Place, 30th Floor
Pittsburgh, PA 15222
(412) 391-5122

Building and equipment grants. Youth organizations; community development; disabled; cultural organizations; social welfare; higher education; minorities; Boys and Girls Club (equipment, renovation); renovation grants

Grants awarded to organizations located in the Pittsburgh vicinity.

Typical grant range: $5,000 to $50,000

775
Harry Plankenhorn Foundation, Inc.
c/o Abram M. Snyder
R.D. 2
Cogan Station, PA 17728

Building grants. Social welfare; youth organizations; disabled; health organizations; American Red Cross (building funds)

Grants awarded to organizations located in Lycoming County.

Typical grant range: $1,000 to $20,000

776
Rockwell International
Corporation Trust
625 Liberty Avenue
Pittsburgh, PA 15222
(412) 565-5803

Building grants. All levels of education; social welfare; community development; child welfare; cultural organizations

Grants awarded to organizations located in areas of company operations.

777
Scott Paper Company Foundation
One Scott Plaza
Philadelphia, PA 19113
(215) 522-6160

Equipment grants. Child welfare; social welfare; disabled; all levels of education

Grants awarded to organizations located in areas of company operations.

Typical grant range: $3,000 to $10,000

778
Ethel Sergeant Clark Smith
Memorial Fund
101 Bryn Mawr Avenue, Suite 200
Bryn Mawr, PA 19010
(215) 525-9667

Building and equipment grants. Cultural
organizations; community development;
women; all levels of education; disabled;
public libraries; youth organizations;
recreation; health organizations;
renovation grants

Grants awarded to organizations located
in Delaware County.

Typical grant range: $5,000 to $40,000

779
W.W. Smith Charitable Trust
101 Bryn Mawr Avenue, Suite 200
Bryn Mawr, PA 19010
(215) 525-9667

Building and equipment grants. Women;
minorities; disabled; elderly; hospitals;
health organizations; homeless; child
welfare; youth organizations; renovation
grants

Typical grant range: $10,000 to $35,000

780
Stackpole-Hall Foundation
44 S. St. Marys Street
St. Marys, PA 15857
(814) 834-1845

Building and equipment grants. Youth
organizations; community development;
hospitals; disabled; higher education;
cultural organizations; renovation grants

Grants awarded to organizations located
in Elk County.

781
Harry C. Trexler Trust
33 S. Seventh St., Suite 205
Allentown, PA 18101
(215) 434-9645

Building grants. Social welfare; hospitals;
child welfare; community development;
disabled; youth organizations; elderly;
cultural organizations; public libraries;
renovation grants

Grants awarded to organizations located
in Lehigh County.

Typical grant range: $12,000 to $30,000

782
Union Pacific Foundation
Martin Tower
Eighth & Eaton Avenues
Bethlehem, PA 18018
(215) 861-3225

Building and equipment grants. Higher
education; environment; social welfare;
cultural organizations; minorities; youth
organizations; women; hospitals; health
organizations; disabled; renovation grants

Grants awarded to organizations located
in areas of company operations.

Typical grant range: $2,000 to $20,000

783
USX Foundation, Inc.
600 Grant Street
Pittsburgh, PA 15219
(412) 433-5237

Building and equipment grants. Child
welfare; disabled; health organizations;
community development; elderly; higher
education; hospitals; youth organizations;
cultural organizations; renovation grants

Grants awarded to organizations located
in areas of company operations.

Typical grant range: $3,000 to $40,000

784
William T. Vogt and Lorine E. Vogt Charitable Foundation
558 W. Montgomery Avenue
Haverford, PA 19041
(215) 527-1650

Building grants. Museums; health organizations; Christian related organizations

Grants awarded to organizations located in Pennsylvania.

Typical grant range: $500 to $4,000

785
Widener Memorial Foundation in Aid of Handicapped Children
665 Thomas Road
P.O. Box 178
Lafayette Hill, PA 19444
(215) 836-7500

Building and equipment grants. Disabled; child welfare; all levels of education; hospitals; health organizations; recreation; renovation grants

Typical grant range: $10,000 to $75,000

786
Wyomissing Foundation, Inc.
1015 Penn Avenue
Wyomissing, PA 19610
(215) 376-7496

Building and equipment grants. Social welfare; higher education; community development; cultural organizations; hospitals; health organizations

Grants awarded to organizations located in Berks County.

RHODE ISLAND

787
Champlin Foundations
410 S. Main Street
Providence, RI 02903
(401) 421-3719

Building and equipment grants. Health organizations; cultural organizations; environment; hospitals; all levels of education; disabled; recreation; elderly; child welfare; women; animal welfare; renovation grants

Grants awarded to organizations located in Rhode Island.

Typical grant range: $10,000 to $100,000

788
Ida Ballou Littlefield Memorial Trust
1500 Fleet Center
Providence, RI 02903
(401) 274-2000

Building and equipment grants. St. Mary's Home for Children (renovation); Geriatric Center (building funds); Rhode Island School of Design (new museum wing); Church (restoration); CARE Educational Center (building funds); Traveler's Aid Society (van); Adult Day Care Services (purchase building); School for the Blind (equipment); Save the Bay (equipment); Historic Society (renovation)

Typical grant range: $5,000 to $20,000

789
Rhode Island Foundation/Rhode Island Community Foundation
70 Elm Street
Providence, RI 02903
(401) 274-4564

Building and equipment grants. Social welfare; homeless; cultural organizations; elderly; disabled; youth organizations; higher education; health organizations; hospitals; community development; child welfare; environment; renovation grants

Grants awarded to organizations located in Rhode Island.

790
Fred M. Roddy Foundation, Inc.
R.I. Hospital Trust National Bank
One Hospital Trust Plaza
Providence, RI 02903
(401) 278-8700

Building grants. Higher education; hospitals; health organizations

791
Textron Charitable Trust
P.O. Box 878
Providence, RI 02901
(401) 457-2430

Building and equipment grants. Cultural organizations; social welfare; health organizations; higher education; community development; minorities; hospitals

Grants awarded to organizations located in areas of company operations.

Typical grant range: $1,000 to $15,000

SOUTH CAROLINA

792
Abney Foundation
P.O. Box 1138
Greenwood, SC 29648
(803) 229-5777

Building grants. Higher education; social welfare; youth organizations

Grants awarded to organizations located in South Carolina.

793
Central Carolina Community Foundation
P.O. Box 11222
Columbia, SC 29211
(803) 254-5601

Building and equipment grants. Community development; cultural organizations; disabled; youth organizations; libraries; recreation; renovation grants

Typical grant range: $1,000 to $5,000

794
Community Foundation of Greater Greenville, Inc.
655 S. Main Street
P.O. Box 6909
Greenville, SC 29606
(803) 233-5925

Equipment grants. Child welfare; community development; disabled; recreation; health organizations

Grants awarded to organizations located in Greenville County.

795
Fullerton Foundation
515 W. Buford Street
Gaffney, SC 29340
(803) 489-6678

Building and equipment grants. Child welfare; hospitals; health organizations; disabled; youth organizations; higher education

Typical grant range: $10,000 to $85,000

796
Gregg-Graniteville Foundation, Inc.
P.O. Box 418
Graniteville, SC 29829
(803) 663-7552

Building and equipment grants. Higher education; disabled; recreation; youth organizations; health organizations; community development; renovation grants

Typical grant range: $1,000 to $12,000

797
Joanna Foundation
P.O. Box 21537
Charleston, SC 29413

Building and equipment grants. Community development; environment; higher education; cultural organizations; disabled; Churches

Grants awarded to organizations located in South Carolina.

798
Post and Courier Foundation
134 Columbus Street
Charleston, SC 29403
(803) 577-7111

Building grants. Health organizations; disabled; community development

Grants awarded to organizations located in the Charleston vicinity.

799
Self Foundation
P.O. Drawer 1017
Greenwood, SC 29648
(803) 941-4063

Building and equipment grants. Hospitals; health organizations; youth organizations; cultural organizations; higher education; disabled; recreation; women; community development; Churches; renovation grants

Grants awarded to organizations located in South Carolina, with an emphasis in the Greenwood vicinity.

Typical grant range: $5,000 to $50,000

800
Spartanburg County Foundation
320 E. Main Street
Spartanburg, SC 29302
(803) 582-0138

Building and equipment grants. Social welfare; disabled; cultural organizations; environment; child welfare; recreation; health organizations; youth organizations; community development; renovation grants

Grants awarded to organizations located in Spartanburg County.

Typical grant range: $1,000 to $12,000

801
Springs Foundation
P.O. Drawer 460
Lancaster, SC 29721
(803) 286-2196

Building and equipment grants. Disabled; environment; cultural organizations; all levels of education; hospitals; recreation; social welfare; community development

Typical grant range: $3,000 to $30,000

802
Summer Foundation
c/o South Carolina Electric and Gas Co.
1426 Main Street, P.O. Box 764
Columbia, SC 29218
(803) 748-3030

Building and equipment grants. Social
welfare; community development;
disabled; child welfare

Grants awarded to organizations located
in South Carolina.

SOUTH DAKOTA

803
South Dakota Community Foundation
207 East Capitol
P.O. Box 296
Pierre, SD 57501
(605) 224-1025

Building and equipment grants. Child
welfare; community development;
minorities; health organizations

Grants awarded to organizations located
in South Dakota.

Typical grant range: $500 to $10,000

TENNESSEE

804
Benwood Foundation, Inc.
1600 American National Bank Bldg.
736 Market Street
Chattanooga, TN 37402
(615) 267-4311

Building and equipment grants. Cultural
organizations; environment; community
development; all levels of education;
hospitals; social welfare; recreation;
renovation grants

Grants awarded to organizations located
in the Chattanooga vicinity.

Typical grant range: $3,000 to $50,000

805
**Community Foundation of Greater
Chattanooga, Inc.**
1600 American National Bank Bldg.
736 Market Street
Chattanooga, TN 37402
(615) 265-0586

Building and equipment grants. All levels
of education; community development;
social welfare; environment; cultural
organizations; renovation grants

Grants awarded to organizations located
in the Chattanooga vicinity.

806
HCA Foundation
c/o Hospital Corp. of America
One Park Plaza, P.O. Box 550
Nashville, TN 37202-0550
(615) 320-2165

Building and equipment grants.
Recreation; higher education; social
welfare; youth organizations; hospice;
health organizations; disabled; women;
cultural organizations; renovation grants

Grants awarded to organizations located
in areas of company operations, with an
emphasis in Nashville.

Typical grant range: $1,000 to $25,000

807
**William P. and Marie R. Lowenstein
Foundation**
100 N. Main Building, Suite 3020
Memphis, TN 38103
(901) 525-5744

Building grants. Jewish Community
Center (building funds)

Grants awarded to organizations located
in Tennessee.

Typical grant range: $250 to $5,000

808
Lyndhurst Foundation
Tallan Building, Suite 701
100 W. Martin Luther King Blvd.
Chattanooga, TN 37402
(615) 756-0767

Building and equipment grants. Cultural
organizations; all levels of education;
environment

Typical grant range: $20,000 to $100,000

809
Maclellan Foundation, Inc.
Provident Building, Suite 501
Chattanooga, TN 37402
(615) 755-1366

Building and equipment grants. Social
welfare; higher education; recreation;
youth organizations; Churches; Ministries
(office equipment)

Grants awarded to organizations located
in the Chattanooga vicinity.

Typical grant range: $30,000 to $100,000

810
R.J. Maclellan Charitable Trust
Provident Building, Suite 501
Chattanooga, TN 37402
(615) 755-1366

Building and equipment grants. Cultural
organizations; recreation; all levels of
education; community development;
youth organizations; Churches; renovation
grants

Grants awarded to organizations located
in the Chattanooga vicinity.

Typical grant range: $15,000 to $125,000

811
Plough Foundation
6077 Primacy Parkway, Suite 230
Memphis, TN 38119
(901) 761-9180

Building and equipment grants. Social
welfare; community development; child
welfare; all levels of education

Grants awarded to organizations located
in the Memphis vicinity.

Typical grant range: $15,000 to $100,000

812
Tonya Memorial Foundation
American National Bank and Trust Co.
736 Market Street
Chattanooga, TN 37402

Building and equipment grants. Hospice;
community development; recreation;
cultural organizations; hospitals; City of
Chattanooga (renovation of auditorium);
Volunteer Community School (building
funds); Museum of Decorative Arts
(equipment)

Grants awarded to organizations located
in the Chattanooga vicinity.

Typical grant range: $5,000 to $200,000

813
Robert Lee Weiss Foundation
c/o First Tennessee Bank, Trust Division
800 South Gay Street
Knoxville, TN 37995

Building and equipment grants. Higher
education; social welfare; disabled;
Churches; Association of Retarded
Citizens (purchase van); Association of
Baptists (building funds); Habitat for
Humanity (expansion of offices)

814
Woods-Greer Foundation
American National Bank and Trust Co.
736 Market Street, P.O. Box 1638
Chattanooga, TN 37401
(615) 757-3203

Building and equipment grants. Cultural
organizations; community development;
higher education; Churches

TEXAS

815
Abell-Hanger Foundation
P.O. Box 430
Midland, TX 79702
(915) 684-6655

Building and equipment grants. Youth
organizations; community development;
social welfare; hospitals; disabled; higher
education; culture; recreation

Grants awarded to organizations located
in Texas.

Typical grant range: $15,000 to $75,000

816
Abercrombie Foundation
5005 Riverway, Suite 500
Houston, TX 77056
(713) 627-2500

Building grants. Hospitals; child welfare;
higher education

Grants awarded to organizations located
in the Houston vicinity.

817
Amarillo Area Foundation, Inc.
700 First National Place I
801 South Fillmore
Amarillo, TX 79101
(806) 376-4521

Building and equipment grants. Hospitals;
health organizations; women; cultural
organizations; community development;
disabled; youth organizations; child
welfare; renovation grants

Typical grant range: $5,000 to $25,000

818
Amini Foundation
8000 IH-Ten West, Suite 820
San Antonio, TX 78230

Equipment grants. Disabled; social
welfare; cultural organizations

Most grants awarded to organizations
located in San Antonio.

819
M.D. Anderson Foundation
1301 Fannin Street, 21st Floor
P.O. Box 809
Houston, TX 77001
(713) 658-2316

Building and equipment grants. Cultural
organizations; youth organizations; social
welfare; higher education; elderly;
hospitals; health organizations; disabled;
renovation grants

Grants awarded to organizations located
in Texas, with an emphasis in the Houston
vicinity.

Typical grant range: $5,000 to $75,000

820
**Austin Community Foundation for
the Capital Area, Inc.**
P.O. Box 5159
Austin, TX 78763
(512) 472-4483

Building and equipment grants. Cultural
organizations; community development;
social services; recreation; youth
organizations; environment; health
organizations; renovation grants

Grants awarded to organizations located
in Travis County.

821
Bosque Foundation
2911 Turtle Creek Blvd., Suite 900
Dallas, TX 75219
(214) 559-0088

Building grants. Health organizations;
hospitals; higher education; disabled;
youth organizations

Grants awarded to organizations located
in Texas.

Typical grant range: $5,000 to $40,000

822
J.S. Bridwell Foundation
807 Eighth Street, Suite 500
Wichita Falls, TX 76301
(817) 322-4436

Building and equipment grants. Higher
education; social welfare; Churches

Grants awarded to organizations located
in Texas.

Typical grant range: $500 to $7,500

823
Brown Foundation, Inc.
2117 Welch Avenue
P.O. Box 130646
Houston, TX 77219
(713) 523-6867

Building and equipment grants. All
levels of education; hospitals; cultural
organizations; social welfare; recreation;
disabled; community development;
renovation grants

Grants awarded to organizations located
in Texas.

Typical grant range: $15,000 to $120,000

824
**H.L. & Elizabeth M. Brown
Foundation**
6300 Ridglea Place, Suite 1118
Ft. Worth, TX 76116

Building and equipment grants. Hospitals;
Military Institute (building funds)

Grants awarded to organizations located
in Texas.

Typical grant range: $500 to $5,000

825
Burkitt Foundation
5847 San Felipe, Suite 4290
Houston, TX 77057
(713) 780-7638

Building grants. Social welfare; all levels
of education; Churches; Junior Service
League (renovation); St. Thomas High
School (building funds); renovation grants

Typical grant range: $1,000 to $7,000

826
Burnett-Tandy Foundation
801 Cherry Street, Suite 1400
Ft. Worth, TX 76102
(817) 877-3344

Building and equipment grants. Youth
organizations; cultural organizations;
homeless; disabled; higher education;
renovation grants

Grants awarded to organizations located
in the Ft. Worth vicinity.

Typical grant range: $7,500 to $75,000

827
Effie and Wofford Cain Foundation
4131 Spicewood Springs Road, Suite A-1
Austin, TX 78759
(512) 346-7490

Building and equipment grants. Higher education; disabled; elderly; recreation; youth organizations; animal welfare; cultural organizations; hospitals; health organizations; community development; Churches; renovation grants

Grants awarded to organizations located in Texas.

Typical grant range: $5,000 to $75,000

828
Gordon and Mary Cain Foundation
Eight Greenway Plaza, Suite 702
Houston, TX 77046
(713) 960-9283

Building grants. Hospitals; child welfare; higher education; health organizations; disabled; renovation grants

Grants awarded to organizations located in Houston.

829
Harry S. and Isabel C. Cameron Foundation
c/o NationsBank
P.O. Box 298502
Houston, TX 77298
(713) 787-4553

Building and equipment grants. Higher education; public libraries; social welfare; youth organizations; disabled; Churches; Resurrection School (equipment); Food Bank (equipment)

Grants awarded to organizations located in Texas.

Typical grant range: $1,000 to $9,000

830
Amon G. Carter Foundation
1212 NCNB Center
P.O. Box 1036
Fort Worth, TX 76101
(817) 332-2783

Building and equipment grants. Social welfare; community development; all levels of education; disabled; cultural organizations; animal welfare; youth organizations; hospitals; elderly; renovation grants

Grants awarded to organizations located in Tarrant County.

Typical grant range: $2,000 to $35,000

831
Cockrell Foundation
1600 Smith, Suite 4600
Houston, TX 77002
(713) 651-1271

Building grants. Cultural organizations; youth organizations; hospitals; health organizations; community development; disabled; Churches; renovation grants

Grants awarded to organizations located in the Houston vicinity.

Typical grant range: $5,000 to $50,000

832
Communities Foundation of Texas, Inc.
4605 Live Oak Street
Dallas, TX 75204
(214) 826-5231

Building and equipment grants. Child welfare; disabled; hospitals; health organizations; social welfare; youth organizations; community development; renovation grants

Grants awarded to organizations located in Dallas.

833
Community Foundation of Abilene
500 Chestnut, Suite 1509
P.O. Box 1001
Abilene, TX 79604
(915) 676-3883

Building and equipment grants. Social welfare; youth organizations; higher education; disabled; elderly; cultural organizations; Goodwill Industries (equipment); Day Nursery of Abilene (office equipment); Meals on Wheels (equipment); renovation grants

Grants awarded to organizations located in the Abilene vicinity.

Typical grant range: $1,000 to $12,000

834
Constantin Foundation
3811 Turtle Creek Blvd., Suite 320-LB 39
Dallas, TX 75219
(214) 522-9300

Building and equipment grants. Cultural organizations; disabled; hospitals; higher education; child welfare; renovation grants

Grants awarded to organizations located in the Dallas vicinity.

835
Cullen Foundation
601 Jefferson, 40th Floor
Houston, TX 77002
(713) 651-8600

Building and equipment grants. Youth organizations; community development; cultural organizations; recreation; all levels of education; hospitals; disabled; renovation grants

Grants awarded to organizations located in Texas.

Typical grant range: $75,000 to $350,000

836
Dallas Foundation
400 S. Record Street, Suite 600
Dallas, TX 75202
(214) 977-6676

Building and equipment grants. Health organizations; hospitals; community development; cultural organizations; recreation; social welfare; disabled; youth organizations; animal welfare; higher education; renovation grants

Grants awarded to organizations located in the Dallas vicinity.

Typical grant range: $15,000 to $50,000

837
Davidson Family Charitable Foundation
310 West Texas, Suite 709
Midland, TX 79701
(915) 687-0995

Building and equipment grants. Hospitals; health organizations; higher education; youth organizations; child welfare; disabled; renovation grants

Grants awarded to organizations located in Texas.

838
Dodge Jones Foundation
P.O. Box 176
Abilene, TX 79604
(915) 673-6429

Building and equipment grants. Higher education; community development; disabled; youth organizations; cultural organizations; recreation; women; health organizations; renovation grants

Grants awarded to organizations located in Abilene.

Typical grant range: $3,000 to $30,000

839
James R. Dougherty, Jr. Foundation
P.O. Box 640
Beeville, TX 78104
(512) 358-3560

Building and equipment grants. Social
welfare; all levels of education; hospitals;
health organizations; women; child
welfare; youth organizations; cultural
organizations; community development;
disabled; St. Joseph's Catholic Church
(building funds); Town and Country
School (equipment); renovation grants

Grants awarded to organizations located
in Texas.

Typical grant range: $1,000 to $4,000

840
Dresser Foundation, Inc.
P.O. Box 718
Dallas, TX 75221
(214) 740-6078

Building grants. Elderly; disabled; higher
education; hospitals; social welfare; youth
organizations; community development

Grants awarded to organizations located
in areas of company operations.

Typical grant range: $1,000 to $15,000

841
Ellwood Foundation
P.O. Box 52482
Houston, TX 77052
(713) 652-0613

Building grants. Higher education;
disabled; health organizations; hospitals;
social welfare; renovation grants

Grants awarded to organizations located
in the Houston vicinity.

Typical grant range: $5,000 to $50,000

842
R.W. Fair Foundation
P.O. Box 689
Tyler, TX 75710
(903) 592-3811

Building and equipment grants. Social
welfare; all levels of education; hospitals;
youth organizations; culture; Churches

Most grants awarded to organizations
located in Texas.

Typical grant range: $10,000 to $45,000

843
William Stamps Farish Fund
1100 Louisiana, Suite 1250
Houston, TX 77002
(713) 757-7313

Building grants. All levels of education;
cultural organizations; social welfare;
health organizations; hospitals; youth
organizations; disabled; Churches;
renovation grants

Grants awarded to organizations located
in Texas.

Typical grant range: $10,000 to $90,000

844
Favrot Foundation
909 Wirt Road, Suite 101
Houston, TX 77024
(713) 956-4009

Building and equipment grants.
Environment; animal welfare; recreation;
community development; disabled; youth
organizations; higher education; health
organizations

Typical grant range: $5,000 to $40,000

845
Feldman Foundation
7800 Stemmons Freeway
P.O. Box 1046
Dallas, TX 75221

Building grants. Social welfare; higher
education; community development;
hospitals; health organizations

Typical grant range: $15,000 to $50,000

846
Leland Fikes Foundation, Inc.
3050 Lincoln Plaza
500 N. Akard
Dallas, TX 75201
(214) 754-0144

Building and equipment grants. Disabled;
cultural organizations; child welfare;
health organizations; hospitals; homeless;
higher education; renovation grants

Grants awarded to organizations located
in Dallas.

Typical grant range: $10,000 to $25,000

847
Fondren Foundation
7 TCT 37
P.O. Box 2558
Houston, TX 77252
(713) 236-4403

Building and equipment grants. Health
organizations; hospitals; social welfare;
community development; women; youth
organizations; cultural organizations;
higher education; recreation; disabled;
animal welfare; Churches; renovation
grants

Grants awarded to organizations located
in Texas.

Typical grant range: $15,000 to $125,000

848
Frees Foundation
5373 W. Alabama, Suite 404
Houston, TX 77056
(713) 623-0515

Building and equipment grants. Youth
organizations; hospitals; social welfare;
minorities; community development

Typical grant range: $2,000 to $50,000

849
George Foundation
207 S. Third Street
P.O. Drawer C
Richmond, TX 77469
(713) 342-6109

Building and equipment grants. Cultural
organizations; disabled; community
development; women; hospitals; youth
organizations

Typical grant range: $10,000 to $60,000

850
Haggar Foundation
6113 Lemmon Avenue
Dallas, TX 75209
(214) 956-0241

Building grants. All levels of education;
hospitals; cultural organizations; child
welfare; renovation grants

Typical grant range: $1,000 to $15,000

851
Ewing Halsell Foundation
711 Navarro Street, Suite 537
San Antonio, TX 78205
(210) 223-2640

Building and equipment grants. Youth
organizations; disabled; community
development; homeless; minorities; health
organizations; higher education; hospitals;
cultural organizations; renovation grants

Grants awarded to organizations located
in Texas.

Typical grant range: $1,000 to $40,000

852

George and Mary Josephine Hamman Foundation
910 Travis Street, Suite 1438
Houston, TX 77002
(713) 658-8345

Building and equipment grants. Social welfare; hospitals; disabled; higher education; recreation; culture; health organizations; Churches

Grants awarded to organizations located in Texas.

853

Hillcrest Foundation
c/o NationsBank, Trust Division
P.O. Box 830241
Dallas, TX 75283

Building and equipment grants. Child welfare; public libraries; cultural organizations; community development; all levels of education; disabled; youth organizations; health organizations; elderly; homeless; renovation grants

Grants awarded to organizations located in Texas, with an emphasis in Dallas.

Typical grant range: $5,000 to $50,000

854

Hoblitzelle Foundation
5956 Sherry Lane, Suite 901
Dallas, TX 75225
(214) 373-0462

Building and equipment grants. Hospitals; community development; child welfare; religious organizations; disabled; youth organizations; culture; higher education; social welfare; homeless; secondary education; science; employment training programs

Grants awarded to organizations located in Texas.

Typical grant range: $15,000 to $75,000

855

Houston Endowment, Inc.
600 Travis, Suite 6400
Houston, TX 77002
(713) 238-8100

Building and equipment grants. Social welfare; colleges and universities; health organizations; disabled; minorities; hospitals; secondary education; libraries; community development; cultural organizations; recreation; elderly

Grants awarded to organizations located in Texas.

Typical grant range: $5,000 to $250,000

856

M.G. and Lillie A. Johnson Foundation, Inc.
P.O. Box 2269
Victoria, TX 77902
(512) 575-7970

Building and equipment grants. Social welfare; youth organizations; hospitals; higher education; health organizations; community development; renovation grants

Typical grant range: $20,000 to $100,000

857

Harris and Eliza Kempner Fund
P.O. Box 119
Galveston, TX 77553
(409) 765-6671

Building and equipment grants. Cultural organizations; minorities; hospice; higher education; environment; social welfare; disabled; renovation grants

Grants awarded to organizations located in the Galveston vicinity.

Typical grant range: $1,500 to $8,500

858
Robert J. Kleberg, Jr. and Helen C. Kleberg Foundation
700 N. St. Mary's Street, Suite 1200
San Antonio, TX 78205
(210) 271-3691

Building and equipment grants. Animal welfare; community development; child welfare; youth organizations; disabled; cultural organizations; higher education; renovation grants

Grants awarded to organizations located in Texas.

859
Eugene McDermott Foundation
3808 Euclid
Dallas, TX 75205
(214) 521-2924

Building and equipment grants. Hospitals; community development; all levels of education; youth organizations; culture; health organizations; disabled; Botanical Garden (renovation); Museum of Art (building funds, purchase museum piece); Southern Methodist University (building funds for theatre); Visiting Nurse Association (building funds)

Grants awarded to organizations located in Dallas.

Typical grant range: $2,500 to $25,000

860
Meadows Foundation, Inc.
Wilson Historic Block
3003 Swiss Avenue
Dallas, TX 75204
(214) 826-9431

Building and equipment grants. Child welfare; culture; youth organizations; community development; public libraries; environment; animal welfare; hospitals; health organizations; disabled; all levels of education; renovation grants

Grants awarded to organizations located in Texas.

Typical grant range: $25,000 to $80,000

861
Moody Foundation
704 Moody National Bank Bldg.
Galveston, TX 77550
(409) 763-5333

Building and equipment grants. Community development; disabled; cultural organizations; social welfare; higher education; health organizations; renovation grants

Grants awarded to organizations located in Texas.

862
Navarro Community Foundation
512 InterFirst Bank Bldg.
P.O. Box 1035
Corsicana, TX 75151
(903) 874-4301

Building grants. Child welfare; all levels of education; youth organizations; community development; Churches

Grants awarded to organizations located in Navarro County.

863
Kathryn O'Connor Foundation
One O'Connor Plaza, Suite 1100
Victoria, TX 77901
(512) 578-6271

Building grants. All levels of education; cultural organizations; hospitals; social welfare; Churches

Typical grant range: $15,000 to $40,000

864
Sid W. Richardson Foundation
309 Main Street
Fort Worth, TX 76102
(817) 336-0494

Building and equipment grants. Homeless;
health organizations; hospitals; recreation;
community development; cultural
organizations; child welfare; elderly;
disabled; youth organizations; higher
education; Association for the Blind
(equipment); Northside Inter-Church
Agency (renovation); Boys and Girls
Clubs (renovation); renovation grants

Grants awarded to organizations located
in Texas.

Typical grant range: $10,000 to $125,000

865
Rockwell Fund, Inc.
1360 Post Oak Blvd., Suite 780
Houston, TX 77056
(713) 629-9022

Building and equipment grants. Social
welfare; cultural organizations; hospitals;
health organizations; disabled; higher
education; youth organizations; Charity
Guild of Catholic Women (building
funds); renovation grants

Grants awarded to organizations located
in the Houston vicinity.

Typical grant range: $10,000 to $25,000

866
Earl C. Sams Foundation, Inc.
101 N. Shoreline Drive, Suite 602
Corpus Christi, TX 78401
(512) 888-6485

Building and equipment grants. Social
welfare; disabled; cultural organizations;
community development

867
San Antonio Area Foundation
530 McCullough, Suite 650
San Antonio, TX 78215
(210) 225-2243

Building and equipment grants. Animal
welfare; cultural organizations; disabled;
higher education; health organizations;
social welfare; environment; Alcoholic
Rehabilitation Center (furniture);
Christian Assistance Ministry (furniture,
renovation); University of Texas, Dept of
Nursing (equipment); Wilderness Park
(renovation); Goodwill Industries
(equipment); renovation grants

Grants awarded to organizations located
in Texas.

Typical grant range: $500 to $15,000

868
Harold Simmons Foundation
Three Lincoln Center
5430 LBJ Freeway, Suite 1700
Dallas, TX 75240

Building grants. Higher education;
youth organizations; elderly; homeless;
community development

Grants awarded to organizations located
in the Dallas vicinity.

869
**Clara Blackford Smith and W. Aubrey
Smith Charitable Foundation**
c/o NationsBank
300 W. Main Street
Denison, TX 75020
(903) 415-2317

Building grants. Social welfare; hospitals;
youth organizations; community
development; higher education; public
libraries; disabled; renovation grants

Most grants awarded to organizations
located in Denison.

870
Strake Foundation
712 Main Street, Suite 3300
Houston, TX 77002
(713) 546-2400

Building and equipment grants. Cultural
organizations; disabled; higher education;
youth organizations; minorities; hospitals;
social welfare

Grants awarded to organizations located
in Texas.

871
Swalm Foundation
8707 Katy Freeway, Suite 300
Houston, TX 77024
(713) 464-1321

Building grants. Health organizations;
disabled; higher education; child welfare;
youth organizations; renovation grants

Grants awarded to organizations located
in Texas.

Typical grant range: $1,000 to $25,000

872
T.L.L. Temple Foundation
109 Temple Blvd.
Lufkin, TX 75901
(409) 639-5197

Building and equipment grants. Cultural
organizations; disabled; elderly; social
welfare; hospitals; health organizations;
women; community development;
recreation; all levels of education

Typical grant range: $10,000 to $100,000

873
Trull Foundation
404 Fourth Street
Palacios, TX 77465
(512) 972-5241

Building and equipment grants. Social
welfare; disabled; all levels of education;
youth organizations; recreation; child
welfare; cultural organizations;
community development; Churches;
renovation grants

874
Vale-Asche Foundation
1010 River Oaks Bank Bldg.
2001 Kirby Drive, Suite 910
Houston, TX 77019
(713) 520-7334

Equipment grants. Disabled; environment;
health organizations; elderly; homeless;
minorities; child welfare; Churches

Grants awarded to organizations located
in Houston.

Typical grant range: $2,000 to $30,000

875
Rachael & Ben Vaughan Foundation
P.O. Box 1579
Corpus Christi, TX 78403
(512) 241-2890

Building and equipment grants.
Environment; cultural organizations;
community development; Churches

876
Crystelle Waggoner Charitable Trust
c/o NationsBank of Texas, N.A.
P.O. Box 1317
Ft. Worth, TX 76101
(817) 390-6114

Building and equipment grants. Social
welfare; elderly; community development;
youth organizations; disabled; cultural
organizations; renovation grants

Grants awarded to organizations located
in Texas.

Typical grant range: $1,000 to $12,000

877
Wortham Foundation
2727 Allen Parkway, Suite 2000
Houston, TX 77019
(713) 526-8849

Building grants. Cultural organizations;
recreation; hospitals; youth organizations;
community development; renovation
grants

Grants awarded to organizations located
in Houston.

878
Lola Wright Foundation
P.O. Box 1138
Georgetown, TX 78627
(512) 869-2574

Building and equipment grants. All levels
of education; elderly; women; youth
organizations; disabled; culture; health
organizations; hospitals; community
development; environment

Grants awarded to organizations located
in Texas.

Typical grant range: $3,000 to $30,000

UTAH

879
**Val A. Browning Charitable
Foundation**
P.O. Box 9936
Ogden, UT 84409
(801) 626-9533

Building grants. Social welfare; health
organizations; hospitals; higher education;
cultural organizations

880
**Robert Harold Burton Private
Foundation**
c/o First Security Bank of Utah, N.A.
P.O. Box 30007
Salt Lake City, UT 84130
(801) 350-5562

Building and equipment grants. Higher
education; recreation; hospitals; cultural
organizations; environment; renovation
grants

Grants awarded to organizations located
in Salt Lake County.

881
Castle Foundation
c/o West One Trust Co.
P.O. Box 3058
Salt Lake City, UT 84110
(801) 534-6085

Building and equipment grants. Cultural
organizations; youth organizations;
recreation; health organizations; higher
education; disabled

Grants awarded to organizations located
in Utah.

882
**Dr. Ezekiel R. and Edna Wattis Dumke
Foundation**
448 S. 400 East, Suite 100
Salt Lake City, UT 84111
(801) 328-3531

Building and equipment grants. Higher
education; health organizations; cultural
organizations; environment; disabled;
community development

Typical grant range: $3,000 to $20,000

883
George S. and Dolores Dore Eccles
Foundation
Deseret Building
79 S. Main Street
Salt Lake City, UT 84111
(801) 246-5336

Building and equipment grants. Cultural
organizations; higher education; women;
child welfare; community development;
youth organizations; renovation grants

Most grants awarded to organizations
located in Utah.

Typical grant range: $5,000 to $90,000

884
Marriner S. Eccles Foundation
701 Deseret Building
79 S. Main Street
Salt Lake City, UT 84111
(801) 322-0116

Equipment grants. Disabled; homeless;
health organizations; social welfare;
cultural organizations; elderly; women;
youth organizations; recreation

Grants awarded to organizations located
in Utah.

Typical grant range: $3,000 to $30,000

885
Willard L. Eccles Charitable
Foundation
P.O. Box 45385
Salt Lake City, UT 84145
(801) 532-1500

Building and equipment grants. Hospitals;
higher education; health organizations

Grants awarded to organizations located
in Utah.

Typical grant range: $5,000 to $75,000

VERMONT

886
Canaan Foundation for
Christian Education
R. R. One
P.O. Box 113
Woodstock, VT 05091
(802) 457-3990

Building and equipment grants. Social
welfare; all levels of education; Churches;
Christian School (equipment, books,
supplies, furniture)

887
Lamson-Howell Foundation
R.D. 2, Box 48
Randolph, VT 05060

Building and equipment grants. Cultural
organizations; community development;
Randolph Youth Baseball (equipment);
Greater Randolph Senior Center (new
roof)

Grants awarded to organizations located
in the Randolph vicinity.

Typical grant range: $500 to $7,500

888
Lintilhac Foundation
100 Harbor Road
Shelburne, VT 05482
(802) 985-4106

Building and equipment grants. Health
organizations; community development;
recreation; environment; disabled; cultural
organizations; renovation grants

889
Mortimer R. Proctor Trust
Green Mountain Bank, Trust Dept.
P.O. Box 669
Rutland, VT 05701
(802) 775-2525

Building and equipment grants.
Community development; elderly;
public libraries; Churches

VIRGINIA

890
Inez Duff Bishop Charitable Trust
Central Fidelity Bank
P.O. Box 27602
Richmond, VA 23261

Building and equipment grants. Social
welfare; hospitals; elderly; community
development; Salvation Army (building
funds); Military Academy (building
funds); renovation grants

Grants awarded to organizations located
in Charlottesville.

Typical grant range: $1,000 to $6,000

891
Community Foundation Serving Richmond & Central Virginia
9211 Forest Hill Ave., Suite 109
Richmond, VA 23235
(804) 330-7400

Building and equipment grants. Elderly;
disabled; health organizations; child
welfare; community development;
cultural organizations; renovation grants

Grants awarded to organizations located
in the Richmond vicinity and central
Virginia.

Typical grant range: $1,000 to $11,000

892
Crestar Bank Charitable Trust
c/o Crestar Bank, N.A.
P.O. Box 27385
Richmond, VA 23261

Building and equipment grants. Youth
organizations; cultural organizations;
higher education; community
development; hospitals

Most grants awarded to organizations
located in Virginia.

893
Freedom Forum
1101 Wilson Blvd.
Arlington, VA 22209

Building and equipment grants. Child
welfare; women; higher education;
disabled; community development;
cultural organizations; recreation;
minorities; elderly; homeless; health
organizations; hospitals; youth
organizations; public libraries;
renovation grants

Typical grant range: $3,000 to $85,000

894
Landmark Charitable Foundation
150 W. Brambleton Avenue
Norfolk, VA 23510

Building grants. Environment; hospitals;
health organizations; social welfare;
cultural organizations; community
development; higher education

Typical grant range: $2,000 to $10,000

895
Mars Foundation
6885 Elm Street
McLean, VA 22101
(703) 821-4900

Building and equipment grants.
Community development; environment;
higher education; disabled; health
organizations; youth organizations

Typical grant range: $1,000 to $12,000

896
Marietta McNeil Morgan & Samuel Tate Morgan, Jr. Foundation
c/o NationsBank, Trust Dept.
P.O. Box 26903
Richmond, VA 23261

Building and equipment grants. Social
welfare; youth organizations; higher
education; community development;
renovation grants

Grants awarded to organizations located
in Virginia.

897
Norfolk Foundation
1410 NationsBank Center
Norfolk, VA 23510
(804) 622-7951

Building and equipment grants.
Environment; recreation; disabled;
community development; hospitals;
cultural organizations; homeless;
youth organizations; child welfare;
elderly; animal welfare

Grants awarded to organizations located
in the Norfolk vicinity.

Typical grant range: $15,000 to $50,000

898
Perry Foundation
P.O. Box 558
Charlottesville, VA 22902
(804) 973-9441

Building and equipment grants. Youth
organizations; elderly; higher education;
child welfare; community development

Grants awarded to organizations located
in Virginia.

899
Reynolds Metals Company Foundation
P.O. Box 27003
Richmond, VA 23261
(804) 281-2222

Building grants. Higher education;
elderly; community development; youth
organizations; disabled; health
organizations; hospitals; social welfare

Grants awarded to organizations located
in areas of company operations, with an
emphasis in Richmond.

900
**C.E. Richardson Benevolent
Foundation**
74 West Main St., Room 211
P.O. Box 1120
Pulaski, VA 24301
(703) 980-6628

Building and equipment grants. Higher
education; social welfare; disabled; youth
organizations; community development;
cultural organizations

Typical grant range: $1,000 to $6,000

901
J. Edwin Treakle Foundation, Inc.
P.O. Box 1157
Gloucester, VA 23061

Building and equipment grants. Health
organizations; community development;
higher education; animal welfare; elderly;
culture; youth organizations; Churches;
Humane Society (purchase storage unit);
Memorial Library (office equipment);
Community Park Committee (building
funds); Fire Department (equipment,
remodeling); Vocational Center (van)

Grants awarded to organizations located
in Virginia.

Typical grant range: $1,000 to $7,500

902
Washington Forrest Foundation
2300 S. Ninth Street
Arlington, VA 22204
(703) 920-3688

Building and equipment grants.
Community development; cultural
organizations; youth organizations;
health organizations; disabled;
Churches; renovation grants

Grants awarded to organizations located
in Northern Virginia.

Typical grant range: $1,000 to $7,000

903
Wheat, First Securities/Butcher & Singer Foundation
P.O. Box 1357
Richmond, VA 23211
(804) 782-3518

Building grants. Health organizations; hospitals; cultural organizations; higher education; child welfare; disabled; renovation grants

Typical grant range: $1,000 to $15,000

WASHINGTON

904
Norman Archibald Charitable Foundation
First Interstate Bank of Washington, N.A.
P.O. Box 21927
Seattle, WA 98111
(206) 292-3543

Building and equipment grants. Social welfare; elderly; disabled; animal welfare; cultural organizations

Most grants awarded to organizations located in the Puget Sound vicinity.

Typical grant range: $1,000 to $11,000

905
E.K. and Lillian F. Bishop Foundation
Seafirst Bank, Charitable Trust Services
P.O. Box 24565, CSC-23
Seattle, WA 98124
(206) 937-0394

Building and equipment grants. Youth organizations; child welfare; cultural organizations; social welfare

Grants awarded to organizations located in Washington.

Typical grant range: $6,500 to $25,000

906
Ben B. Cheney Foundation, Inc.
1201 Pacific Ave., Suite 1600
Tacoma, WA 98402
(206) 572-2442

Building and equipment grants. Social welfare; disabled; youth organizations; animal welfare; performing arts; health organizations; museums; child welfare; Buckley Senior Citizens (van); Lutheran School (playground equipment); Crista Ministries (renovation); Food Bank (equipment)

Typical grant range: $2,000 to $45,000

907
Comstock Foundation
819 Washington Trust Financial Center
West 717 Sprague Ave.
Spokane, WA 99204
(509) 747-1527

Building and equipment grants. Social welfare; health organizations; hospitals; youth organizations; community development; cultural organizations

Grants awarded to organizations located in Washington.

Typical grant range: $1,000 to $30,000

908
Greater Tacoma Community Foundation
P.O. Box 1995
Tacoma, WA 98401
(206) 383-5622

Building and equipment grants. Social welfare; cultural organizations; health organizations

Grants awarded to organizations located in Pierce County.

909
Matlock Foundation
1201 Third Avenue, Suite 4900
Seattle, WA 98101
(206) 224-5196

Building and equipment grants. Social
welfare; cultural organizations; health
organizations; community development;
disabled; renovation grants

910
Medina Foundation
1300 Norton Building
801 Second Avenue, 13th Floor
Seattle, WA 98104
(206) 464-5231

Building and equipment grants. Disabled;
social welfare; community development;
youth organizations

Grants awarded to organizations located
in the Seattle vicinity.

Typical grant range: $5,000 to $20,000

911
M.J. Murdock Charitable Trust
703 Broadway, Suite 710
Vancouver, WA 98660
(206) 694-8415

Building and equipment grants. Social
welfare; performing arts; museums;
higher education; disabled; youth
organizations; Mental Health Center
(building funds); Boys and Girls Club
(building funds)

Typical grant range: $10,000 to $200,000

912
Norcliffe Foundation
First Interstate Center
999 Third Avenue, Suite 1006
Seattle, WA 98104

Building and equipment grants. Social
welfare; hospitals; health organizations;
youth organizations; elderly

Grants awarded to organizations located
in the Puget Sound area.

Typical grant range: $500 to $20,000

913
Seafirst Foundation
P.O. Box 34661
Seattle, WA 98124
(206) 358-3443

Building grants. Hospitals; disabled;
social welfare; elderly; child welfare;
performing arts; museums; AIDS;
renovation grants

Grants awarded to organizations located
in Washington.

Typical grant range: $5,000 to $20,000

914
Seattle Foundation
425 Pike Street, Suite 510
Seattle, WA 98101
(206) 622-2294

Building and equipment grants. Social
welfare; community development; health
organizations; Library for the Blind and
Physically Handicapped (equipment);
Korean Community Counseling Center
(equipment); renovation grants

Grants awarded to organizations located
in Seattle.

Typical grant range: $3,000 to $20,000

915
Skinner Foundation
1326 Fifth Avenue, Suite 711
Seattle, WA 98101
(206) 623-6480

Building and equipment grants. Social
welfare; health organizations; disabled;
women; cultural organizations; youth
organizations; renovation grants

Grants awarded to organizations located
in areas of company operations (Skinner
Corporation).

Typical grant range: $1,000 to $11,000

916
Weyerhaeuser Company Foundation
CHIF 31
Tacoma, WA 98477
(206) 924-3159

Building and equipment grants. Social welfare; health organizations; elderly; child welfare; cultural organizations; animal welfare; renovation grants

Grants awarded to organizations located in areas of company operations.

Typical grant range: $3,000 to $15,000

WEST VIRGINIA

917
Beckley Area Foundation, Inc.
P.O. Box 1092
Beckley, WV 25802

Building and equipment grants. Elementary school (books and overhead projector); Girl Scouts (equipment); Women's Resource Center (equipment); Homeless Shelter (equipment); YMCA (equipment, renovation); Little League (building funds); State Park Foundation (playground equipment); Hospice Care (equipment); Literacy Program (books)

Most grants awarded in Beckley County and Raleigh County.

Typical grant range: $500 to $6,000

918
Clay Foundation, Inc.
1426 Kanawha Blvd., East
Charleston, WV 25301
(304) 344-8656

Building and equipment grants. Health organizations; homeless; elderly; child welfare; Churches; United Way (building funds); Habitat for Humanity (building funds); Nature Conservancy (purchase land); renovation grants

Grants awarded to organizations located in West Virginia.

Typical grant range: $5,000 to $50,000

919
Greater Kanawha Valley Foundation
1426 Kanawha Blvd., East
Charleston, WV 25301
(304) 346-3620

Building and equipment grants. Performing arts; museums; community development; recreation; social welfare; disabled; Catholic High School (renovation); YMCA (building funds)

Grants awarded to organizations located in Greater Kanawha Valley.

Typical grant range: $1,000 to $14,000

920
Huntington Foundation, Inc.
P.O. Box 2548
Huntington, WV 25726

Building and equipment grants. Elderly; child welfare; recreation; abused women; Boys Club (renovation)

Grants awarded to organizations located in West Virginia.

921
Bernard McDonough Foundation, Inc.
1000 Grand Central Mall
P.O. Box 1825
Parkersburg, WV 26102
(304) 485-4494

Building and equipment grants. Social welfare; recreation; performing arts; disabled; higher education; Commission on Aging (van); Educational Foundation (building funds); Child Care Center (furnace and air conditioning system)

Grants awarded to organizations located in West Virginia.

Typical grant range: $1,000 to $20,000

167

922
Parkersburg Community Foundation
402 Juliana Street
P.O. Box 1762
Parkersburg, WV 26102
(304) 428-4438

Building and equipment grants. Social
welfare; child welfare; performing arts;
animal welfare; secondary education;
Habitat for Humanity (building funds);
renovation grants

Grants awarded to organizations located
in the Parkersburg vicinity.

WISCONSIN

923
Helen Bader Foundation
777 E. Wisconsin Avenue, Suite 3275
Milwaukee, WI 53202
(414) 224-6464

Building grants. Child welfare; elderly;
disabled; University of Rochester Medical
Center (renovation); Sunrise Nursing
Home for the Blind (building funds);
renovation grants

924
**Lynde and Harry Bradley
Foundation, Inc.**
777 E. Wisconsin Avenue, Suite 2285
Milwaukee, WI 53202
(414) 291-9915

Building and equipment grants. All
Children's Playground (equipment);
American Architectural Foundation
(renovation); Goodwill Industries
(renovation)

Typical grant range: $20,000 to $125,000

925
Frank G. Brotz Family Foundation, Inc.
3518 Lakeshore Road
P.O. Box 551
Sheboygan, WI 53081
(414) 458-2121

Building grants. Hospitals; health
organizations; cultural organizations;
youth organizations

Grants awarded to organizations located
in Wisconsin.

926
**Community Foundation for the Fox
Valley Region, Inc.**
P.O. Box 563
Appleton, WI 54912
(414) 830-1290

Building and equipment grants. Child
welfare; community development; health
organizations; disabled

Grants awarded to organizations located
in the Fox Valley area.

927
Consolidated Papers Foundation, Inc.
231 First Avenue North
P.O. Box 8050
Wisconsin Rapids, WI 54495
(715) 422-3368

Building and equipment grants. Hospitals;
health organizations; social welfare; higher
education; youth organizations

Grants awarded to organizations located
in Wisconsin.

928
Patrick & Anna M. Cudahy Fund
P.O. Box 11978
Milwaukee, WI 53211
(708) 866-0760

Building and equipment grants. Social
welfare; homeless; environment; disabled;
youth organizations

Typical grant range: $3,000 to $25,000

929
Elizabeth Elser Doolittle Charitable Trust No. 1
c/o Foley & Lardner
777 E. Wisconsin Avenue
Milwaukee, WI 53202

Building and equipment grants. Social welfare; environment; culture; County Historical Society (renovation)

Grants awarded to organizations located in Wisconsin.

930
Ralph Evinrude Foundation, Inc.
c/o Quarles and Brady
411 E. Wisconsin Avenue
Milwaukee, WI 53202
(414) 277-5000

Building and equipment grants. Health organizations; social welfare; recreation; elderly; youth organizations; renovation grants

Grants awarded to organizations located in the Milwaukee vicinity.

Typical grant range: $500 to $4,000

931
First Wisconsin Foundation, Inc.
777 E. Wisconsin Avenue
Milwaukee, WI 53202
(414) 765-4292

Building and equipment grants. Social welfare; community development; cultural organizations

Grants awarded to organizations located in the Milwaukee vicinity.

932
Grede Foundation, Inc.
P.O. Box 26499
Milwaukee, WI 53226
(414) 257-3600

Building grants. Hospitals; health organizations; social welfare; youth organizations

Grants awarded to organizations located in Wisconsin.

933
Janesville Foundation, Inc.
121 N. Parker Drive
P.O. Box 8123
Janesville, WI 53547
(608) 752-1032

Building and equipment grants. City of Janesville (purchase land); Day Care Center (equipment); School District (renovation); College (renovate library); Boys Baseball (building funds)

Grants awarded to organizations located in the Janesville area.

Typical grant range: $3,000 to $15,000

934
Johnson Controls Foundation
5757 N. Green Bay Avenue
P.O. Box 591
Milwaukee, WI 53201
(414) 228-2219

Building grants. Social welfare; hospitals; disabled; cultural organizations

Grants awarded to organizations located in areas of company operations.

Typical grant range: $500 to $10,000

935
Johnson's Wax Fund, Inc.
1525 Howe Street
Racine, WI 53403
(414) 631-2826

Building grants. Environment; hospitals; health organizations; culture; Public Library

Grants awarded to organizations located in areas of company operations, with an emphasis in Wisconsin.

Typical grant range: $2,000 to $40,000

936
La Crosse Community Foundation
P.O. Box 578
La Crosse, WI 54602
(608) 782-3223

Building and equipment grants. Social
welfare; child welfare; disabled;
renovation grants

Grants awarded to organizations located
in La Crosse County.

Typical grant range: $500 to $15,000

937
Madison Community Foundation
615 E. Washington Avenue
Madison, WI 53703
(608) 255-0503

Building and equipment grants. Child
welfare; recreation; disabled; elderly;
homeless; Habitat for Humanity (building
funds)

Grants awarded to organizations located
in the Madison vicinity.

Typical grant range: $1,000 to $25,000

938
Faye McBeath Foundation
1020 North Broadway
Milwaukee, WI 53202
(414) 272-2626

Building and equipment grants. Youth
organizations; disabled; abused women;
hospitals; community development; health
organizations; Girl Scouts (building
funds); Blood Center (building funds);
Goodwill Industries (renovation)

Grants awarded to organizations located
in Wisconsin, with an emphasis in
Milwaukee.

Typical grant range: $10,000 to $40,000

939
Milwaukee Foundation
1020 North Broadway
Milwaukee, WI 53202
(414) 272-5805

Building and equipment grants. Health
organizations; disabled; elderly; social
welfare; performing arts; museums; child
welfare; homeless; Public Libraries;
renovation grants

Grants awarded to organizations located
in the Milwaukee vicinity.

940
L.E. Phillips Family Foundation, Inc.
3925 N. Hastings Way
Eau Claire, WI 54703
(715) 839-2139

Building and equipment grants. Hospitals;
community development; recreation;
youth organizations; higher education;
Public Libraries; Jewish related
organizations; renovation grants

Typical grant range: $500 to $11,000

941
Rexnord Foundation, Inc.
P.O. Box 2022
Milwaukee, WI 53201
(414) 643-3000

Building grants. Youth organizations;
community development; cultural
organizations

Grants awarded to organizations located
in areas of company operations, with an
emphasis in Milwaukee.

942
Walter Schroeder Foundation, Inc.
1000 North Water St., 13th Fl.
Milwaukee, WI 53202
(414) 287-7177

Building and equipment grants. Hospitals;
higher education; social welfare

Grants awarded to organizations located
in Milwaukee County.

943
Siebert Lutheran Foundation, Inc.
2600 N. Mayfair Road, Suite 390
Wauwatosa, WI 53226
(414) 257-2656

Building and equipment grants. Lutheran
related organizations including elderly,
child welfare, all levels of education and
Churches; renovation grants

Grants awarded to organizations located
in Wisconsin.

Typical grant range: $3,500 to $10,000

944
A.O. Smith Foundation, Inc.
P.O. Box 23965
Milwaukee, WI 53223
(414) 359-4100

Building and equipment grants. Hospitals;
health organizations; youth organizations;
social welfare; cultural organizations;
Public Libraries; renovation grants

Most grants awarded to organizations
located in the Milwaukee vicinity.

945
Stackner Family Foundation, Inc.
411 E. Wisconsin Avenue
Milwaukee, WI 53202
(414) 277-5000

Building and equipment grants. Social
welfare; child welfare; minorities; health
organizations

Grants awarded to organizations located
in the Milwaukee vicinity.

Typical grant range: $1,500 to $12,000

946
**Wausau Area Community
Foundation, Inc.**
500 Third Street, Suite 316
Wausau, WI 54403
(715) 845-9555

Building and equipment grants. Social
welfare; cultural organizations; health
organizations; community development;
disabled; Wausau Police Department
(equipment); Girl Scouts (building funds);
renovation grants

Grants awarded to organizations located
in the Wausau vicinity.

Typical grant range: $300 to $3,000

WYOMING

947
Newell B. Sargent Foundation
P.O. Box 18
Worland, WY 82401

Building and equipment grants. Higher
education; cultural organizations; public
libraries; disabled; elderly; community
development; Rescue Mission (building
funds); Western Pleasure Dancers (sound
equipment); Save the Wigwam Theatre
(restoration of building); Meals on Wheels
(building funds)

Grants awarded to organizations located
in Wyoming.

Typical grant range: $300 to $3,500

948
Paul Stock Foundation
P.O. Box 2020
Cody, WY 82414
(307) 587-5275

Building grants. Hospitals; social welfare;
culture; youth organizations

Grants awarded to organizations located
in Wyoming.

Federal Programs

12.001 INDUSTRIAL EQUIPMENT LOANS TO EDUCATIONAL INSTITUTIONS
(Tools for Schools)

FEDERAL AGENCY: DEFENSE LOGISTICS AGENCY, DEPARTMENT OF DEFENSE

AUTHORIZATION: Public Law 93-155, 50 U.S.C. 451.

OBJECTIVES: To develop skilled manpower as an industrial preparedness measure.

TYPES OF ASSISTANCE: Use of Property, Facilities, and Equipment.

USES AND USE RESTRICTIONS: Qualified educational institutions and training schools may be loaned idle metal working machines.

ELIGIBILITY REQUIREMENTS:

Applicant Eligibility: Qualified nonprofit educational institutions and training schools that conduct vocational programs contributing materially to national defense skills.

Beneficiary Eligibility: Trainees enrolled in vocational training programs and students engaged in college and university engineering programs.

Credentials/Documentation: None.

APPLICATION AND AWARD PROCESS:

Preapplication Coordination: None. This program is excluded from coverage under E.O. 12372.

Application Procedure: A letter of request should be sent to Commander, Defense General Supply Center, DGSC-OM, Richmond, VA 23297-5000.

Award Procedure: Not applicable.

Deadlines: None.

Range of Approval/Disapproval Time: Approximately 2 weeks for application, up to 5 months for property to be shipped.

Appeals: None.

Renewals: Reapplication.

ASSISTANCE CONSIDERATIONS:

Formula and Matching Requirements: Equipment, if available, is loaned without charge to qualified educational institutions and vocational training schools. The recipient must provide funds for maintenance, packing, crating, handling, transportation, and installation.

Length and Time Phasing of Assistance: Not applicable.

POST ASSISTANCE REQUIREMENTS:

Reports: None.

Audits: The Defense General Supply Center conducts inspections to evaluate program objectives, equipment maintenance, degree of utilization, and adherence to course curricula.

Records: None.

172

FINANCIAL INFORMATION:

Account Identification: 97-0100-0-1-051.

Obligations: (Total value of property at acquisition value on loan) FY 92 $39,974,000; FY 93 est $36,531,000; and FY 94 est $36,037,000.

Range and Average of Financial Assistance: Average loan is seven machines with an approximate total acquisition value of $60,810.

PROGRAM ACCOMPLISHMENTS: At the end of fiscal year 1992 there were 761 loans covering 5,331 items with an acquisition value of $46,822,640.

REGULATIONS, GUIDELINES, AND LITERATURE: Pamphlet published by Defense General Supply Center entitled "Tools for Schools."

INFORMATION CONTACTS:

Regional or Local Office: Commander, Defense General Supply Center, Richmond, VA 23297-5000. Telephone: (804) 275-3374; DSN: 695-3374.

Headquarters Office: Directorate of Supply Operations, Defense Logistics Agency, Cameron Station, Alexandria, VA 22304-6100. Telephone: (703) 274-6253.

EXAMPLES OF FUNDED PROJECTS: Not applicable.

CRITERIA FOR SELECTING PROPOSALS: Not applicable.

14.157 SUPPORTIVE HOUSING FOR THE ELDERLY (202)

FEDERAL AGENCY: HOUSING, DEPARTMENT OF HOUSING AND URBAN DEVELOPMENT

AUTHORIZATION: Housing Act of 1959, as amended; Housing and Community Development Act of 1974, as amended, Title II; Public Law 86-372, 12 U.S.C. 1701q, 73 Stat. 654, 667; as amended by National Affordable Housing Act, Public Law 101-507, 42 USC 12701.

OBJECTIVES: To expand the supply of housing with supportive services for the elderly.

TYPES OF ASSISTANCE: Project Grants.

USES AND USE RESTRICTIONS: Capital advances shall be used to finance the construction or rehabilitation of a structure or portion thereof, or the acquisition of a structure from the Resolution Trust Corporation to provide supportive housing for the elderly, which may include the cost of real property acquisition, site improvement, conversion, demolition, relocation and other expenses of supportive housing for the elderly. Project rental assistance is used to cover the difference between the HUD-approved operating cost per unit and the amount the tenant pays.

ELIGIBILITY REQUIREMENTS:

Applicant Eligibility: Private nonprofit corporations and consumer cooperatives. Public bodies and their instrumentalities are not eligible Section 202 applicants.

Beneficiary Eligibility: Beneficiaries of housing developed under this program must be elderly (62 years of age or older)

Credentials/Documentation: The nonprofit sponsor/owner must receive certification of eligibility from HUD. The owner must submit financial statements to support its ability to provide a capital investment of 1/2 of 1 percent of the HUD-approved capital advance amount, up to a maximum of $25,000 for national sponsors or $10,000 if not a national sponsor. This program is excluded from coverage under OMB Circular No. A-87.

APPLICATION AND AWARD PROCESS:

Preapplication Coordination: This program is excluded from coverage under OMB Circular No. A-102. An environmental assessment is required for this program. This program is eligible for coverage under E.O. 12372, "Intergovernmental Review of Federal Programs." An applicant should consult the office or official designated as the single point of contact in his or her State for more information on the process the State requires to be followed in applying for assistance, if the State has selected the program for review.

Application Procedure: A Notice of Fund Availability is published in the Federal Register each fiscal year announcing the availability of funds to HUD Regional or Field Offices. Applicants must submit a Request for Fund Reservation, using HUD Form 92015-CA, in response to the Notice of Fund Availability (or a Funding Notification issued by the local HUD Field Office). This program is excluded from coverage under OMB Circular No. A-110.

Award Procedure: Applications are reviewed and selected for funding within the funding allocation of the particular HUD Field Office or Regional Office. Those selected for funding must meet basic program requirements including, but not limited to: eligibility as a nonprofit entity, ability to meet the minimum capital investment and prior experience in housing or related service activities. The Request for Capital Advance Financing, using HUD Form 92013, is reviewed to determine acceptability of project site and market, correctness of zoning, effect on environment, value of site and financial feasibility.

Deadlines: Applications must be submitted within the time period specified in the Notice of Fund Availability (or Funding Notification), usually 6 to 10 weeks.

Range of Approval/Disapproval Time: At the fund reservation stage, the sponsor usually is advised of the decision within 4 to 5 months from the end of the application period, but in any event, usually by the end of the same fiscal year (September 30).

Appeals: None.

Renewals: None.

ASSISTANCE CONSIDERATIONS:

Formula and Matching Requirements: This program has maintenance of effort (MOE) requirements, see funding agency for further details. Statistical factors used for allocating funds include a measure of total elderly rental households, including the very low income elderly renters, and a measure of the number of one- and two-person elderly renter households with incomes at or below the very low income standard with housing deficiencies, consisting primarily of households paying more than 30 percent of their incomes for rent.

Length and Time Phasing of Assistance: The capital advance is not repayable so long as the project is available to very low income elderly for 40 years. Project Rental Assistance Contract payments may not exceed 20 years. Projects are expected to start construction within 18 months of the date of the fund reservation, with limited provision for extensions. Funds will be advanced on a monthly basis during construction for work in place.

POST ASSISTANCE REQUIREMENTS:

Reports: Any change in the owner during the period of the advance must be approved by HUD. All owners will be required to submit an annual financial statement to HUD.

Audits: HUD reserves the right to audit the accounts of the owner in order to determine compliance and conformance with HUD regulations and standards.

Records: Regular financial reports are required. Owners must service and maintain records in accordance with acceptable mortgage practices and HUD regulations. Owners also must supply those records necessary to indicate compliance with the project rental assistance contract.

FINANCIAL INFORMATION:

Account Identification: 86-4115-0-3-371.

Obligations: (Reservations for Capital Grants, Rental Assistance and Service Coordinators) FY 92 $1,581,699,584; FY 93 est $1,351,415,201; and FY 94 est $1,145,000,000.

Range and Average of Financial Assistance: Approximate average award $3,235,300 in FY 92.

PROGRAM ACCOMPLISHMENTS: Cumulative totals through September 30, 1992 are 231,620 units funded for a total of $10,863,945,100. For fiscal year 1992, under the capital advance program $741.6 million for 12,379 units.

REGULATIONS, GUIDELINES, AND LITERATURE: 24 CFR 885; HUD Handbook 4571.1 Rev. 2 (loans); 24 CFR 889 (capital advances); HUD Handbooks 4571.3 and 4571.5 (capital advances).

INFORMATION CONTACTS:

Headquarters Office: Housing for the Elderly and Handicapped People Division, Office of Elderly and Assisted Housing, Housing, Department of Housing and Urban Development, Washington, DC 20410. Telephone: (202) 708-2730. (Use the same number for FTS).

EXAMPLES OF FUNDED PROJECTS: Not applicable.

CRITERIA FOR SELECTING PROPOSALS: Not applicable.

14.181 SUPPORTIVE HOUSING FOR PERSONS WITH DISABILITIES (811)

FEDERAL AGENCY: HOUSING, DEPARTMENT OF HOUSING AND URBAN DEVELOPMENT

AUTHORIZATION: National Affordable Housing Act, Public Law 101-625, 42 USC 8013, 104 Stat. 4324, 4331.

OBJECTIVES: To provide for supportive housing and related facilities for persons with disabilities.

TYPES OF ASSISTANCE: Project Grants.

USES AND USE RESTRICTIONS: Capital advances may be used to finance the construction or rehabilitation of supportive housing for persons with disabilities, including the purchase of buildings with or without rehabilitation for use as group homes. Project rental assistance is used to cover any part of the HUD-approved operating costs of the facility that is not met from project income.

ELIGIBILITY REQUIREMENTS:

Applicant Eligibility: Nonprofit corporations.

Beneficiary Eligibility: Beneficiaries of housing developed under this program must be very low income physically disabled, developmentally disabled or chronically mentally ill persons (18 years of age or older).

Credentials/Documentation: The nonprofit sponsor and owner must receive certification of eligibility from HUD. The owner must submit financial statements to support its ability to provide a minimum capital investment of 1/2 of 1 percent of the capital advance amount, up to a maximum of $10,000. This program is excluded from coverage under OMB Circular No. A-87.

APPLICATION AND AWARD PROCESS:

Preapplication Coordination: At the fund reservation processing stage, a copy of each application will be forwarded to the appropriate state or local agency for a review of the supportive services plan. A certification from the agency as to whether the provision of services identified in the sponsor's application is well designed to meet the needs of the anticipated occupancy must be forwarded to the HUD Field Office. This program is excluded from coverage under OMB Circular No. A-102. An environmental assessment is required for applications containing evidence of site control. This program is eligible for coverage under E.O. 12372, "Intergovernmental Review of Federal Programs." An applicant should consult the office or official designated as the single point of contact in his or her State for more information on the process the State requires to be followed in applying for assistance, if the State has selected the program for review.

Application Procedure: A Notice of Fund Availability is published in the Federal Register each fiscal year announcing the availability of funds to HUD Regional or Field Offices. Applicants must submit a Request for Fund Reservation in response to an invitation published by the local HUD Field Office. This program is excluded from coverage under OMB Circular No. A-110.

Award Procedure: Applications are reviewed and selected for funding within the funding allocation of the particular HUD Field Office or Regional Office. Those selected for funding must meet basic program requirements including, but not limited to: eligibility as a nonprofit entity, financial capacity and prior experience in housing or related service activities.

Deadlines: Applications must be submitted within the time period specified in the invitation, usually 6 to 10 weeks.

Range of Approval/Disapproval Time: At the fund reservation stage, the sponsor usually is advised of the decision within 4 to 5 months from the end of the application period.

Appeals: None.

Renewals: None.

ASSISTANCE CONSIDERATIONS:

Formula and Matching Requirements: This program has maintenance of effort (MOE) requirements; see funding agency for further details. Statistical factors used for fund allocation include a measure of the disabled population with incomes below 50 percent the median family income from the source survey of Income and Education, Census. Statistical factors used for eligibility do not apply for this program.

Length and Time Phasing of Assistance: The capital advance is not repayable if the project is available for very low income persons with disabilities for 40 years. Project Rental Assistance Contract payments may not exceed 20 years. Projects are expected to start construction within 18 months of the date of the fund reservation, with limited provision for extensions. Funds will be advanced on a monthly basis during construction for work in place.

POST ASSISTANCE REQUIREMENTS:

Reports: Any change in the owner during the 40-year period must be approved by HUD. All owners will be required to submit an annual financial statement to HUD.

Audits: HUD reserves the right to audit the accounts of the owners in order to determine compliance and conformance with HUD regulations and standards.

Records: Regular financial reports are required. Owners must service and maintain records in accordance with acceptable mortgage practices and HUD regulations. Owners also must supply those records necessary to indicate compliance with the project rental assistance contract.

FINANCIAL INFORMATION:

Account Identification: 86-4588-0-3-371.

Obligations: (Reservations for Capital Grants and Rental Assistance) FY 92 $375,583,650; FY 93 est $357,096,834; and FY 94 est $193,754,000.

Range and Average of Financial Assistance: Not applicable.

PROGRAM ACCOMPLISHMENTS: For fiscal year 1992, $375.6 million for 3,234 units.

REGULATIONS, GUIDELINES, AND LITERATURE: 24 CFR, 890; HUD Handbooks 4571.2 and 4571.4.

INFORMATION CONTACTS:

Headquarters Office: Housing for Elderly and Handicapped People Division, Office of Elderly and Assisted Housing, Housing, Department of Housing and Urban Development, Washington, DC 20410. Telephone: (202) 708-2730. Use the same number for FTS.

EXAMPLES OF FUNDED PROJECTS: Not applicable.

CRITERIA FOR SELECTING PROPOSALS: Not applicable.

15.918 DISPOSAL OF FEDERAL SURPLUS REAL PROPERTY FOR PARKS, RECREATION, AND HISTORIC MONUMENTS   (Surplus Property Program)

FEDERAL AGENCY: NATIONAL PARK SERVICE, DEPARTMENT OF THE INTERIOR

AUTHORIZATION: Federal Property and Administrative Services Act of 1949, Section 203(k), 63 Stat. 385 as amended, 40 U.S.C. 484, Public Law 91-485; Federal Lands for Parks and Recreation, 16 U.S.C. 4601-5.

OBJECTIVES: To transfer surplus Federal real property for public park and recreation use or for historic monument use.

TYPES OF ASSISTANCE: Use of Property, Facilities, and Equipment.

USES AND USE RESTRICTIONS: Surplus real property may be conveyed for public park and recreation use at discounts up to 100 percent of fair market value and for historic monument purposes without monetary consideration. Property conveyed for park and recreation use or historic monument purposes must be used for these purposes in perpetuity or be reverted to Federal ownership.

ELIGIBILITY REQUIREMENTS:

Applicant Eligibility: Only State or local units of government are eligible to apply for surplus real property for public park and recreation and historic monument purposes, and, must agree to manage the property in the public interest and for public use.

Beneficiary Eligibility: Only State or local units of government are eligible to apply for surplus real property for public park and recreation and historic monument purposes, and, must agree to manage the property in the public interest and for public use.

Credentials/Documentation: The applicant must submit a proposed program of use for the property and evidence of its ability to finance the program. This program is excluded from coverage under OMB Circular No. A-87.

APPLICATION AND AWARD PROCESS:

Preapplication Coordination: Park and recreation and historic monument applications are coordinated by the National Park Service, Department of the Interior, and the General Services Administration, or in the case of legislated military base closures, the Department of Defense. This program is excluded from coverage under OMB Circular No. A-102 and E.O.12372.

Application Procedure: Applications for park and recreation use and historic monuments are submitted to the National Park Service Regional Office. Application forms are issued by the National Park Service. This program is excluded from coverage under OMB Circular Nos. A-102 and A-110.

Award Procedure: Upon approval of a park and recreation application the National Park Service will request GSA or DOD military service in the case of base closures, to assign the property to the Secretary of the Interior for transfer. Upon approval of an application, the National Park Service recommends that DOD or GSA transfer the property to the National Park Service for transfer to the applicant.

Deadlines: The National Park Service must notify the General Services Administration (or DOD) within 20 calendar days after the date of the notice of determination of surplus if it has an eligible applicant interested in acquiring the property. The National Park Service must request assignment of property from GSA (or DOD) within 25 calendar days after the expiration of the 20 day period.

Range of Approval/Disapproval Time: From 3 to 6 months.

Appeals: None.

Renewals: None.

ASSISTANCE CONSIDERATIONS:

Formula and Matching Requirements: Not applicable.

Length and Time Phasing of Assistance: Not applicable.

POST ASSISTANCE REQUIREMENTS:

Reports: Recipients of surplus properties are required to submit biennial compliance reports on the use of the property.

Audits: The National Park Service conducts periodic on-site compliance inspections to assure that the properties are being utilized for the purposes for which they are conveyed. Properties in noncompliance may be reverted back to the Federal Government.

Records: The National Park Service maintains official records concerning the property.

FINANCIAL INFORMATION:

Account Identification: 14-1042-0-1-303.

Obligations: (Salaries and expenses) FY 92 $267,500; FY 93 est $272,000; and FY 94 est $180,000.

Range and Average of Financial Assistance: Not applicable.

PROGRAM ACCOMPLISHMENTS: Since 1949, over 1,260 properties comprising over 140,000 acres have been transferred to State and local governments for park and recreation purposes. In fiscal year 1992, 9 properties (approximately 108 acres) were transferred for park and recreation purposes.

REGULATIONS, GUIDELINES, AND LITERATURE: "Disposal of Surplus Real Property," booklet published by the General Service Administration (no charge). Section 203 (K) (2) and 203 (K) (3) of the Federal Property and Administrative Service Act of 1949, as amended (40 U.S.C. 484 (K) (2) and (K) (3).

INFORMATION CONTACTS:

Headquarters Office: National Park Service, Recreation Resource Assistance Division, Department of the Interior, P.O. Box 37127, Washington, DC 20013-7127. Contacts: Wendy E. Ormont (Park and Recreation Program). Telephone: (202) 343-3759. Tom Jester (Historic Monument Program). Telephone: (202) 343-9587.

EXAMPLES OF FUNDED PROJECTS: Nature Study Areas - Wildlife Conservation Areas; Intensively Developed Play Areas; State and Regional Parks; Arts/Crafts Youth and Senior Citizen Areas; Historic Monuments (Buildings) and/or Archeological Areas.

CRITERIA FOR SELECTING PROPOSALS: Suitability of real property for the proposed use and the ability of the applicant local unit of government to carry out the proposed program of use.

39.002 DISPOSAL OF FEDERAL SURPLUS REAL PROPERTY

FEDERAL AGENCY: GENERAL SERVICES ADMINISTRATION

AUTHORIZATION: Federal Property and Administrative Services Act of 1949, Section 203, as amended, 63 Stat. 385, 40 U.S.C. 484; Surplus Property Act of 1944, Section 13(g), as amended, 50 U.S.C. 1622(g); Public Law 80-537, as amended, 62 Stat. 240, 16 U.S.C. 667b-d; Section 218, Public Law 91-646, 84 Stat. 1902, 42 U.S.C. 4638; Stewart B. McKinney Homeless Assistance Act of 1987, Title V, as amended, 42 U.S.C. 11411, Public Laws 100-77, 100-628, and 101-645.

OBJECTIVES: To dispose of surplus real property by lease, permits, sale, exchange, or donation.

TYPES OF ASSISTANCE: Sale, Exchange, or Donation of Property and Goods.

USES AND USE RESTRICTIONS: Surplus real and related personal property may be conveyed for: public park or recreation use and public health or educational purposes at discounts up to 100 percent; public airport purposes, wildlife conservation, correctional facility, replacement housing and for historic monument purposes without monetary consideration; and for general public purposes without restrictions at a negotiated price of not less than the estimated fair market value of the property. Properties are made available for discount conveyance where the public purposes to be served reflect the highest and best use of the property. Properties determined suitable by the Department of Housing and Urban Development may be made available by permit, lease, or deed for homeless assistance use. Restrictions: Surplus real property conveyed for public park or recreation use, historic monument, public airport use, correctional facility use and wildlife conservation use must be used for the purposes so conveyed in perpetuity. Property conveyed for health (including homeless) or education use must be used for those purposes for a period of not less than 30 years. Properties made available for homeless use by lease or permit must be used for that purpose for a period of not less than one year, unless the provider requests a shorter term. Surplus real property which is not deeded to public bodies or made available for homeless purposes is generally offered for sale to the public on a competitive bid basis.

ELIGIBILITY REQUIREMENTS:

Applicant Eligibility: State and local government agencies are eligible to apply for surplus real property for park, recreation, correctional facility, historic monument, public airport, health, educational, homeless, replacement housing, and general public purposes. Eligibility for property for wildlife conservation use, other than for migratory birds, is limited to the States. Tax-supported and nonprofit medical and educational institutions which have been held exempt from taxation under 501(c) (3) of the Internal Revenue Code are also eligible to apply for property for health, educational and homeless use.

Beneficiary Eligibility: General public.

Credentials/Documentation: The applicant must submit a proposed program of use of the property and evidence of its ability to finance the program.

APPLICATION AND AWARD PROCESS:

Preapplication Coordination: Applicants for property coordinate with other Federal agencies as follows: health and homeless use—Department of Health and Human Services; education—Department of Education; public airport purposes—Federal Aviation Administration; park or recreational and historic monument use—National Park Service, Department of the Interior; wildlife conservation—Fish and Wildlife Service, Department of the Interior; correctional facility use—Office of Justice Programs, Department of Justice; replacement housing—any Federal agency having a requirement for property involving housing for displaced persons in connection with a Federal or federally assisted project.

Application Procedure: Applications for health and homeless assistance use are submitted to the Department of Health and Human Services (HHS) which requests assignment of the property from GSA; applications for educational use are submitted to the Department of Education which requests assignment of the property from GSA; applications for park and recreation use are submitted to the National Park Service, Department of the Interior which requests assignment of the property from GSA, applications for correctional use are submitted to the Office of Justice Programs, Department of Justice. Applications for other uses are submitted to GSA, which then obtains the recommendation of the Federal agency which sponsors the use program.

Award Procedure: When possible, awards are made through the participating agency. Other awards are made to State or local units of government by the Administrator of GSA.

Deadlines: Advice of interest must be submitted within 20 days from date notice of availability of the property was released. Reasonable time thereafter is allowed for the filing of applications.

Range of Approval/Disapproval Time: From 1 to 3 months.

Appeals: None.

Renewals: None.

ASSISTANCE CONSIDERATIONS:

Formula and Matching Requirements: Not applicable.

Length and Time Phasing of Assistance: Not applicable.

POST ASSISTANCE REQUIREMENTS:

Reports: The Federal agencies sponsoring the use programs are responsible for enforcing compliance with the restrictions, except that GSA is responsible for compliance with respect to conveyances for wildlife conservation and correctional facility use.

Audits: The Federal agencies sponsoring the use program and GSA are responsible for audits.

Records: Not applicable.

FINANCIAL INFORMATION:

Account Identification: 47-0533-0-1-804.

Obligations: (Salaries and expenses) FY 92 $13,950,000; FY 93 est $13,933,000; and FY 94 est $15,756,000.

Range and Average of Financial Assistance: Not applicable.

PROGRAM ACCOMPLISHMENTS: The Disposal Program was as follows: Actual for fiscal year 1992: Donations and other discounts - 52 properties having an actual value of $70 million; Sales - 267 properties generating proceeds of $23 million; Estimate for fiscal year 1993: Sales, donations and other discounts - 337 properties having an estimated value of $131 million; Fiscal year 1994 estimates: Sales, donations and other discounts - 337 properties having an estimated value of $131 million.

REGULATIONS, GUIDELINES, AND LITERATURE: "Disposal of Surplus Real Property" - no charge; 41 CFR 101-47, Utilization and Disposal of Real Property, "U.S. Real Property Sales List," - no charge.

INFORMATION CONTACTS:

Headquarters Office: Assistant Commissioner, Office of Real Estate Policy and Sales, Federal Property Resources Service, General Services Administration, Washington, DC 20405. Telephone: (202) 501-0084.

EXAMPLES OF FUNDED PROJECTS: Not applicable.

CRITERIA FOR SELECTING PROPOSALS: Not applicable.

39.003 DONATION OF FEDERAL SURPLUS PERSONAL PROPERTY

FEDERAL AGENCY: GENERAL SERVICES ADMINISTRATION

AUTHORIZATION: Federal Property and Administrative Services Act of 1949, Section 203(j), Public Law 81-152, as amended, Public Law 94-519, 40 U.S.C. 484(j); Surplus Property Act of 1944, Section 13(g), as amended, 50 U.S.C. 1622(g); Older Americans Act of 1965, Section 213, as amended, 42 U.S.C. 3020d; Section 502, Public Law 100-77.

OBJECTIVES: To transfer surplus property to the States for donation to State and local public agencies for public purposes or to qualifying nonprofit, tax-exempt activities; to public airports; and to educational activities of special interest to the armed services.

TYPES OF ASSISTANCE: Sale, Exchange, or Donation of Property and Goods.

USES AND USE RESTRICTIONS: Surplus items are used by State and local public agencies for carrying out or promoting one or more public purposes, such as conservation, parks and recreation, education, public health, public safety, economic development and programs for older individuals; by certain nonprofit, tax-exempt activities for public health or educational purposes, including research for such purposes, and for use in programs for older individuals; or by public airports for airport development, operation or maintenance. Federal restrictions require that all surplus property be placed into use by the donee within 1 year of acquisition and be used at least for 1 year thereafter. Other restrictions, terms and conditions are imposed by the agencies determining eligibility (shown under Applicant Eligibility, section below). The following items are representative of those donated: office machines and supplies, furniture, hardware, textiles, special purpose motor vehicles, boats, airplanes, and construction equipment. Items not donated are made available for sale to the general public.

ELIGIBILITY REQUIREMENTS:

Applicant Eligibility: (a) State participation is contingent upon the acceptance by the General Services Administration (GSA) of a State plan of operation as being in conformance with Public Law 94-519. This State plan must establish a State agency which is responsible for the distribution of Federal surplus personal property to eligible recipients within the State on a fair and equitable basis. Eligible donee categories for the distribution of property through the State Agencies for Surplus Property are defined as: (1) Public agencies which include any (i) State or department, agency, or instrumentality thereof; (ii) political subdivision of the State, including any unit of local government or economic development district, or any department, agency or instrumentality thereof; (iii) instrumentality created by compact or other agreement between State or political subdivisions; (iv) multijurisdictional sub-State district established by or pursuant to State law; and (v) Indian tribe, band, group, pueblo, or community located on a State reservation. Eligibility for public agencies is determined by the State Agency for Surplus Property. (2) Nonprofit, tax-exempt activities such as schools, colleges, universities, public libraries, schools for the mentally retarded or physically handicapped, educational radio or TV stations, child care centers, museums, medical institutions, hospitals, clinics, health centers, drug abuse treatment centers, providers of assistance to the homeless, and programs for older individuals. Eligibility for nonprofit institutions and organizations is determined by the State Agency for Surplus Property. (b) Service educational activities, including the American Red Cross, Center for Excellence in Education, Boy Scouts of America, Boys and Girls Clubs of America, Camp Fire Incorporated, Girl Scouts of the United States of America, Big Brothers/Big Sisters of America, National Ski Patrol System, Naval Sea Cadet Corps, Operation Raleigh, United Service Organizations, United States Olympic Committee, Little League Baseball, National Association for Equal Opportunity in Higher Education, Young Marines of the Marine Corps League, and schools with military-connected programs. Eligibility is determined by the Assistant Secretary of Defense

(Production and Logistics). (c) Public airports. Eligibility is determined by the Federal Aviation Administration. (d) Non-eligible institutions and organizations include institutions such as animal hospitals, summer camps or playgrounds that are not part of a public agency or a school, Sunday schools, churches and nonprofit tax-exempt public health and education money-funding organizations that provide grants, scholarships and funds to support approved or accredited public health and educational institutions but do not themselves operate such programs.

Beneficiary Eligibility: State and local public agencies; nonprofit educational or public health institutions or organizations, including providers of assistance to the homeless; nonprofit and public programs for the elderly; educational activities of special interest to the armed services; and public airports.

Credentials/Documentation: Contact appropriate State or Federal agency shown under Applicant Eligibility section of this program.

APPLICATION AND AWARD PROCESS:

Preapplication Coordination: (1) Public agencies, nonprofit educational and public health applicants, providers of assistance to the homeless, and programs for the elderly coordinate with the State Agency for Surplus Property. (2) Service Educational Activity schools and national organizations coordinate with their sponsoring military service or national headquarters. (3) Public airports coordinate with the regional Airports District Office of the Federal Aviation Administration. The coordinating agency which determines donee eligibility may request GSA to issue a screener's card to the donee which would authorize a designee to screen surplus property at specific location(s).

Application Procedure: Contact appropriate agency shown under Preapplication Coordination section of this program.

Award Procedure: Upon determination of eligibility, applicant maintains contact with the appropriate agency shown under Preapplication Coordination section of this program.

Deadlines: None.

Range of Approval/Disapproval Time: Not applicable.

Appeals: Applicants participating through State agencies for surplus property may appeal a determination of ineligibility through the State agency for review by GSA.

Renewals: Not applicable.

ASSISTANCE CONSIDERATIONS:

Formula and Matching Requirements: Not applicable.

Length and Time Phasing of Assistance: Not applicable.

POST ASSISTANCE REQUIREMENTS:

Reports: Prescribed by agencies shown under Applicant Eligibility section of this program.

Audits: Prescribed by agencies shown under Applicant Eligibility section of this program.

Records: Prescribed by agencies shown under Applicant Eligibility section of this program.

FINANCIAL INFORMATION:

Account Identification: 47-0116-0-1-804.

Obligations: (Salaries and expenses) FY 92 $9,635,000; FY 93 est $9,630,000; and FY 94 est $9,884,000.

Range and Average of Financial Assistance: Not applicable.

PROGRAM ACCOMPLISHMENTS: In fiscal year 1992, surplus personal property with an original government acquisition cost of $640.0 million was donated. Fiscal year 1993 is estimated at $730 million. Fiscal year 1994 estimates are $810 million.

REGULATIONS, GUIDELINES, AND LITERATURE: 41 CFR 101-44, "Donation of Personal Property," available for purchase from Superintendent of Documents, Government Printing Office, Washington, DC 20402. Pamphlet, "Federal Surplus Personal Property Donation Programs," available from General Services Administration at no charge.

INFORMATION CONTACTS:

Regional or Local Office: Individual units of Service Educational Activities national organizations such as Boy Scout or Girl Scout troops, Boys and Girls Clubs, etc., should contact their regional or national headquarters; Service Educational Activity Schools should contact their sponsoring military service.

Headquarters Office: Director, Property Management Division, Office of Transportation and Property Management, Federal Supply Service, General Services Administration, Washington, DC 20406. Telephone: (703) 305-5234. Information concerning the designation of Service Education Activities can be obtained from the Assistant Secretary of Defense, Production and Logistics, The Pentagon, Washington, DC, 20301.

EXAMPLES OF FUNDED PROJECTS: Not applicable.

CRITERIA FOR SELECTING PROPOSALS: Not applicable.

64.013 VETERANS PROSTHETIC APPLIANCES (Prosthetics Services)

FEDERAL AGENCY: VETERANS HEALTH ADMINISTRATION, DEPARTMENT OF VETERANS AFFAIRS

AUTHORIZATION: 38 U.S.C. Sections 1162, 1701, 1710, 1712, 1713, 1714, 1717, 1719, 1723, 1724, 3104, 3901, 3902, 3903, and 8123.

OBJECTIVES: To provide, through purchase and/or fabrication, prosthetic and related appliances, equipment and services to disabled veterans so that they may live and work as productive citizens.

TYPES OF ASSISTANCE: Sale, Exchange, or Donation of Property and Goods.

USES AND USE RESTRICTIONS: Appliances and services are provided only for the use and benefit of the disabled veteran to whom they are furnished. The program also includes the replacement and repair of appliances and training in the use of artificial limbs, artificial eyes, wheelchairs, aids for blind, hearing aids, braces, orthopedic shoes, eyeglasses, crutches and canes, medical equipment, implants, and medical supplies, and automotive adaptive equipment.

ELIGIBILITY REQUIREMENTS:

Applicant Eligibility: Any disabled veteran or authorized representative on his behalf meeting the criteria below may apply for prosthetic appliances or services.

Beneficiary Eligibility: Disabled veterans eligible for VA outpatient treatment for service-connected or nonservice-connected conditions requiring prosthetic services; veterans receiving hospital care in VA facilities or at VA expense, or receiving domiciliary, or nursing home care in VA facilities; veterans in receipt of 50 percent compensation for service-connected disabilities or special monthly compensation or increased pension based on being housebound or the need for regular aid and attendance; veterans in receipt of compensation for disabilities resulting from hospitalization, medical or surgical treatment, or the pursuit of a cause of vocational rehabilitation; veterans of World War I; or former prisoner of war. Ineligible veterans are those not eligible for outpatient care or nonservice-connected veterans residing or sojourning in foreign lands.

Credentials/Documentation: None.

APPLICATION AND AWARD PROCESS:

Preapplication Coordination: None.

Application Procedure: Eligible veteran may request prosthetics services by reporting in person at any VA Medical Center as well as by correspondence, telephone, or community physician prescription.

Award Procedure: Not applicable.

Deadlines: None.

Range of Approval/Disapproval Time: Usually immediately, although delays of 30 to 60 days have occurred in unusual cases.

Appeals: A veteran who is administratively refused prosthetics services by a local VA health care facility may appeal to the Secretary of Veterans Affairs. Determinations of the Veterans Health Administration involving the need or nature of medical treatment as distinguished from legal or basic eligibility for medical services, are not appealable.

Renewals: None.

ASSISTANCE CONSIDERATIONS:

Formula and Matching Requirements: Not applicable.

Length and Time Phasing of Assistance: For veterans eligible for outpatient medical treatment and those in receipt of special monthly compensation or increased pension based on the need for regular aid and attendance, assistance is maintained for as long as eligibility continues (usually for life). Veterans receiving hospital, domiciliary, or nursing home care, assistance is available until discharge from such care.

POST ASSISTANCE REQUIREMENTS:

Reports: None.

Audits: Not applicable.

Records: Not applicable.

FINANCIAL INFORMATION:

Account Identification: 36-0160-0-1-703.

Obligations: (Value and repair of prosthetic appliances) FY 92 $189,465,000; FY 93 est $195,610,000 and FY 94 est $212,500,000.

Range and Average of Financial Assistance: $10 to $25,000; $114.

PROGRAM ACCOMPLISHMENTS: The program has provided 1,500,000 prosthetic item/services in the form of prosthetic appliances, sensory aids, medical equipment, medical supplies, implants, therapeutic devices and repair services during fiscal year 1992. Approximately the same prosthetic item/services will be provided in fiscal year 1993.

REGULATIONS, GUIDELINES, AND LITERATURE: 38 CFR 17.115, 17.115a, 17.115b, 17.115c, 17.115d, 17.116, 17.118, 17.119, 17.119a, 17.119b, 17.119c, 17.119d.

INFORMATION CONTACTS:

Headquarters Office: Director, Prosthetic and Sensory Aids (117C), Department of Veterans Affairs, Washington, DC 20420. Telephone: (202) 535-7293.

EXAMPLES OF FUNDED PROJECTS: Not applicable.

CRITERIA FOR SELECTING PROPOSALS: Not applicable.

68.001 NATIONAL GALLERY OF ART EXTENSION SERVICE

FEDERAL AGENCY: NATIONAL GALLERY OF ART

AUTHORIZATION: 20 U.S.C. 71-75.

OBJECTIVES: To provide educational material (slide programs, videocassettes, and films) on the Gallery's collections and exhibitions, free of charge except for transportation costs, to schools, colleges, and libraries across the Nation.

TYPES OF ASSISTANCE: Use of Property, Facilities, and Equipment.

USES AND USE RESTRICTIONS: Audio-visual materials for the use in art education programs, and humanities curricula.

ELIGIBILITY REQUIREMENTS:

Applicant Eligibility: Schools, colleges, libraries, clubs, museums, community organizations, and individuals.

Beneficiary Eligibility: Public and private nonprofit institutions and organizations.

Credentials/Documentation: None.

APPLICATION AND AWARD PROCESS:

Preapplication Coordination: None.

Application Procedure: Write to the headquarters office for list of available materials; order forms provided.

Award Procedure: Not applicable.

Deadlines: Not applicable.

Range of Approval/Disapproval Time: Not applicable.

Appeals: Not applicable.

Renewals: Not applicable.

ASSISTANCE CONSIDERATIONS:

Formula and Matching Requirements: Not applicable.

Length and Time Phasing of Assistance: Not applicable.

POST ASSISTANCE REQUIREMENTS:

Reports: Data on use of materials.

Audits: None.

Records: None.

FINANCIAL INFORMATION:

Account Identification: 33-0200-0-1-503.

Obligations: (Salaries and Expenses) FY 92 $793,000; FY 93 est $833,000; and FY 94 est $875,000.

Range and Average of Financial Assistance: Not applicable.

PROGRAM ACCOMPLISHMENTS: In fiscal year 1992, audiovisual art education materials relating to the nation's collection of paintings and sculptures and to the Gallery's special exhibitions were shown 120,778 times. In fiscal years 1993 and 1994 the number of showings and audiences are estimated to remain in this range, due to diminishing levels of use of program materials by public television audiences. In fiscal year 1992, Extension Programs on the Gallery's collections and exhibitions were seen by a reported 44,949,419 persons. Audience figures for fiscal year 1993 will be lower, due to a decline in availability of films and video programs for public and educational television broadcast and to changes, mergers, and acquisition of educational networks by commercial, for-profit companies. The use of these resource materials in the educational community and for continuing and lifelong learning will remain high.

REGULATIONS, GUIDELINES, AND LITERATURE: None.

INFORMATION CONTACTS:

Regional or Local Office: None.

Headquarters Office: Department of Education Resources, Extension Programs Section, National Gallery of Art, Washington, DC 20565. Telephone: (202) 737-4215. Contact: Ruth Perlin, Telephone: (202) 842-6273 (FTS 8-737-6600).

EXAMPLES OF FUNDED PROJECTS: Not applicable.

CRITERIA FOR SELECTING PROPOSALS: Not Applicable.

81.022 USED ENERGY-RELATED LABORATORY EQUIPMENT GRANTS
(Used Equipment Grants)

FEDERAL AGENCY: OFFICE OF SCIENCE EDUCATION AND TECHNICAL INFORMATION, DEPARTMENT OF ENERGY

AUTHORIZATION: Atomic Energy Act of 1954, Section 31(a) and (b), as amended, Public Law 83-703, 68 Stat. 919, 42 U.S.C. 2051; Energy Reorganization Act of 1974, Title I, Section 107, Public Law 93-438, 88 Stat. 1240, 42 U.S.C. 5817; Department of Energy Organization Act of 1977, as amended, Public Law 95-91, 42 U.S.C. 7101.

OBJECTIVES: To assist United States institutions of higher education in equipping their science and engineering laboratories for energy-related research and/or instructional purposes.

TYPES OF ASSISTANCE: Sale, Exchange, or Donation of Property and Goods.

USES AND USE RESTRICTIONS: Used energy-related laboratory equipment is granted to nonprofit educational institutions of higher learning for use in energy-oriented Research or instructional programs in the life, physical, and environmental sciences and engineering.

ELIGIBILITY REQUIREMENTS:

Applicant Eligibility: Nonprofit educational institutions of higher learning, such as universities, colleges, junior colleges, hospitals, and technical institutes or museums located in the United States and interested in establishing or upgrading energy oriented educational and research programs in the life, physical, and environmental sciences and engineering may apply.

Beneficiary Eligibility: Nonprofit institutions of higher education benefit.

Credentials/Documentation: Proposal should include identification of institution and school and/or department where equipment would be used; the objectives to be met through use of the equipment; a detailed listing of the equipment requested; a brief description of energy-oriented course offerings and numbers of graduate and undergraduate students enrolled; data on qualifications of faculty members to make effective use of the equipment; reference to any prior grant for equipment (financial or otherwise) to the same or to a related department; and the name, title, and signature of the person preparing the proposal; and appropriate official university signature(s). This program is excluded from coverage under OMB Circular No. A-87.

APPLICATION AND AWARD PROCESS:

Preapplication Coordination: Representatives of eligible institutions may review lists of equipment eligible for a grant which is maintained at DOE installations located throughout the United States. Installation addresses are listed in "Instruction and Information on Used Energy-Related Laboratory Equipment Grants for Educational Institutions of Higher Learning." (DOE/ER-00423 Revised 8/85). These listings of eligible equipment are also available from two other sources which are also noted in the cited publication: (1) An institution may access the "Eligible Equipment Grant Access Data System" that is maintained at DOE Headquarters on a microcomputer; or (2) the "Energy Related Laboratory Equipment Catalog" is available for $69.00 a year for a 12 month subscription from the Government Printing Office. This program is excluded from coverage under OMB Circular No. A-102. This program is excluded from coverage under E.O. 12372.

Application Procedure: Written proposal to the DOE field office responsible for the site where the specific equipment is known to be located. This program is subject to the provisions of OMB Circular No. A-110.

Award Procedure: Award is on basis of first-received, first-qualified proposal.

Deadlines: None.

Range of Approval/Disapproval Time: From 30 to 60 days.

Appeals: A written appeal must be submitted within 15 days after a freeze is placed on an item.

Renewals: Not applicable.

ASSISTANCE CONSIDERATIONS:

Formula and Matching Requirements: Not applicable.

Length and Time Phasing of Assistance: None.

POST ASSISTANCE REQUIREMENTS:

Reports: At the end of the first year of use, institution must report on the manner in which equipment was used in establishment, expansion, or enhancement of energy research and/ or energy related courses.

Audits: On a selective basis.

Records: None.

FINANCIAL INFORMATION:

Account Identification: 89-0224-0-1-271.

Obligations: Not identifiable.

Range and Average of Financial Assistance: Not applicable.

PROGRAM ACCOMPLISHMENTS: The number of awards made depends on the amount and type of equipment excised during the year. In fiscal year 1992, approximately 700 pieces of equipment with an original acquisition cost of $8,400,000 were awarded to 82 institutions of higher learning.

REGULATIONS, GUIDELINES, AND LITERATURE: "Energy Related Laboratory Equipment Catalog". "Instruction and information on Used Energy-Related Laboratory Equipment Grants for Educational Institutions of Higher Learning," available without costs, lists officials at approximately 15 DOE offices and installations where list of equipment available through this program may be reviewed.

INFORMATION CONTACTS:

Headquarters Office: Larry L. Barker, Postsecondary Programs Division, Office of University and Science Education Programs, Office of Science Education and Technical Information, DOE, Washington, DC 20585. Telephone: (202) 586-8947. Use same number for FTS.

EXAMPLES OF FUNDED PROJECTS: Not applicable.

CRITERIA FOR SELECTING PROPOSALS: Not applicable.

81.077 UNIVERSITY RESEARCH INSTRUMENTATION

FEDERAL AGENCY: OFFICE OF SCIENCE EDUCATION AND TECHNICAL INFORMATION, DEPARTMENT OF ENERGY

AUTHORIZATION: Atomic Energy Act of 1954, as amended, Section 31 (a) and (b), Public Law 83-703; Department of Energy Organization Act of 1977, as amended, Section 209, Public Law 95-91; Energy and Water Development Appropriations Act of 1991.

OBJECTIVES: To assist universities and colleges in strengthening their capabilities to conduct long-range research in specific energy research and development areas of direct interest to DOE through the acquisition of specialized research instrumentation.

TYPES OF ASSISTANCE: Project Grants.

USES AND USE RESTRICTIONS: Program emphasis will be placed on assisting institutions to obtain the major research instruments (costing $100,000 and above) that are required to advance research principally in specially designated areas which are of special interest to DOE. In fiscal year 1994, the URI program funds are concerned with capital equipment needed for on-campus research among the following areas: biological and environmental; chemical sciences; engineering; materials sciences; mechanistic plant and microbial research; and energy efficiency and renewable energy.

ELIGIBILITY REQUIREMENTS:

Applicant Eligibility: Institutions of higher education which demonstrated their capabilities to conduct research in the designated areas and which, during the past two years, have received a minimum of $150,000 from the DOE program offices or National Laboratories for research in the area(s) for which the equipment will be used.

Beneficiary Eligibility: Benefiting are public nonprofit institutions (universities and colleges).

Credentials/Documentation: This program is excluded from coverage under OMB Circular No. A-87.

APPLICATION AND AWARD PROCESS:

Preapplication Coordination: This program is excluded from coverage under OMB Circular No. A-102. This program is excluded from coverage under E.O. 12372.

Application Procedure: Written application is submitted to the Department of Energy in accordance with the Notice of Program Announcement. This program is subject to the provisions of OMB Circular No. A-110.

Award Procedure: Proposals will be evaluated using the criteria outlined in the Program Announcement by Federal and nonfederal employees who are experienced in the designated research areas. In addition to technical merit, consideration will be given to research and program balance.

Deadlines: Proposal receipt is approximately 60 days after the beginning of the fiscal year.

Range of Approval/Disapproval Time: About 120 days.

Appeals: None.

Renewals: Assistance will be available for one year (equipment support only). If the equipment requires more than one year for delivery, no-cost extensions may be requested.

ASSISTANCE CONSIDERATIONS:

Formula and Matching Requirements: No formal requirements, but cost-sharing is strongly encouraged.

Length and Time Phasing of Assistance: The support provided is limited to purchasing the equipment with a grant term of one year.

POST ASSISTANCE REQUIREMENTS:

Reports: Annual reports for two years describing accomplishments of research conducted with the equipment obtained with DOE's funds, including fiscal reports outlining expenditure of both Federal and cost-sharing funds.

Audits: On a selective basis, audits are performed.

Records: None.

FINANCIAL INFORMATION:

Account Identification: 89-0224-0-1-271.

Obligations: (Grants) FY 92 $4,700,000; FY 93 est $5,200,000; and FY 94 est $5,200,000.

Range and Average of Financial Assistance: Grants are from $100,000 and above; $200,000 is the average award.

PROGRAM ACCOMPLISHMENTS: In fiscal year 1993, 24 awards were made.

REGULATIONS, GUIDELINES, AND LITERATURE: Federal Register announcement of June 7, 1983, Vol. 48, No. 110, 26328-26331. Federal Register announcement of October 18, 1983, Vol. 48, No. 202, Pages 48277-48281; Federal Register announcement of December 15, 1983, Vol. 48, No. 242, Pages 55774-55775, "Guide for the Preparation of Applications for the University Research Instrumentation Program."

INFORMATION CONTACTS:

Regional or Local Office: Oak Ridge Operations Office, Contract Management Branch, Procurement and Contracts Division, Oak Ridge, TN 37830. Telephone: (615) 576-0999. Use the same number for FTS.

Headquarters Office: Contact: Michael L. Wolfe, Postsecondary Programs Division, Office of University and Science Education Programs (ET-31), Office of Science Education and Technical Information, DOE, Washington, DC 20585. Telephone: (202) 586-8949. Use the same number for FTS.

EXAMPLES OF FUNDED PROJECTS: Mass spectrometers, confocal laser scanning light microscopes, laser diagnostic systems, fermentation facilities, positron emission tomography scanners.

CRITERIA FOR SELECTING PROPOSALS: (1) Technical merit and accomplishments of an institution's research programs in the applicable energy areas; (2) expertise of the faculty associated with the principal research areas and the degree of faculty experience with similar equipment; and (3) importance of equipment in energy research.

84.031 HIGHER EDUCATION—INSTITUTIONAL AID

FEDERAL AGENCY: OFFICE OF ASSISTANT SECRETARY FOR POSTSECONDARY EDUCATION, DEPARTMENT OF EDUCATION

AUTHORIZATION: Higher Education Act of 1965, Title III, as amended, Public Law 89-329; Public Law 98-95; Public Law 99-498; Public Laws 100-369 and 102-325, 20 U.S.C. 1051-1069h.

OBJECTIVES: To help eligible colleges and universities to strengthen their management and fiscal operations and to assist such institutions to plan, develop, or implement activities including endowment building that promise to strengthen the academic quality of their institutions.

TYPES OF ASSISTANCE: Project Grants.

USES AND USE RESTRICTIONS: Eligible institutions may apply under: a) The Strengthening Institutions Program; b) the Historically Black Colleges and Universities (HBCU) program; and c) the Endowment Challenge Grant Program. The first program provides funds to eligible institutions to plan, develop, and implement activities for development of faculty, funds and administrative management, development and improvement of academic programs, acquisition of equipment for use in strengthening academic programs and institutional management, and joint use of facilities such as libraries, laboratories, and student services. The second program provides funds to undergraduate and graduate HBCUs. Funds may be used for purchase, rental, or lease of scientific equipment; construction, maintenance, renovation, improvement in classroom, library and other instructional facilities; support of faculty exchanges and fellowships;

academic instruction in disciplines in which Blacks are underrepresented, purchase of library books, periodicals, and other educational materials; tutoring, counseling, and student services; funds and administrative management; acquisition of equipment for use in funds management; and joint use of facilities. Under the graduate HBCU program funds may also be used to establish or maintain endowments. Funds may not be used for activities other than those in an approved application, activities that are inconsistent with any applicable State plan of higher education or State plan for desegregation, a school or department of divinity or any religious worship or sectarian activity; general operating and maintenance expenses; indirect costs; construction costs (except under Part B); or supplanting of other funds available to the institution. The Endowment Challenge Grant Program provides matching funds to establish or increase endowment funds to eligible institutions and to promote fundraising activities which will foster increased independence.

ELIGIBILITY REQUIREMENTS:

Applicant Eligibility: An institution of higher education that qualifies as eligible using criteria as specified in the regulations. Under the Strengthening Institutions Program, and the Endowment Challenge Grant Program, both specific and basic requirements as stated in the program regulations must be met. Eligible applicants include institutions that have: (1) A low average per FTE educational and general expenditure; (2) a substantial percentage of students having Pell Grants or other Federal need-based financial aid. However, a waiver of the low educational and general expenditure requirement and the needy student enrollment requirement may be granted to institutions meeting the criteria specified in the existing regulations. Under the HBCU program certain historically Black institutions that were established prior to 1964, whose principal mission was, and is, the education of Black Americans are eligible. A listing of those institutions is published in program regulations; these HBCUs are also eligible under the Endowment Challenge Grant Program.

Beneficiary Eligibility: Applicant institutions of higher education, including those in the territories and possessions that meet statutory eligibility requirements will benefit.

Credentials/Documentation: Institutions must document that they are accredited by a nationally recognized accrediting agency or that they are making satisfactory progress toward such accreditation. A four year institution must have authority to award a bachelor's degree. A two year institution must offer a program acceptable for full credit towards a bachelor's degree, or a two year program in engineering, mathematics, or the physical or biological sciences designed to prepare the student to work as a technician at a semiprofessional level. This program is excluded from coverage under OMB Circular No. A-87.

APPLICATION AND AWARD PROCESS:

Preapplication Coordination: This program is excluded from coverage under OMB Circular No. A-102. This program is eligible for coverage under E.O. 12372, "Intergovernmental Review of Federal Programs." An applicant should consult the office or official designated as the single point of contact in his or her State for more information on the process the State requires to be followed in applying for assistance, if the State has selected the program for review.

Application Procedure: Under the Strengthening Institutions Program and the Endowment Challenge Grant Program, first, submit a Request for Designation as an Eligible Institution (ED Form 1049) to the Application Control Center, ROB-3, Room 3633 Attention: 84.031H (Title III Designation), 7th and D Streets, SW., Washington DC 20202-4725, by the date published separately in the Federal Register. Second, if the institution is an eligible applicant, submit a completed application to Application Control Center, Department of Education, ROB-3, Room 3633, 7th and D Streets, SW., Washington, DC 20202-4725. For proper identification and distribution, an Attention line must be used: Attention: 84.031A, 84.031B, or 84.031C depending on the program applied for (see above). The grant application forms for the programs are ED Forms 851A, 852, or E40-20P respectively. This program is subject to the provisions of OMB Circular No. A-110.

Award Procedure: Strengthening Institutions Programs applications are evaluated by external reviewers who are experts in postsecondary education. The Secretary makes final awards based on the recommendations submitted by the Division of Institutional Development, Office of Postsecondary Education. Notification of grant approval to the institutions of higher education is provided by Grants Management Services.

Deadlines: Deadline dates for each program are published in the Federal Register for both eligibility and project grants.

Range of Approval/Disapproval Time: About six months.

Appeals: None.

Renewals: Under the Strengthening Institutions Program priority is given to applicants who are not already receiving a grant. Under the Endowment Challenge Grant Program an institution may receive additional Endowment Grants after five years, or after 10 years dependent on the amount of the appropriation. Institutions which are applying for a renewable grant under the Strengthening Institutions Program, or applying for an Endowment Challenge Grant, must reapply for eligibility.

ASSISTANCE CONSIDERATIONS:

Formula and Matching Requirements: Under the HBCU program, eligible graduate institutions that have project grants over $500,000 must match the entire Federal share on a dollar-for-dollar basis. Under the Endowment Challenge Grant Program, awards require a match of one dollar institutional funds to two dollars of Federal funds.

Length and Time Phasing of Assistance: Under the Strengthening Institutions Program, planning grants are for a period of up to one year, development grants are for a period of five years. Under the HBCU Programs, grants are awarded up to five years. A grantee must wait out 10 years before applying for another Endowment grant if the appropriation is equal to or less than $20.0 million; a grantee must wait out five years if the appropriation exceeds $20.0 million. An institution must wait 20 years before it can spend the grant/ corpus for other than endowment purposes. However, grantees may spend up to 50 percent of the income annually produced by the endowment corpus for any purpose.

POST ASSISTANCE REQUIREMENTS:

Reports: As required by the Special Grant Terms and Conditions.

Audits: Subject to a Federal audit any time during the term of the grant and within a period of three years after the termination of Federal support.

Records: Must be retained for five years after the end of the fiscal year during which the expenditures were made or until the grantee is notified that the records are no longer needed.

FINANCIAL INFORMATION:

Account Identification: 91-0201-0-1-502.

Obligations: (Grants) Strengthening Institutions: FY 92 $87,831,000; FY 93 est $86,257,000; and FY 94 est $88,297,000. Strengthening HBCUs: FY 92 $111,711,000; FY 93 est $109,709,000; and FY 94 est $112,672,000. Endowment grants: FY 92 $7,500,000; FY 93 est $7,366,000; and FY 94 est $7,565,000.

Range and Average of Financial Assistance: Under the Strengthening Institutions Program, planning grants ranged up to $35,000. Ranges for development grants are announced in closing date notices. Under the HBCU Program, grants may not be less than $500,000 and range according to formula allotments. Under the Endowment Challenge grant program, grants are from a minimum of $50,000 to a maximum of $1,500,000 depending upon the appropriation.

PROGRAM ACCOMPLISHMENTS: There were 202 continuation grants made in fiscal year 1993, under the Strengthening Institutions program. In fiscal year 1993, 14 planning grants and 59 new grants were made. Under the HBCU program in both fiscal years 1992 and 1993, 103 grants are anticipated. Under the Endowment program for fiscal year 1992, 20 awards were made. In fiscal year 1993, 17 are anticipated.

REGULATIONS, GUIDELINES, AND LITERATURE: 34 CFR 607, 608, 609, and 628. The Education Department General Administrative Regulations also applies to the first two programs. They do not apply to the Endowment Challenge Grant Program unless so cited in the regulations for the Endowment Grant Program.

INFORMATION CONTACTS:

Regional or Local Office: Not applicable.

Headquarters Office: Institutional Aid Programs, Office of Postsecondary Education, Department of Education, 400 Maryland Avenue, SW., Washington, DC 20202. Contact: Dr. Caroline J. Gillin. Telephone: (202) 708-8816.

EXAMPLES OF FUNDED PROJECTS: The Education Department awarded grants: (1) To develop a management information system at the applicant institution; (2) to develop curriculum; (3) to develop management capabilities among administrators; (4) to develop computer-assisted instruction; and (5) to develop funds management procedures.

CRITERIA FOR SELECTING PROPOSALS: (a) Under the Strengthening Institutions Program, the Secretary appoints review panels to provide comments and recommend ratings for the applications. The reviewers numerically rate each application assigned and provide the Secretary with comments on each. Criteria are published in the Federal Register along with the point value for each criterion. Under the Endowment Challenge Grant Program, eligible institutions must provide the latest available data concerning the institution's current endowment status which would be data of the year preceding the year of application for assistance. The selection criteria include five factors, the first two of which are considerations: (1) Whether the institution had a Strengthening Institutions project or a project under the HBCU program within the last five years of the application year (20 points); (2) need for an endowment as measured by a lack of endowment funds (20 points); (3) need for an endowment grant as measured by a lack of resources which is determined by the current funds revenues by source for the fiscal year prior to the year of application, i.e., fiscal year 1992 data for a fiscal year 1993 application (50 points); (4) past efforts to build or maintain an endowment fund based on data for the preceding four years prior to application (25 points); and (5) the source of the proposed matching funds (15 points). Points are determined from the data submitted. Institutions must establish annual eligibility to participate in the program in each year in which the institution seeks an award. Institutions are advised to read the program regulations, 34 CFR 628.30-32, which explains the funding criteria more fully.

84.040 IMPACT AID—CONSTRUCTION

FEDERAL AGENCY: OFFICE OF ASSISTANT SECRETARY FOR ELEMENTARY AND SECONDARY EDUCATION, DEPARTMENT OF EDUCATION

AUTHORIZATION: Public Law 81-815.

OBJECTIVES: To provide assistance for the construction of urgently needed minimum school facilities: in school districts that have had substantial increases in school membership as a result of new or increased Federal activities (Section 5); for children residing on Federal property where State or local funds cannot be spent on the education of federally connected children (Section 10); for school districts comprised mainly of Indian lands or that provide a free public education to children who reside on Indian lands (Section 14(a) and (b)) and for districts that are comprised mainly of Federal property and that have inadequate facilities (Section 14 (c)).

TYPES OF ASSISTANCE: Project Grants.

USES AND USE RESTRICTIONS: To construct and equip minimum school facilities as specified in the project application and approved by the Secretary. In most instances, subject to program office review and approval, the receiving district determines the type, size, and location of the facilities to be constructed, hires the architect, and supervises the construction as if it were financed by local funds. In the case of Section 10 the Department directly oversees construction projects.

ELIGIBILITY REQUIREMENTS:

Applicant Eligibility: Section 5 provides construction assistance if a school district has experienced or will be experiencing a substantial increase in the number of federally connected children during a four-year increase period. Section 10 requires the Department of Education to provide school facilities for federally connected children when State or local laws preclude the expenditure of State and local funds for providing school facilities for children residing on Federal property. Section 14(a) provides construction assistance to school districts if (1) At least 15 of the school district's children, constituting at least one-third of the school district's total membership, reside on Indian lands, (2) Indian lands constitute at least one-third of the land area of the school district, or (3) the school district provides free public education for at least 100 children who reside on Indian lands outside of the school district; the tax-exempt status of Indian lands substantially and continually impairs the school district from financing needed school facilities; the school district makes a reasonable tax effort to raise funds for financing school facilities and avails itself of State and other sources of financial assistance for this purpose; and the school district has insufficient funds available from all sources to provide classrooms and classroom equipment for at least five percent of its enrollment. Section 14(b) provides construction assistance to school districts if (1) At least 15 of the district's children, constituting at least 10 percent of the total membership in the school district, reside on Indian lands, (2) Indian lands constitute 10 percent of the land area of the school district, or (3) the school district educates at least 100 children who reside on Indian lands outside of the school district; and the tax-exempt status of Indian land substantially and continually impairs the school district from financing needed school facilities. Section 14(c) provides construction assistance to school districts if (1) At least 20 of the district's children, representing at least thirty-three and one-third percent of its total membership, have inadequate or no facilities; Federal property constitutes at least thirty-three and one-third percent of the land area of the school district; the nontaxable status of Federal property within the district substantially and continually impairs the district's ability to finance school facilities; the

195

school district makes a reasonable tax effort to raise funds for school facilities and avail itself of State and other sources of assistance for this purpose; and the school district has insufficient funds from all other sources to provide minimum school facilities for at least five percent of its membership.

Beneficiary Eligibility: Public elementary and secondary school children will benefit.

Credentials/Documentation: Costs will be determined in accordance with OMB Circular No. A-87 for State and local governments.

APPLICATION AND AWARD PROCESS:

Preapplication Coordination: Except for Section 10, the standard application forms as furnished by the Federal agency and required by OMB Circular No. A-102 must be used for this program. The official in charge of the affected Federal installation requests assistance directly from the Department under Section 10. An environmental impact statement is required for this program. This program is eligible for coverage under E.O. 12372, "Intergovernmental Review of Federal Programs." An applicant should consult the office or official designated as the single point of contact in his or her State for more information on the process the State requires to be followed in applying for assistance, if the State has selected the program for review.

Application Procedure: Preapplications and applications are submitted to the Secretary of Education through the State educational agency as specified in notices published in the Federal Register. A local educational agency may secure advice and a preapplication form from its State department of education. This program is excluded from coverage under OMB Circular No. A-110.

Award Procedure: The Department of Education makes final decisions to award grants or fund projects.

Deadlines: Established each year by notices published in the Federal Register, usually on or about June 30.

Range of Approval/Disapproval Time: Varies from two months to one year after filing date; approval is dependent upon meeting eligibility criteria and availability of funds.

Appeals: Subject to hearings under the provisions of Sections 6(c) and 11(a) of Public Law 81-815.

Renewals: Approved construction projects may be revised during construction subject to appropriate approvals.

ASSISTANCE CONSIDERATIONS:

Formula and Matching Requirements: Section 5 payments are based on a percentage of the State's average per pupil cost of school construction in the second year of the four year increase period covered by the project request. Awards under other sections of the Act may not exceed the cost of constructing minimum school facilities for federally connected children. See CFR 221.60 through 221.63 for additional details.

Length and Time Phasing of Assistance: Except for Section 10, after firm preliminary sketches and other requirements of the Act have been met, a project is approved and 10 percent of the total approved amount is paid. When the basic contract has been let, an additional 50 percent is certified for payment and 30 percent additional is paid when the project is approximately 50 percent completed. The remaining 10 percent is paid after the project has been completed. Except for the initial 10 percent payment, applicants must request additional payments at the appropriate stage of the project. Under Section 10, the Department generally makes payments directly to contractors.

POST ASSISTANCE REQUIREMENTS:

Reports: In accordance with OMB Circular No. A-102 (Attachments H and I) and Education Department General Administrative Regulations (EDGAR) for direct project grant and contract programs, Part 100a, Subpart F. See 34 CFR 74, Subpart H, Standards for Grantees Financial Management Systems.

Audits: In accordance with the provisions of OMB Circular No. A-128, "Audits of State and Local Governments," State and local governments that receive financial assistance of $100,000 or more within the State's fiscal year shall have an audit made for that year. State and local governments that receive between $25,000 and $100,000 within the State's fiscal year shall have an audit made in accordance with Circular No. A-128, or in accordance with Federal laws and regulations governing the programs in which they participate.

Records: In accordance with OMB Circular No. A-102 (Attachment C) and Education Department General Administrative Regulations, for direct project grant and contract programs, Part 100a, Subpart F. See 34 CFR 74, Subpart H, Standards for Grantees Financial Management Systems.

FINANCIAL INFORMATION:

Account Identification: 91-0102-0-1-501.

Obligations: (Grants) FY 92 $43,155,000; FY 93 est $15,076,000; and FY 94 est $3,000,000.

Range and Average of Financial Assistance: $2,000 to $12,000,000; average not applicable.

PROGRAM ACCOMPLISHMENTS: In fiscal year 1993, regular program funds will initiate approximately four to five new construction projects, including life safety repairs and replacements.

REGULATIONS, GUIDELINES, AND LITERATURE: Regulations are in Title 34 CFR 219 and 221.

INFORMATION CONTACTS:

Regional or Local Office: Not applicable.

Headquarters Office: Impact Aid Program, Office of Elementary and Secondary Education, Department of Education, 400 Maryland Ave., SW., Washington, DC 20202-6244. Contact: Charles E. Hansen. Telephone: (202) 401-3637.

EXAMPLES OF FUNDED PROJECTS: Additions of classrooms to existing buildings. Repairs of schools to incorporate access to the physically handicapped and ensure the safety of building users. Construction of school facilities on Indian lands.

CRITERIA FOR SELECTING PROPOSALS: Except for Section 10, based on priority indices established by a combination of: 1) Ratio of federally connected children eligible for payment to the total membership in the district; and 2) ratio of the number of children unhoused (without school facilities) to the total membership. For Section 10, projects are funded according to relative urgency of need.

84.216 CAPITAL EXPENSES
(Chapter 1 - Capital Expenses)

FEDERAL AGENCY: OFFICE OF ELEMENTARY AND SECONDARY EDUCATION, DEPARTMENT OF EDUCATION

AUTHORIZATION: Elementary and Secondary Education Act of 1965, Title I, Chapter 1, Section 1017(d), 20 U.S.C. 2727.

OBJECTIVES: To help local educational agencies pay for the additional capital costs, incurred since July 1, 1985, associated with providing equitable Chapter 1 services to eligible private school children, in compliance with the decision in Aguilar vs. Felton.

TYPES OF ASSISTANCE: Formula Grants; Project Grants.

USES AND USE RESTRICTIONS: Funds are used for such costs as the purchase, lease, and renovation of real and personal property (including but not limited to mobile educational units and leasing of neutral sites or spaces), insurance, maintenance costs, transportation, and comparable goods and services.

ELIGIBILITY REQUIREMENTS:

Applicant Eligibility: State educational agencies (SEAs) may apply. LEAs are subgrantees.

Beneficiary Eligibility: Educationally deprived children benefit.

Credentials/Documentation: None.

APPLICATION AND AWARD PROCESS:

Preapplication Coordination: None. This program is excluded from coverage under E.O. 12372.

Application Procedure: State educational agencies submit one-time assurances to the Department of Education in accordance with Section 200.10 of the program regulations. A local educational agency may apply to its State educational agency in accordance with Section 200.57.

Award Procedure: The Department of Education awards grants to SEAs on a formula basis. SEAs distribute funds to LEA on the basis of need.

Deadlines: Deadlines are established by each State.

Range of Approval/Disapproval Time: The range varies with each State.

Appeals: An LEA whose application is disapproved by its SEA may appeal to the SEA and than to the Department of Education under Section 425 of the General Education Provisions Act.

Renewals: Not applicable.

ASSISTANCE CONSIDERATIONS:

Formula and Matching Requirements: Funds are allocated to States based on their proportion of private school children served under Chapter 1 in school year 1984-85. There is no matching requirement.

Length and Time Phasing of Assistance: Funds are available for one fiscal year. Unexpended funds may be carried forward to the next fiscal year.

POST ASSISTANCE REQUIREMENTS:

Reports: None.

Audits: In accordance with the Education Department General Administration Regulations in the Appendix to 34 CFR 80, State and local governments that receive financial assistance of $100,000 or more within the State's fiscal year shall have an audit made for that year. State and local governments that receive between $25,000 and $100,000 within the State's fiscal year shall have an audit made in accordance with the Appendix to Part 80, or in accordance with Federal laws and regulations governing the programs in which they participate.

Records: In accordance with the General Education Provisions Act and the Education Department General Administrative Regulation, certain project records must be maintained for five years.

FINANCIAL INFORMATION:

Account Identification: 91-0900-0-1-501.

Obligations: (Grants) FY 92 $42,433,000; FY 93 est $39,734,000; and FY 94 est $39,734,000.

Range and Average of Financial Assistance: For 1993, $10,335 to $8,540,265; $764,876.

PROGRAM ACCOMPLISHMENTS: Grant awards are issued to the 50 States, the District of Columbia, and Puerto Rico.

REGULATIONS, GUIDELINES, AND LITERATURE: 34 CFR 200 and the Chapter 1 Policy Manual are available from the Department of Education.

INFORMATION CONTACTS:

Regional or Local Office: Not applicable.

Headquarters Office: Department of Education, Compensatory Education Programs, Office of Elementary and Secondary Education, Department of Education, 400 Maryland Avenue, SW., Room 2043, Washington, DC 20202-6132. Contact: Mary Jean LeTendre. Telephone: (202) 401-1682.

EXAMPLES OF FUNDED PROJECTS: Funds are used for such costs as rental of classroom space in neutral sites; rental or purchase of mobile vans; and transportation of private school students to public schools or neutral sites.

CRITERIA FOR SELECTING PROPOSALS: This is a formula grant program.

88.001 ARCHITECTURAL AND TRANSPORTATION BARRIERS COMPLIANCE BOARD (ATBCB)

FEDERAL AGENCY: ARCHITECTURAL AND TRANSPORTATION BARRIERS COMPLIANCE BOARD

AUTHORIZATION: Rehabilitation Act of 1973, Section 502, as amended, Public Law 93-112, 29 U.S.C. 792; Architectural Barriers Act of 1968, as amended, Public Law 90-480; Public Law 94-541, 42 U.S.C. 4151 et seq; Americans with Disabilities Act of 1990, Public Law 101-336.

OBJECTIVES: To enforce Federal laws requiring accessibility for persons with disabilities in certain federally funded buildings and facilities throughout the Nation; set guidelines and requirements for accessibility standards prescribed by Federal agencies under the Americans with Disabilities Act and the Architectural Barriers Act; provide technical assistance to organizations and agencies, and individuals requesting help in explaining the guidelines and requirements and in solving accessible design and construction problems; conduct research to determine appropriate specifications for accessibility.

TYPES OF ASSISTANCE: Dissemination of Technical Information.

USES AND USE RESTRICTIONS: Technical information and assistance on creating a barrier free environment is available to Federal, State and local government agencies and to private organizations and individuals.

ELIGIBILITY REQUIREMENTS:

Applicant Eligibility: Requests for information may be made by the general public as well as all agencies of Federal, State, and local government.

Beneficiary Eligibility: General public, all levels of government, and private organizations will benefit.

Credentials/Documentation: This program is excluded from coverage under OMB Circular No. A-87.

APPLICATION AND AWARD PROCESS:

Preapplication Coordination: This program is excluded from coverage under E.O. 12372.

Application Procedure: Requests for information and assistance should be sent to Director, Office of Technical and Information Services, Architectural and Transportation Barriers Compliance Board, Suite 1000, 1331 F Street, NW., Washington, DC 20004-1111. Telephone: (202) 272-5434 (voice); (202) 272-5449 (TDD); Toll-free 1-800-USA-ABLE (voice or TDD). This program is excluded from coverage under OMB Circular No. A-110.

Award Procedure: Not applicable.

Deadlines: Not applicable.

Range of Approval/Disapproval Time: Not applicable.

Appeals: Not applicable.

Renewals: Not applicable.

ASSISTANCE CONSIDERATIONS:

Formula and Matching Requirements: Not applicable.

Length and Time Phasing of Assistance: Not applicable.

POST ASSISTANCE REQUIREMENTS:

Reports: Not applicable.

Audits: Not applicable.

Records: Not applicable.

FINANCIAL INFORMATION:

Account Identification: 95-3200-0-1-751.

Obligations: (Salaries and expenses) FY 92 $3,300,000; FY 93 est $3,348,000; and FY 94 est $3,000,000.

Range and Average of Financial Assistance: Not applicable.

PROGRAM ACCOMPLISHMENTS: In fiscal year 1992, responded to approximately 19,000 telephone requests for Americans with Disabilities Act (ADA) technical assistance; distributed approximately 10,500 technical information packages to the public; mailed nearly 41,000 copies of 32 Access Board publications; distributed over 32,000 copies of the ADA Accessibility Guidelines; finalized technical bulletins on detectable warnings and visual alarms; completed the ADA Accessibility Guidelines Checklist; completed ADA Accessibility Guidelines manuals on buses, rapid rail, light rail, commuter rail, intercity rail, over-the- road buses, high-speed rail, automated guideway transit systems, and trams systems; completed a transportation access course with slides and workbooks; completed training videos on the ADA Accessibility Guidelines and the Uniform Federal Accessibility Standards; sponsored or participated in 62 ADA Accessibility Guidelines training sessions; participated in meetings with representatives of model building code groups, the American National Standards Institute (ANSI) Committee, State building code officials, and the Department of Justice to coordinate development of ADA Accessibility Guidelines and ANSI; issued a Federal Register notice requesting comments on the Access Board's five-year technical assistance/research plan and ADA related research projects; acted on four petitions under the Administrative Procedures Act to review aspects of ADA regulations; closed 153 Architectural Barriers Act complaints between October 1, 1991, and September 30, 1992; received 145 new cases during the year.

REGULATIONS, GUIDELINES, AND LITERATURE: General information publications, "Uniform Federal Accessibility Standards," technical assistance papers, Americans with Disabilities Act guidelines, pamphlets, and the agency's annual report to the President and Congress are available.

INFORMATION CONTACTS:

Regional or Local Office: Not applicable.

Headquarters Office: Director, Office of Technical and Information Services, Architectural and Transportation Barriers Compliance Board, Suite 1000, 1331 F Street, NW., Washington, DC 20004-1111. Telephone: (202) 272-5434 (voice); (202) 272-5449 (TDD); Toll-free 1-800-USA-ABLE (voice or TDD).

EXAMPLES OF FUNDED PROJECTS: Not applicable.

CRITERIA FOR SELECTING PROPOSALS: Not applicable.

93.224 COMMUNITY HEALTH CENTERS

FEDERAL AGENCY: HEALTH RESOURCES AND SERVICES ADMINISTRATION, PUBLIC HEALTH SERVICE, DEPARTMENT OF HEALTH AND HUMAN SERVICES

AUTHORIZATION: Public Health Service Act, Section 330, as amended, Public Law 99-280.

OBJECTIVES: To support the development and operation of community health centers which provide primary health services, supplemental health services and environmental health services to medically underserved populations. Priorities will be focused on providing services in the most medically underserved areas on maintaining existing centers which are serving high priority populations. Centers must have demonstrated sound capacities in the following areas: fiscal and management capabilities; monitoring and assessment of project performance; development and implementation of mechanisms for improving quality of care; and maximization of third-party reimbursement levels, through improved project administration and management.

TYPES OF ASSISTANCE: Project Grants.

USES AND USE RESTRICTIONS: Applications should be designed to improve the availability, accessibility and organization of health care within medically underserved communities. Funds may also be used for acquiring, constructing and modernizing existing buildings, including amortizing the principal of and paying the interest on loans, and for related equipment in excess of $100,000.

ELIGIBILITY REQUIREMENTS:

Applicant Eligibility: Public or nonprofit private agency, institution, or organization and a limited number of State and local governments. Profit-making organizations are not eligible.

Beneficiary Eligibility: Population groups in medically underserved areas.

Credentials/Documentation: Costs will be determined in accordance with OMB Circular No. A-87 for State and local governments. For others, costs will be determined in accordance with HHS Regulations, 45 CFR, Part 74, Subpart Q.

APPLICATION AND AWARD PROCESS:

Preapplication Coordination: Necessary coordination varies; Contact the HHS Regional Offices for details. This program is eligible for coverage under E.O. 12372, "Intergovernmental Review of Federal Programs." An applicant should consult the office or official designated as the single point of contact in his or her State for more information on the process the State requires to be followed in applying for assistance, if the State has selected the program for review. This program is subject to the requirements of the Public Health System Impact Statement.

Application Procedure: Application forms are available from the regional offices. The standard application forms, furnished by PHS and required by 45 CFR, Part 92, must be used by State and local government applicants. State and local governments must prepare a Form HHS 5161, Application for Federal Assistance (Nonconstruction), fully documenting the need for the grant and the proposed amount for the project. Other nonprofit organizations must complete Form PHS-5194, Grant Application for Health Services, documenting the need for and the proposed amount of the grant. Applications must be given to designated organizations for review and approval. This program is subject to the provisions of 45 CFR, Part 92 for State and local governments, and 45 CFR Part 74 for nonprofit organizations. Applications are subject to review pursuant to 45 CFR, Part 100.

Award Procedure: An objective review committee reviews applications for merit and recommends approval or disapproval. Final decisions are made by the Director of the Bureau of Primary Health Care, Health Resources and Services Administration.

Deadlines: Contact Headquarters Office for application deadlines.

Range of Approval/Disapproval Time: From 90 to 120 days.

Appeals: None.

Renewals: Same as Application Procedure.

ASSISTANCE CONSIDERATIONS:

Formula and Matching Requirements: This program has no statutory formula. The applicant must assume part of the project costs determined on a case-by-case basis. Statement of availability is required as indicated in the appropriate program.

Length and Time Phasing of Assistance: The initial period of support may be up to 5 years. The project may be renewed for additional years of support based on its progress and the need for additional Federal support.

POST ASSISTANCE REQUIREMENTS:

Reports: All grantees must submit a financial status report 90 days after the end of each budget period and a final financial status report 90 days after the end of the project period. Basic data, cost accounting, and reporting or monitoring systems will be compatible with federally established national reporting requirements for health services delivery projects.

Audits: In accordance with the provisions of OMB Circular No. A-128, "Audits of State and Local Governments," State and local governments that receive financial assistance of $100,000 or more within the State's fiscal year shall have an audit made for that year. State and local governments that receive between $25,000 and $100,000 within the State's fiscal year shall have an audit made in accordance with Circular No. A-128, or in accordance with Federal laws and regulations governing the programs in which they participate. For nongovernmental grant recipients, audits are to be carried out in accordance with the provisions set forth in OMB Circular No. A-133. In addition, grants and cooperative agreements are subject to inspection and audits by DHHS and other Federal officials.

Records: HHS and the Comptroller General of the United States or any of their authorized representatives, shall have the right of access to any books, documents, papers, or other records of a grantee, subgrantee, contractor, or subcontractor, which are pertinent to the HHS grant, in order to make audits, examinations, excerpts and transcripts. Grantees are required to maintain grant accounting records 3 years after the end of a budget period. If any litigation, claim, negotiation, audit or other action involving the records has been started before the expiration of the 3-year period, the records shall be retained until completion of the action and resolution of all issues which arise from it, or until the end of the regular 3-year period, whichever is later.

FINANCIAL INFORMATION:

Account Identification: 75-0350-0-1-550.

Obligations: (Grants) FY 92 $532,000,000; FY 93 $558,800,000; and FY 94 est $617,300,000.

Range and Average of Financial Assistance: $25,000 to $4,000,000; $1,203,731.

PROGRAM ACCOMPLISHMENTS: The main thrust of Section 330 has been to support Community Health Centers (CHC) in urban and rural medically underserved areas. In addition, the Bureau of Primary Health Care identifies the most needy communities/populations through State-based planning action sites. In fiscal year 1992, 549 community health centers were funded, providing services at 1,425 sites and serving 5.86 million people. It is anticipated that some new community health centers will be funded in fiscal years 1993 and 1994.

REGULATIONS, GUIDELINES, AND LITERATURE: PHS Grants Policy Statement, DHHS Publication No. (OASH) 90-50,000, (Rev.) October 1, 1990; 42 CFR 51 C.

INFORMATION CONTACTS:

Headquarters Office: Program Contact: Director, Division of Community and Migrant Health Care Services, Bureau of Primary Health Care, Health Resources and Services Administration, Public Health Service, Department of Health and Human Services, Room 7A-55, Parklawn Building, 5600 Fishers Lane, Rockville, MD 20857. Telephone: (301) 443-2260. Grants Management Contact: Grants Management Officer, Bureau of Primary Health Care, Health Resources and Services Administration, Public Health Service, Department of Health and Human Services, 12100 Parklawn Drive, Rockville, MD. 20857. Telephone: (301) 443-5902. (Use same numbers for FTS.)

EXAMPLES OF FUNDED PROJECTS: (1) Community health centers; (2) health networks to support systems of care; (3) a community health program; and (4) planning grants.

CRITERIA FOR SELECTING PROPOSALS: (1) Relative merit of grant proposals as measured against the Bureau's funding criteria; (2) specific program guidelines; (3) service to high priority population; (4) demonstrated sound fiscal and management capabilities: and (5) past management performance of the applicant.

93.291 SURPLUS PROPERTY UTILIZATION
(Federal Property Assistance Program)

FEDERAL AGENCY: OFFICE OF THE ASSISTANT SECRETARY FOR HEALTH, PUBLIC HEALTH SERVICE, DEPARTMENT OF HEALTH AND HUMAN SERVICES

AUTHORIZATION: Federal Property and Administrative Services Act of 1949, Section 203(k), Public Law 81-152, 40 U.S.C. 484, as amended; Stewart B. McKinney Homeless Assistance Act of 1987, as amended, 104 Stat. 4673.

OBJECTIVES: To convey or lease all surplus Federal real properties made available by the disposal agency which are needed and usable by eligible organizations and institutions to carry out health programs.

TYPES OF ASSISTANCE: Sale, Exchange, or Donation of Property and Goods.

USES AND USE RESTRICTIONS: Real property must be used for eligible health purposes including research. It may consist of land with or without buildings and other improvements or buildings only. A discount of up to 100 percent based on the proposed-use program is granted. This discount applied against the fair value of the property, is earned by approved use over a prescribed period of 30 years for land with or without improvements, and a lesser time for leased facilities and improvements which are sold without land. Allowance of less than 100 percent requires payment of the difference in cash at the time of conveyance. Property must be used for the purpose for which conveyed, and may not be sold, leased, mortgaged, or encumbered without consent of the Department.

ELIGIBILITY REQUIREMENTS:

Applicant Eligibility: States, their political subdivisions and instrumentalities; tax-supported public health institutions, and nonprofit institutions which (except for institutions which lease property to assist the homeless under Title V of Public Law 100-77) have been held exempt from taxation under Section 501(c) (3) of the 1986 Internal Revenue Code.

Beneficiary Eligibility: Anyone attending, working with or for, or served by the eligible applicants. Examples of potentially eligible use programs are hospitals, public health clinics, water and sewer systems, institutions for the rehabilitation of mentally or physically handicapped, health research institutions, homeless assistance facilities, and other institutions with basic health programs.

Credentials/Documentation: Applicants must demonstrate current need for properties they request and the ability to carry out the proposed program.

APPLICATION AND AWARD PROCESS:

Preapplication Coordination: Notice of availability of surplus real property is sent by Public Health Service Headquarters to all known potentially interested institutions. When applying for real property, an informal preapplication conference either in person or by telephone is recommended. At that time, consultation and assistance are available to aid in the preparation of an application. Applicants are required to submit factors for consideration of potential environmental impact, in accordance with the Environmental Questionnaire furnished with the application instructions. This program is excluded from coverage under E.O. 12372.

Application Procedure: Applicants interested in acquiring Federal real properties must contact the Public Health Service Headquarters.

Award Procedure: Real property is awarded to the applicant whose programs of use are determined to be in the highest public interest. Land (with or without improvements) is conveyed by quitclaim deed or lease; buildings for off-site removal are by agreement of sale.

Deadlines: Any organization interested in acquiring real property must notify the Public Health Service Headquarters Office within 15 days after notice of availability, or in the case of acquiring properties for homeless purposes, within 60 days after publication by Department of Housing and Urban Development in the Federal Register.

Range of Approval/Disapproval Time: Normally, approval or disapproval is made within 30 days after an application has been submitted for real property. For properties to assist homeless individuals under Title V of the McKinney Act, approval or disapproval is made 25 days after a complete application is received.

Appeals: An applicant may appeal a decision to the Office of the Assistant Secretary for Health, Division of Health Facilities Planning.

Renewals: Not applicable.

ASSISTANCE CONSIDERATIONS:

Formula and Matching Requirements: This program has no statutory formula or matching requirements.

Length and Time Phasing of Assistance: Deed restrictions run for a period of 30 years and Agreements of Sale are normally for 5 years, after which the transferee has clear title to the property. Restrictions on leased property run for the period of the lease.

POST ASSISTANCE REQUIREMENTS:

Reports: Transferees/lessees are required to make an annual utilization report to the Public Health Service Headquarters Office and the property is also visited by Public Health Service personnel.

Audits: The Department's Audit agency makes periodic audits of the headquarters operation and may make spot checks of utilization by real property transferees.

Records: Transferees of real property, who expend funds to rebuild, refurbish, or to otherwise improve property under restrictions, should maintain records of these costs in the event they wish to dispose of the property prior to termination of the restriction period.

FINANCIAL INFORMATION:

Account Identification: 75-1101-0-1-550.

Obligations: (Salaries and Expenses) FY 92 $146,000; FY 93 $153,000; and FY 94 est $157,000.

Range and Average of Financial Assistance: Not applicable.

PROGRAM ACCOMPLISHMENTS: During fiscal year 1992, Federal surplus real property having an acquisition cost of $668,385 was transferred for public health purposes. This represents 8 transfers of 89.54 acres of land, and 4 buildings. It is estimated that over $500,000 in real property will be transferred in fiscal year 1993 for public health purposes.

REGULATIONS, GUIDELINES, AND LITERATURE: Title 45, Subtitle A, Part 12, Disposal and Utilization of Surplus Real Property for Public Health Purposes. Literature: The following pamphlet is available from the Public Health Service Headquarters Office: "How to Acquire Federal Surplus Real Property for Public Health Purposes," at no charge.

INFORMATION CONTACTS:

Regional or Local Office: None.

Headquarters Office: Kathleen Furey Martin, Director, Division of Health Facilities Planning, Office of the Assistant Secretary for Health, Public Health Service, Department of Health and Human Services, Parklawn Building, Room 17A 10, 5600 Fishers Lane, Rockville, MD 20857. Telephone: (301) 443-2265. (Use same number for FTS.)

EXAMPLES OF FUNDED PROJECTS: Land and buildings are provided for hospitals, clinics, public health administration, water and sewer system development, facilities to assist homeless individuals, and rehabilitation programs.

CRITERIA FOR SELECTING PROPOSALS: All applications must establish eligibility of the institution, its programs, and the proposed use to meet the program needs. A public benefit allowance formula, uniformly applied, determines the respective benefits of each program. Basic allowance of 50 percent is allowed to institutions meeting the following: (1) proof of current need; (2) ability to operate and maintain; (3) suitability of facilities or adaptability for conversion; (4) requirement for utilization through period of restrictions; and (5) nondiscrimination because of race, color, sex, age, handicap, or national origin. Additional allowances are made for tax support, accreditation, hardship, integrated research, outpatient services, public services, and training programs. For competing programs, the one showing the greatest public benefit is selected. Where property can be divided, as many compatible programs as possible are accommodated.

Appendix A

TYPES OF FEDERAL ASSISTANCE

A. Formula Grants—Allocations of money to states or their subdivisions in accordance with a distribution formula prescribed by law or administrative regulation, for activities of a continuing nature not confined to a specific project.

B. Project Grants—The funding, for fixed or known periods, of specific projects or the delivery of specific services or products without liability for damages for failure to perform. Project grants include fellowships, scholarships, research grants, training grants, traineeships, experimental and demonstration grants, evaluation grants, planning grants, technical assistance grants, survey grants, construction grants, and unsolicited contractual agreements.

C. Direct Payments for Specified Use—Financial assistance from the Federal government provided directly to individuals, private firms, and other private institutions to encourage or subsidize a particular activity by conditioning the receipt of the assistance on a particular performance by the recipient. This does not include solicited contracts for the procurement of goods and services for the Federal government.

D. Direct Payments with Unrestricted Use—Financial assistance from the Federal government provided directly to beneficiaries who satisfy Federal eligibility requirements with no restrictions being imposed on the recipient as to how the money is spent. Included are payments under retirement, pension, and compensation programs.

E. Direct Loans—Financial assistance provided through the lending of Federal monies for a specific period of time, with a reasonable expectation of repayment. Such loans may or may not require the payment of interest.

F. Guaranteed/Insured Loans—Programs in which the Federal government makes an arrangement to indemnify a lender against part or all of any defaults by those responsible for repayment of loans.

G. Insurance—Financial assistance provided to assure reimbursement for losses sustained under specified conditions. Coverage may be provided directly by the Federal government or through private carriers and may or may not involve the payment of premiums.

H. Sale, Exchange, or Donation of Property and Goods—Programs which provide for the sale, exchange, or donation of Federal real property, personal property, commodities, and other goods including land, buildings, equipment, food and drugs. This does not include the loan of, use of, or access to Federal facilities or property.

I. Use of Property, Facilities, and Equipment—Programs which provide for the loan of, use of, or access to Federal facilities or property wherein the federally-owned facilities or property do not remain in the possession of the recipient of the assistance.

J. Provision of Specialized Services—Programs which provide Federal personnel to directly perform certain tasks for the benefit of communities or individuals. These services may be performed in conjunction with nonfederal personnel, but they involve more than consultation, advice, or counseling.

K. Advisory Services and Counseling—Programs which provide Federal specialists to consult, advise, or counsel communities or individuals, to include conferences, workshops, or personal contacts. This may involve the use of published information, but only in a secondary capacity.

L. Dissemination of Technical Information—Programs which provide for the publication and distribution of information or data of a specialized technical nature frequently through clearinghouses or libraries. This does not include conventional public information services designed for general public consumption.

M. Training—Programs which provide instructional activities conducted directly by a Federal agency for individuals not employed by the Federal government.

N. Investigation of Complaints—Federal administrative agency activities that are initiated in response to requests, either formal or informal, to examine or investigate claims of violations of Federal statutes, policy, or procedure. The origination of such claims must come from outside the Federal government.

O. Federal Employment—Programs which reflect the government-wide responsibilities of the Office of Personnel Management in the recruitment and hiring of Federal civilian agency personnel.

Appendix B
The Foundation Center

The Foundation Center is an independent national service organization established by foundations to provide an authoritative source of information on private philanthropic giving. In fulfilling its mission, The Foundation Center disseminates information on private giving through public service programs, publications and through a national network of library reference collections for free public use. The New York, Washington, DC, Atlanta, Cleveland and San Francisco reference collections operated by The Foundation Center offer a wide variety of services and comprehensive collections of information on foundations and grants. The Cooperating Collections are libraries, community foundations and other nonprofit agencies that provide a core collection of Foundation Center publications and a variety of supplementary materials and services in subject areas useful to grantseekers.

Many of the network members make available sets of private foundation information returns (IRS Form 990-PF) for their state and/or neighboring states which are available for public use. A complete set of U.S. foundation returns can be found at the New York and Washington, DC, offices of the Foundation Center. The Atlanta, Cleveland, and San Francisco offices contain IRS Form 990-PF returns for the southeastern, midwestern, and western states, respectively.

Those collections marked with a bullet (•) have sets of private foundation returns (IRS Form 990-PF) for their states or regions, available for public reference.

Because the collections vary in their hours, materials and services, IT IS RECOMMENDED THAT YOU CALL EACH COLLECTION IN ADVANCE.

To check on new locations or current information, call toll-free 1-800-424-9836.

Reference Collections
• The Foundation Center
79 Fifth Ave., 8th Fl.
New York, NY 10003
(212) 620-4230
• The Foundation Center
312 Sutter St., Suite 312
San Francisco, CA 94108
(415) 397-0902
• The Foundation Center
1001 Connecticut Ave., N.W.
Washington, DC 20036
(202) 331-1400
• The Foundation Center
Kent H. Smith Library
1422 Euclid, Suite 1356
Cleveland, OH 44115
(216) 861-1933
• The Foundation Center
Suite 150, Grand Lobby
Hurt Building, 50 Hurt Plaza
Atlanta, GA 30303

**COOPERATING
COLLECTIONS**
Alabama
• Birmingham Public Library
Government Documents
2100 Park Place
Birmingham, AL 35203
(205) 226-3600

Huntsville Public Library
915 Monroe Street
Huntsville, AL 35801
(205) 532-5940
• University of South Alabama
Library Building
Mobile, AL 36688
(205) 460-7025
• Auburn University at
Montgomery Library
7300 University Drive
Montgomery, AL 36117
(205) 244-3653
Alaska
• University of Alaska at
Anchorage, Library
3211 Providence Drive
Anchorage, AK 99508
(907) 786-1848
Juneau Public Library
292 Marine Way
Juneau, AK 99801
(907) 586-5267
Arizona
• Phoenix Public Library
Business and Sciences Unit
12 E. McDowell Road
Phoenix, AZ 85004
(602) 262-4636

• Tucson Pima Library
101 N. Stone Avenue
Tucson, AZ 85701
(602) 791-4010
Arkansas
• Westark Community College
Borham Library
5210 Grand Avenue
Fort Smith, AR 72913
(501) 785-7133
• Central Arkansas Library Sys.
700 Louisiana Street
Little Rock, AR 72201
(501) 370-5952
Pine Bluff-Jefferson County
Library System
200 East Eighth
Pine Bluff, AR 71601
(501) 534-2159
California
• Ventura Co. Comm. Foundation
Funding and Information
Resource Center
1355 Del Norte Road
Camarillo, CA 93010
(805) 988-0196
• California Community Foundation
Funding Information Center
606 S. Olive Street, Suite 2400
Los Angeles, CA 90014
(213) 413-4042

Community Foundation for
Monterey County
177 Van Buren
Monterey, CA 93940
(408) 375-9712
Grant and Resource Center of
Northern California
Building C, Suite A
2280 Benton Drive
Redding, CA 96003
(916) 244-1219
Riverside City and County
Public Library
3581 7th Street
Riverside, CA 92502
(714) 782-5201
Nonprofit Resource Center
Sacramento Public Library
828 I Street, 2nd Floor
Sacramento, CA 95812
(916) 552-8817
• San Diego Community Foundation
Funding Information Center
101 W. Broadway, Suite 1120
San Diego, CA 92101
(619) 239-8815
• Nonprofit Development
Center Library
1762 Technology Dr., #225
San Jose, CA 95110
(408) 452-8181
• Peninsula Community Foundation
Funding Information Library
1700 S. El Camino Real, R301
San Mateo, CA 94402
(415) 358-9392
• Volunteer Center of Greater
Orange County
Nonprofit Management Assistance Ctr
1000 E. Santa Ana Blvd., Suite 200
Santa Ana, CA 92701
(714) 953-1655
• Santa Barbara Public Library
40 East Anapamu
Santa Barbara, CA 93101
(805) 962-7653
Santa Monica Public Library
1343 Sixth Street
Santa Monica, CA 90401
(310) 458-8600
Sonoma County Library
3rd & E Streets
Santa Rosa, CA 95404
(707) 545-0831

Colorado
Pikes Peak Library District
20 North Cascade Avenue
Colorado Springs, CO 80901
(719) 531-6333
• Denver Public Library
Social Sciences and Genealogy
1357 Broadway
Denver, CO 80203
(303) 640-8870
Connecticut
Danbury Public Library
170 Main Street
Danbury, CT 06810
(203) 797-4527
• Hartford Public Library
500 Main Street
Hartford, CT 06103
(203) 293-6000
D.A.T.A.
70 Audubon Street
New Haven, CT 06510
(203) 772-1345
Delaware
• University of Delaware
Hugh Morris Library
Newark, DE 19717
(302) 831-2432
District of Columbia
• The Foundation Center
1001 Connecticut Avenue, NW
Washington, DC 20036
(202) 331-1400
Florida
Volusia County Library Center
City Island
Daytona Beach, FL 32014
(904) 255-3765
• Nova University
Einstein Library
3301 College Avenue
Ft. Lauderdale, FL 33314
(305) 475-7050
Indian River Comm. College
Charles S. Miley Learning
Resource Center
3209 Virginia Avenue
Ft. Pierce, FL 34981
(407) 468-4757
• Jacksonville Public Library
Grants Resource Center
122 North Ocean Street
Jacksonville, FL 32202
(904) 630-2665

• Miami-Dade Public Library
Humanities/Social Science
101 W. Flagler Street
Miami, FL 33130
(305) 375-5015
• Orlando Public Library
Social Sciences Department
101 E. Central Blvd.
Orlando, FL 32801
(407) 425-4694
Selby Public Library
1001 Boulevard of the Arts
Sarasota, FL 34236
(813) 951-5501
• Tampa-Hillsborough County
Public Library
900 N. Ashley Drive
Tampa, FL 33602
(813) 273-3628
Community Foundation for
Palm Beach and Martin Counties
324 Datura Street, Suite 340
West Palm Beach, FL 33401
(407) 659-6800
Georgia
• Atlanta-Fulton Public Library
Foundation Collection
Ivan Allen Department
1 Margaret Mitchell Square
Atlanta, GA 30303
(404) 730-1900
Dalton Regional Library
310 Cappes Street
Dalton, GA 30720
(706) 278-4507
Hawaii
• University of Hawaii
Hamilton Library
2550 The Mall
Honolulu, HI 96822
(808) 956-7214
Hawaii Community Foundation
Hawaii Resource Center
222 Merchant Street, 2nd Floor
Honolulu, HI 96813
(808) 537-6333
Idaho
• Boise Public Library
715 S. Capitol Blvd.
Boise, ID 83702
(208) 384-4024
• Caldwell Public Library
1010 Dearborn Street
Caldwell, ID 83605
(208) 459-3242

Illinois

• Donors Forum of Chicago
53 W. Jackson Blvd., #430
Chicago, IL 60604
(312) 431-0265

• Evanston Public Library
1703 Orrington Avenue
Evanston, IL 60201
(708) 866-0305

Rock Island Public Library
401 19th Street
Rock Island, IL 61201
(309) 788-7627

• Sangamon State University
Library
Shepherd Road
Springfield, IL 62794
(217) 786-6633

Indiana

• Allen County Public Library
900 Webster Street
Fort Wayne, IN 46802
(219) 424-0544

Indiana University
Northwest Library
3400 Broadway
Gary, IN 46408
(219) 980-6582

• Indianapolis-Marion County
Public Library
Social Sciences
40 E. St. Clair Street
Indianapolis, IN 46206
(317) 269-1733

Iowa

• Cedar Rapids Public Library
Funding Center Collection
500 First Street, SE
Cedar Rapids, IA 52401
(319) 398-5123

• Southwestern Community
College
Learning Resource Center
1501 W. Townline Road
Creston, IA 50801
(515) 782-7081

• Public Library of Des Moines
100 Locust Street
Des Moines, IA 50309
(515) 283-4152

Kansas

• Topeka and Shawnee County
Public Library
1515 W. Tenth Avenue
Topeka, KS 66604
(913) 233-2040

• Wichita Public Library
223 South Main Street
Wichita, KS 67202
(316) 262-0611

Kentucky

Western Kentucky University
Helm-Cravens Library
Bowling Green, KY 42101
(502) 745-6125

• Louisville Free Public Library
301 York Street
Louisville, KY 40203
(502) 574-1611

Louisiana

• East Baton Rouge Parish Library
Centroplex Branch Grants Collection
120 St. Louis Street
Baton Rouge, LA 70802
(504) 389-4960

Beauregard Parish Library
205 S. Washington Avenue
De Ridder, LA 70634
(318) 463-6217

• New Orleans Public Library
Business and Science Division
219 Loyola Avenue
New Orleans, LA 70140
(504) 596-2580

• Shreve Memorial Library
424 Texas Street
Shreveport, LA 71120
(318) 226-5894

Maine

• University of Southern Maine
Office of Sponsored Research
246 Deering Avenue, Room 628
Portland, ME 04103
(207) 780-4871

Maryland

• Enoch Pratt Free Library
Social Science and History
Department
400 Cathedral Street
Baltimore, MD 21201
(301) 396-5430

Massachusetts

• Associated Grantmakers
of Massachusetts
Suite 840
294 Washington Street
Boston, MA 02108
(617) 426-2606

• Boston Public Library
Social Science Reference
666 Boylston Street
Boston, MA 02117
(617) 536-5400

Western Mass. Funding
Resource Center
65 Elliot Street
Springfield, MA 01101
(413) 732-3175

• Worcester Public Library
Grants Resource Center
Salem Square
Worcester, MA 01608
(508) 799-1655

Michigan

• Alpena County Library
211 N. First Street
Alpena, MI 49707
(517) 356-6188

• University of Michigan
Graduate Library
Reference & Research Services Dept.
Ann Arbor, MI 48109
(313) 664-9373

• Battle Creek Community Foundation
Southwest Michigan Funding
Resource Center
2 Riverwalk Centre
34 W. Jackson Street
Battle Creek, MI 49017
(616) 962-2181

• Henry Ford Centennial Library
Adult Services
16301 Michigan Avenue
Dearborn, MI 48126
(313) 943-2330

• Wayne State University
Purdy-Kresge Library
5265 Cass Avenue
Detroit, MI 48202
(313) 577-6424

• Michigan State University Libraries
Social Sciences/Humanities
Main Library
East Lansing, MI 48824
(517) 353-8818

• Farmington Comm. Library
32737 W. 12 Mile Road
Farmington Hills, MI 48018
(313) 553-0300

• University of Michigan
Flint Library
Flint, MI 48502
(313) 762-3408

• Grand Rapids Public Library
Business Department, 3rd Floor
60 Library Plaza NE
Grand Rapids, MI 49503
(616) 456-3600
• Michigan Technological University
Van Pelt Library
1400 Townsend Drive
Houghton, MI 49931
(906) 487-2507
Sault Ste. Marie Area
Public Schools
Office of Compensatory
Education
460 W. Spruce Street
Sault Ste. Marie, MI 49783
(906) 635-6619
• Northwestern Michigan College
Mark & Helen Osterin Library
1701 E. Front Street
Traverse City, MI 49684
(616) 922-1060

Minnesota
• Duluth Public Library
520 W. Superior Street
Duluth, MN 55802
(218) 723-3802
Southwest State University
Library
Marshall, MN 56258
(507) 537-6176
• Minneapolis Public Library
Sociology Department
300 Nicollet Mall
Minneapolis, MN 55401
(612) 372-6555
Rochester Public Library
11 First Street, SE
Rochester, MN 55904
(507) 285-8002
Saint Paul Public Library
90 W. Fourth Street
Saint Paul, MN 55102
(612) 292-6307

Mississippi
• Jackson/Hinds Library System
300 N. State Street
Jackson, MS 39201
(601) 968-5803

Missouri
• Clearinghouse for Midcontinent
Foundations
University of Missouri
5315 Rockhill Road
Kansas City, MO 64110
(816) 235-1176

• Kansas City Public Library
311 E. 12th Street
Kansas City, MO 64106
(816) 235-9650
• Metropolitan Association for
Philanthropy, Inc.
Suite 20
5615 Pershing Avenue
St. Louis, MO 63112
(314) 361-3900
• Springfield-Greene County
Library
397 E. Central Street
Springfield, MO 65802
(417) 869-9400

Montana
• Eastern Montana College Library
Special Collections-Grants
1500 N. 30th Street
Billings, MT 59101
(406) 657-1662
Bozeman Public Library
220 E. Lamme
Bozeman, MT 59715
(406) 586-4787
• Montana State Library
Library Services
1515 E. 6th Avenue
Helena, MT 59620
(406) 444-3004

Nebraska
• University of Nebraska
Love Library
14th and R Streets
Lincoln, NE 68588
(402) 472-2848
• W. Dale Clark Library
Social Sciences Department
215 S. 15th Street
Omaha, NE 68102
(402) 444-4826

Nevada
• Las Vegas-Clark County
Library District
833 Las Vegas Blvd. North
Las Vegas, NV 89101
(702) 382-5280
• Washoe County Library
301 S. Center Street
Reno, NV 89501
(702) 785-4010

New Hampshire
• New Hampshire Charitable Fund
One South Street
Concord, NH 03302
(603) 225-6641

• Plymouth State College
Herbert H. Lamson Library
Plymouth, NH 03264
(603) 535-2258

New Jersey
Cumberland County Library
New Jersey Room
800 E. Commerce Street
Bridgeton, NJ 08302
(609) 453-2210
• Free Public Library of Elizabeth
11 S. Broad Street
Elizabeth, NJ 07202
(908) 354-6060
County College of Morris
Learning Resource Center
214 Center Grove Road
Randolph, NJ 07869
(201) 328-5296
• New Jersey State Library
Governmental Reference Services
185 W. State Street
Trenton, NJ 08625
(609) 292-6220

New Mexico
Albuquerque Community
Foundation
3301 Menual N.E., Suite 16
Albuquerque, NM 87176
(505) 883-6240
• New Mexico State Library
Information Services
325 Don Gaspar
Santa Fe, NM 87503
(505) 827-3824

New York
• New York State Library
Humanities Reference
Cultural Education Center
Empire State Plaza
Albany, NY 12230
(518) 474-5355
Suffolk Coop Library System
627 N. Sunrise Service Road
Bellport, NY 11713
(516) 286-1600
New York Public Library
Fordham Branch
2556 Bainbridge Avenue
Bronx, NY 10458
(212) 220-6575
Brooklyn-In-Touch Information Ctr.
Room 2504
One Hanson Place
Brooklyn, NY 11243
(718) 230-3200

• Buffalo and Erie County
Public Library
History Department
Lafayette Square
Buffalo, NY 14203
(716) 858-7103
Huntington Public Library
338 Main Street
Huntington, NY 11743
(516) 427-5165
Queens Borough Public Library
Social Sciences Division
89-11 Merrick Blvd.
Jamaica, NY 11432
(718) 990-0700
• Levittown Public Library
One Bluegrass Lane
Levittown, NY 11756
(516) 731-5728
New York Public Library
Countee Cullen Branch Library
104 West 136th Street
New York, NY 10030
(212) 491-2070
• The Foundation Center
79 Fifth Avenue
New York, NY 10003
(212) 620-4230
Adriance Memorial Library
Special Services Department
93 Market Street
Poughkeepsie, NY 12601
(914) 485-3445
• Rochester Public Library
Business, Economics and Law
115 South Avenue
Rochester, NY 14604
(716) 428-7328
Onondaga Co. Public Library
447 S. Salina Street
Syracuse, NY 13202
(315) 448-4700
Utica Public Library
303 Genesee Street
Utica, NY 13501
(315) 735-2279
• White Plains Public Library
100 Martine Avenue
White Plains, NY 10601
(914) 442-1480
North Carolina
• Asheville-Buncombe Technical
Community College
Learning Resources Center
14 College Street
P.O. Box 1888
Asheville, NC 28801
(704) 254-4960

• The Duke Endowment
200 S. Tryon Street, #1100
Charlotte, NC 28202
(704) 376-0291
Durham County Public Library
301 N. Roxboro Street
Durham, NC 27702
(919) 560-0110
• State Library of North Carolina
Government and Business Services
Archives Building
109 E. Jones Street
Raleigh, NC 27601
(919) 733-3270
• The Winston-Salem Foundation
310 W. 4th Street, Suite 229
Winston-Salem, NC 27101
(919) 725-2382
North Dakota
• North Dakota State University
The Library
Fargo, ND 58105
(701) 237-8886
Ohio
Stark County District Library
Humanities
715 Market Avenue North
Canton, OH 44702
(216) 452-0665
• Public Library of Cincinnati
and Hamilton County
Grants Resource Center
800 Vine Street-Library Square
Cincinnati, OH 45202
(513) 369-6940
• The Foundation Center
Kent H. Smith Library
1442 Euclid Building, Suite 1356
Cleveland, OH 44115
(216) 861-1933
Columbus Metro. Library
Business and Technology
96 S. Grant Ave.
Columbus, OH 43215
(614) 645-2590
• Dayton and Montgomery County
Public Library
215 E. Third Street
Dayton, OH 45402
(513) 227-9500 ext. 211
• Toledo-Lucas County
Public Library
Social Science Department
325 Michigan Street
Toledo, OH 43624
(419) 259-5245

Youngstown & Mahoning
County Library
305 Wick Avenue
Youngstown, OH 44503
(216) 744-8636
Muskinghum County Library
220 N. 5th Street
Zanesville, OH 43701
(614) 453-0391
Oklahoma
• Oklahoma City University
Dulaney Browne Library
2501 N. Blackwelder
Oklahoma City, OK 73106
(405) 521-5072
• Tulsa City-Co. Library System
400 Civic Center
Tulsa, OK 74103
(918) 596-7944
Oregon
Oregon Inst of Technology Library
3201 Campus Drive
Klamath Falls, OR 97601
(503) 885-1773
Pacific Non-Profit Network
Grantsmanship Resource Library
33 N. Central, Suite 211
Medford, OR 97501
(503) 779-6044
• Multnomah County Library
Government Documents
801 S.W. Tenth Avenue
Portland, OR 97205
(503) 248-5123
Oregon State Library
State Library Building
Salem, OR 97310
(503) 378-4277
Pennsylvania
Northampton Community College
Learning Resources Center
3835 Green Pond Road
Bethlehem, PA 18017
(215) 861-5360
Erie County Library System
27 S. Park Row
Erie, PA 16501
(814) 451-6927
Dauphin County Library System
Central Library
101 Walnut Street
Harrisburg, PA 17101
(717) 234-4961
Lancaster County Public Library
125 N. Duke Street
Lancaster, PA 17602
(717) 394-2651

• Free Library of Philadelphia
Regional Foundation Center
Logan Square
Philadelphia, PA 19103
(215) 686-5423
• Carnegie Library of Pittsburgh
Foundation Collection
4400 Forbes Avenue
Pittsburgh, PA 15213
(412) 622-1917
Pocono Northeast Development Fund
James Pettinger Memorial Library
1151 Oak Street
Pittston, PA 18640
(717) 655-5581
Reading Public Library
100 S. Fifth Street
Reading, PA 19602
(215) 655-6355
Martin Library
159 Market Street
York, PA 17401
(717) 846-5300

Rhode Island
• Providence Public Library
150 Empire Street
Providence, RI 02906
(401) 521-7722

South Carolina
• Charleston County Library
404 King Street
Charleston, SC 29403
(803) 723-1645
• South Carolina State Library
1500 Senate Street
Columbia, SC 29211
(803) 734-8666

South Dakota
Nonprofit Grants Assistance Center
Business and Education Institute
Washington Street, East Hall
Dakota State University
Madison, SD 57042
(605) 256-5555
• South Dakota State Library
800 Governors Drive
Pierre, SD 57501
(605) 773-5070
(800) 592-1841 (SD residents)
Sioux Falls Area Foundation
141 N. Main Ave., Suite 310
Sioux Falls, SD 57102
(605) 336-7055

Tennessee
• Knox County Public Library
500 W. Church Avenue
Knoxville, TN 37902
(615) 544-5700
• Memphis & Shelby County
Public Library
1850 Peabody Avenue
Memphis, TN 38104
(901) 725-8877
• Nashville Public Library
Business Information Division
225 Polk Avenue
Nashville, TN 37203
(615) 862-5843

Texas
Community Foundation of Abilene
Funding Information Library
500 N. Chestnut, Suite 1509
Abilene, TX 79604
(915) 676-3883
• Amarillo Area Foundation
700 First National Place
801 S. Fillmore
Amarillo, TX 79101
(806) 376-4521
• Hogg Foundation for
Mental Health
Will C. Hogg Building, Suite 301
Inner Campus Drive
University of Texas
Austin, TX 78713
(512) 471-5041
Texas A & M University
Library-Reference Dept.
6300 Ocean Drive
Corpus Christi, TX 78412
(512) 994-2608
• Dallas Public Library
Urban Information
1515 Young Street
Dallas, TX 75201
(214) 670-1487
El Paso Community Foundation
1616 Texas Commerce Building
El Paso, TX 79901
(915) 533-4020
• Funding Information Center
Texas Christian University Library
2800 S. University Drive
Ft. Worth, TX 76129
(817) 921-7664

• Houston Public Library
Bibliographic Information
Center
500 McKinney Avenue
Houston, TX 77002
(713) 236-1313
• Longview Public Library
222 W. Cotton Street
Longview, TX 75601
(903) 237-1352
Lubbock Area Foundation
502 Texas Commerce Bank Bldg.
Lubbock, TX 79401
(806) 762-8061
• Funding Information Center
530 McCullough, Suite 600
San Antonio, TX 78212
(210) 227-4333
North Texas Center for Nonprofit
Management
624 Indiana, Suite 307
Wichita Falls, TX 76301
(817) 322-4961

Utah
• Salt Lake City Public Library
209 E. 500 South
Salt Lake City, UT 84111
(801) 524-8200

Vermont
• Vermont Department of
Libraries
Reference & Law Info. Services
109 State Street
Montpelier, VT 05609
(802) 828-3268

Virginia
• Hampton Public Library
4207 Victoria Blvd.
Hampton, VA 23669
(804) 727-1312
• Richmond Public Library
Business, Science & Technology
Department
101 E. Franklin Street
Richmond, VA 23219
(804) 780-8223
• Roanoke City Public
Library System
Central Library
706 S. Jefferson Street
Roanoke, VA 24016
(703) 981-2477

Washington
• Mid-Columbia Library
405 S. Dayton
Kennewick, WA 99336
(509) 586-3156
• Seattle Public Library
Science, Social Science
1000 Fourth Avenue
Seattle, WA 98104
(206) 386-4620
• Spokane Public Library
Funding Information Center
West 811 Main Avenue
Spokane, WA 99201
(509) 838-3364
• United Way of Pierce County
Center for Nonprofit Development
734 Broadway
P.O. Box 2215
Tacoma, WA 98401
(206) 597-6686
Greater Wenatchee Community
Foundation at the Wenatchee
Public Library
310 Douglas Street
Wenatchee, WA 98807
(509) 662-5021
West Virginia
• Kanawha County Public Library
123 Capital Street
Charleston, WV 25301
(304) 343-4646
Wisconsin
• University of Wisconsin
Memorial Library
728 State Street
Madison, WI 53706
(608) 262-3242
• Marquette University Memorial
Library
Funding Information Center
1415 W. Wisconsin Avenue
Milwaukee, WI 53233
(414) 288-1515
Wyoming
• Natrona County Public Library
307 East 2nd Street
Casper, WY 82601
(307) 237-4935
• Laramie County Community
College
Instructional Resource Center
1400 E. College Drive
Cheyenne, WY 82007
(307) 778-1206

• Campbell County Public Library
2101 4-J Road
Gillette, WY 82716
(307) 682-3223
• Teton County Library
320 South King Street
Jackson, WY 83001
(307) 733-2164
Rock Springs Library
400 C Street
Rock Springs, WY 82901
(307) 362-6212

Puerto Rico
University of Puerto Rico
Ponce Technological College
Library
Box 7186
Ponce, PR 00732
(809) 844-8181
Universidad Del Sagrado
Corazon
M.M.T. Guevara Library
Santurce, PR 00914
(809) 728-1515 ext. 357

Appendix C

The Grantsmanship Center

The Grantsmanship Center is the world's oldest and largest training organization for the nonprofit sector. Since it was founded in 1972, the Center has trained more than 50,000 staff members of public and private agencies in grantsmanship, program management and fundraising.

The five-day Grantsmanship Training Program, first offered in 1972 and continuously updated, began a new era in training seminars and workshops for nonprofit agencies. Over 30,000 nonprofit agency staff members have attended this demanding, week-long workshop. It covers all aspects of researching for grants, writing grant proposals, and negotiating with funding sources.

The Grant Proposal Writing Workshop, an intensive three-day laboratory, teaches you how to write a good proposal and plan better programs at the same time, using the Grantsmanship Center's program planning and proposal writing format.

The Center also produces publications on grantsmanship, planning, fundraising, management, and personnel issues for nonprofit agencies. Its Program Planning and Proposal Writing booklet is now a classic in the field and has been used by hundreds of thousands of successful grant seekers.

For detailed information about The Grantsmanship Center's training programs, publications, and other services to the nonprofit sector, write to The Grantsmanship Center, Dept. DD, P.O. Box 17220, Los Angeles, CA 90017 and ask for a free copy of *The Whole Nonprofit Catalog*.

Index to Foundations

(Alphabetical)

Citations are by entry number

S

Y

Z

Index to Foundations

(Subject Index)

Citations are by entry number

ANIMAL WELFARE—11, 26, 29, 49, 161, 209, 215, 216, 229, 248, 250, 255, 290, 299, 304, 390, 398, 406, 436, 437, 441, 472, 496, 519, 537, 555, 563, 597, 631, 638, 666, 693, 751, 773, 787, 827, 830, 836, 844, 847, 858, 860, 867, 897, 901, 904, 906, 916, 922

COMMUNITY DEVELOPMENT—3, 5, 9, 11, 14, 16, 19, 20, 27, 35, 38, 39, 41, 42, 43, 49, 65, 66, 68, 75, 77, 82, 93, 100, 104, 106, 107, 109, 110, 115, 117, 126, 127, 128, 130, 132, 135, 136, 138, 140, 141, 142, 143, 145, 146, 147, 149, 153, 154, 169, 175, 177, 180, 186, 187, 188, 193, 196, 205, 206, 213, 222, 223, 232, 239, 243, 244, 245, 247, 248, 249, 257, 258, 261, 262, 264, 267, 270, 274, 275, 276, 280, 285, 290, 295, 300, 303, 304, 308, 313, 318, 320, 322, 329, 330, 331, 335, 338, 342, 345, 349, 350, 356, 357, 360, 361, 362, 363, 365, 367, 369, 372, 373, 376, 380, 382, 385, 387, 389, 390, 391, 392, 393, 394, 395, 396, 397, 398, 399, 401, 403, 404, 405, 406, 408, 410, 411, 414, 415, 419, 420, 421, 422, 424, 425, 427, 428, 432, 435, 439, 440, 441, 442, 443, 448, 449, 450, 454, 457, 458, 459, 461, 463, 464, 465, 468, 472, 473, 474, 478, 479, 482, 486, 488, 489, 493, 495, 496, 497, 498, 499, 502, 503, 504, 506, 509, 513, 514, 516, 518, 519, 520, 521, 523, 525, 526, 527, 531, 532, 534, 537, 539, 540, 542, 544, 548, 551, 553, 555, 556, 558, 559, 560, 562, 563, 567, 568, 569, 573, 574, 575, 576, 579, 580, 583, 586, 587, 589, 590, 592, 595, 605, 607, 608, 610, 612, 613, 615, 616, 617, 619, 621, 625, 626, 633, 639, 640, 641, 643, 644, 645, 648, 649, 650, 654, 655, 657, 659, 662, 664, 665, 667, 668, 669, 671, 674, 675, 676, 677, 678, 680, 683, 684, 685, 686, 690, 691, 693, 696, 698, 700, 701, 702, 704, 705, 706, 708, 709, 710, 714, 716, 718, 719, 720, 723, 726, 727, 728, 729, 730, 731, 733, 734, 735, 737, 738, 740, 741, 742, 743, 744, 746, 747, 751, 753, 754, 755, 757, 758, 759, 760, 766, 768, 771, 772, 773, 774, 776, 778, 780, 781, 783, 786, 789, 791, 793, 794, 796, 797, 798, 799, 800, 801, 802, 803, 804, 805, 810, 811, 812, 814, 815, 817, 820, 823, 827, 830, 831, 832, 833, 835, 836, 838, 839, 840, 844, 845, 847, 848, 849, 851, 853, 854, 855, 856, 858, 859, 860, 861, 862, 864, 866, 868, 869, 872, 873, 875, 876, 877, 878, 882, 883, 887, 888, 889, 890, 891, 892, 893, 894, 895, 896, 897, 898, 899, 900, 901, 902, 907, 909, 910, 914, 919, 926, 931, 938, 940, 941, 946, 947

CULTURAL ORGANIZATIONS—1, 3, 4, 5, 6, 7, 8, 9, 10, 11, 12, 14, 15, 18, 21, 22, 24, 25, 26, 27, 29, 30, 31, 32, 33, 34, 35, 37, 40, 41, 42, 43, 44, 45, 46, 47, 50, 51, 54, 55, 57, 59, 61, 64, 65, 68, 69, 70, 71, 73, 74, 75, 76, 77, 78, 81, 82, 83, 84, 85, 87, 88, 89, 92, 93, 96, 97, 98, 99, 100, 101, 102, 103, 104, 105, 107, 109, 110, 111, 113, 114, 115, 116, 117, 118, 120, 123, 125, 126, 127, 131, 132, 133, 134, 136, 137, 138, 139, 141, 142, 143, 145, 147, 151, 153, 154, 160, 161, 162, 164, 166, 167, 169, 170, 173, 175, 176, 181, 186, 187, 189, 191, 192, 195, 196, 197, 199, 200, 204, 207, 208, 209, 211, 212, 213, 214, 215, 217, 222, 223, 224, 235, 238, 239, 240, 242, 245, 247, 249, 250, 251, 253, 255, 258, 259, 260, 261, 262, 269, 271, 272, 273, 274, 275, 279, 280, 281, 282, 283, 284, 288, 289, 290, 292, 293, 294, 295, 298, 299, 301, 302, 303, 311, 313, 317, 325, 333, 336, 337, 345, 346, 347, 348, 349, 350, 351, 356, 357, 359, 361, 365, 366, 367, 368, 369, 370, 371, 372, 373, 374, 375, 376, 377, 380, 381, 382, 383, 384, 385, 386, 387, 388, 390, 391, 392, 393, 394, 395, 396, 398, 399, 400, 401, 402, 403, 406, 407, 408, 410, 412, 414, 415, 416, 417, 419, 420, 421, 423, 424, 425, 426, 427, 430, 431, 432, 433, 434, 435, 436, 439, 440, 443, 445, 446, 447, 448, 450, 453, 456, 457, 458, 459, 462, 463, 464, 465, 466, 467, 468, 469, 471, 472, 473, 474, 475, 476, 477, 478, 479, 480, 481, 482, 485, 488, 489, 490, 492, 493, 495, 497, 498, 499, 500, 501, 503, 504, 508, 512, 513, 514, 515, 517, 518, 520, 521, 523, 525, 526, 527, 530, 531, 532, 534, 536, 537, 540, 541, 546, 547, 548, 549, 550, 551, 552, 553, 555, 556, 557, 559, 562, 563, 566, 568, 569, 570, 573, 574, 576, 578, 579, 580, 583, 584, 585, 586, 587,

592, 593, 594, 595, 596, 597, 599, 602, 604, 605, 607, 608, 609, 610, 611, 612, 613, 615, 616, 617, 619, 620, 621, 622, 624, 626, 628, 629, 630, 631, 632, 633, 634, 635, 636, 637, 638, 639, 641, 644, 645, 648, 650, 653, 654, 656, 658, 659, 661, 662, 663, 664, 665, 666, 667, 668, 669, 670, 671, 673, 674, 677, 678, 679, 680, 681, 682, 684, 685, 686, 687, 688, 691, 692, 693, 695, 696, 697, 698, 699, 700, 701, 702, 703, 704, 705, 706, 707, 708, 709, 710, 712, 713, 714, 716, 717, 718, 720, 721, 723, 724, 726, 727, 728, 729, 730, 731, 732, 734, 735, 736, 737, 739, 740, 741, 742, 743, 747, 748, 749, 751, 752, 754, 755, 756, 758, 760, 761, 762, 763, 766, 767, 768, 771, 772, 773, 774, 776, 778, 780, 781, 782, 783, 784, 786, 787, 789, 791, 793, 797, 799, 800, 801, 804, 805, 806, 808, 810, 812, 814, 815, 817, 818, 819, 820, 823, 826, 827, 830, 831, 833, 834, 835, 836, 838, 839, 842, 843, 846, 847, 849, 850, 851, 852, 853, 854, 855, 857, 858, 859, 860, 861, 863, 864, 865, 866, 867, 870, 872, 873, 875, 876, 877, 878, 879, 880, 881, 882, 883, 884, 887, 888, 891, 892, 893, 894, 897, 900, 901, 902, 903, 904, 905, 906, 907, 908, 909, 911, 913, 915, 916, 919, 921, 922, 925, 929, 931, 934, 935, 939, 941, 944, 946, 947, 948

DISABLED—4, 6, 7, 8, 9, 10, 11, 14, 15, 19, 21, 23, 24, 26, 27, 28, 29, 31, 32, 33, 34, 35, 40, 41, 43, 44, 45, 51, 54, 57, 58, 59, 60, 65, 66, 68, 69, 71, 72, 73, 74, 75, 76, 77, 78, 79, 81, 82, 83, 88, 89, 90, 94, 97, 100, 102, 104, 115, 118, 120, 121, 124, 126, 127, 135, 142, 143, 145, 150, 152, 153, 155, 159, 161, 162, 163, 165, 166, 167, 168, 169, 171, 173, 174, 177, 178, 183, 187, 191, 196, 199, 201, 202, 205, 207, 209, 211, 213, 214, 215, 216, 218, 228, 232, 233, 237, 242, 249, 250, 254, 255, 256, 257, 259, 260, 262, 264, 267, 269, 271, 272, 274, 276, 280, 281, 283, 284, 289, 290, 291, 292, 295, 296, 301, 305, 306, 307, 308, 309, 317, 322, 323, 325, 332, 334, 339, 340, 341, 342, 343, 344, 345, 346, 349, 352, 353, 354, 355, 356, 360, 363, 369, 370, 371, 374, 382, 386, 387, 393, 394, 395, 402, 403, 404, 406, 407, 412, 413, 415, 416, 417, 419, 422, 423, 424, 425, 428, 431, 432, 433, 434, 436, 437, 438, 439, 440, 442, 443, 444, 445, 446, 449, 450, 451, 452, 454, 455, 457, 458, 459, 460, 462, 463, 465, 467, 468, 469, 470, 473, 476, 478, 483, 484, 485, 487, 491, 493, 495, 498, 499, 503, 504, 505, 507, 509, 511, 512, 513, 514, 515, 516, 518, 519, 523, 527, 528, 529, 530, 532, 534, 535, 537, 539, 540, 542, 543, 544, 545, 546, 547, 548, 549, 551, 552, 553, 554, 555, 556, 557, 558, 559, 560, 561, 562, 563, 564, 566, 568, 569, 570, 571, 572, 575, 576, 577, 581, 582, 583, 584, 586, 587, 588, 590, 591, 592, 593, 594, 595, 596, 597, 599, 600, 601, 602, 603, 606, 607, 610, 611, 612, 613, 614, 616, 619, 620, 623, 625, 626, 627, 628, 630, 631, 632, 633, 634, 638, 640, 642, 644, 645, 647, 648, 650, 652, 653, 655, 656, 657, 658, 661, 662, 663, 665, 666, 667, 669, 670, 672, 673, 675, 676, 677, 678, 679, 680, 682, 683, 685, 686, 687, 689, 690, 691, 692, 693, 695, 696, 697, 698, 701, 702, 703, 704, 705, 706, 707, 708, 709, 715, 716, 717, 718, 720, 722, 725, 728, 729, 730, 731, 732, 733, 734, 737, 739, 740, 741, 742, 743, 744, 745, 747, 750, 751, 752, 753, 754, 755, 757, 758, 759, 760, 762, 763, 764, 765, 766, 767, 768, 769, 771, 772, 774, 775, 777, 778, 779, 780, 781, 782, 783, 785, 788, 789, 793, 794, 795, 796, 797, 798, 799, 800, 801, 802, 806, 813, 815, 817, 818, 819, 821, 823, 826, 827, 828, 829, 830, 831, 832, 833, 834, 835, 836, 837, 838, 839, 840, 841, 843, 844, 846, 847, 849, 851, 852, 853, 854, 855, 857, 858, 859, 860, 861, 864, 865, 866, 867, 869, 870, 871, 872, 873, 874, 876, 878, 881, 882, 884, 888, 891, 893, 895, 897, 899, 900, 902, 903, 904, 906, 909, 910, 911, 913, 914, 915, 919, 921, 923, 924, 926, 928, 934, 936, 937, 938, 939, 946, 947

EDUCATION (other than higher education)—7, 10, 19, 21, 29, 30, 34, 43, 44, 45, 47, 48, 51, 54, 65, 68, 69, 70, 79, 80, 81, 83, 87, 92, 93, 95, 105, 106, 109, 113, 114, 118, 126, 134, 140, 141, 144, 151, 153, 160, 168, 170, 173, 182, 183, 187, 197, 199, 201, 209, 211, 214, 219, 220, 223, 224, 226, 261, 272, 275, 281, 286, 287, 292, 294, 295, 300, 304, 309, 319, 327, 328, 329, 331, 332, 333, 335, 336, 342, 344, 364, 387, 405, 408, 410, 420, 421, 428, 439, 441, 442, 462, 476, 477, 479, 495, 505, 508, 510, 513, 522, 534, 537, 540, 541, 552, 559, 561, 562, 564, 568, 573, 579, 580, 583, 585, 590, 591, 592, 594, 597, 604, 605, 608, 610, 617, 620, 623, 630, 631, 633, 656, 661, 665, 669, 678, 684, 688, 689, 696, 700, 701, 705, 708, 710, 715, 716, 719, 732, 738, 739, 746, 753, 756, 762, 771, 772, 773, 776, 777, 778, 781, 785, 787, 788, 793, 801, 804, 805, 808, 810, 811, 823, 825, 829, 830, 835, 839, 842, 843, 850, 853, 854, 855, 859, 860, 862, 863, 869, 872, 873, 878, 886, 889, 893, 901, 906, 914, 917, 919, 921, 922, 933, 935, 939, 940, 943, 944, 947

230

ELDERLY—3, 6, 8, 11, 24, 29, 31, 32, 35, 39, 41, 44, 45, 46, 51, 56, 60, 61, 66, 68, 70, 72, 73, 77, 78, 82, 83, 104, 106, 108, 111, 112, 118, 140, 143, 146, 152, 153, 156, 161, 165, 169, 171, 177, 183, 184, 198, 204, 211, 214, 220, 221, 248, 254, 263, 264, 277, 290, 293, 296, 300, 304, 305, 317, 352, 353, 354, 356, 363, 379, 386, 393, 395, 396, 400, 407, 408, 415, 417, 418, 426, 430, 436, 441, 443, 447, 450, 454, 458, 465, 472, 473, 476, 478, 483, 484, 489, 490, 491, 497, 498, 503, 509, 512, 513, 516, 517, 518, 520, 523, 534, 535, 537, 547, 549, 550, 551, 554, 555, 557, 558, 559, 563, 566, 568, 571, 572, 575, 576, 577, 586, 590, 594, 600, 601, 604, 606, 610, 611, 612, 615, 616, 619, 620, 624, 626, 630, 631, 638, 645, 650, 652, 653, 654, 655, 657, 662, 663, 665, 666, 668, 673, 674, 678, 680, 689, 693, 696, 697, 704, 709, 715, 717, 720, 725, 729, 731, 732, 739, 740, 946, 750, 751, 753, 755, 756, 759, 762, 770, 771, 772, 779, 781, 783, 787, 788, 789, 819, 827, 830, 833, 840, 853, 855, 864, 868, 872, 874, 876, 878, 884, 887, 889, 890, 891, 893, 897, 898, 899, 901, 904, 906, 912, 916, 918, 920, 921, 923, 930, 937, 939, 943, 947

ENVIRONMENT—10, 28, 36, 66, 68, 74, 83, 84, 109, 114, 127, 130, 142, 144, 146, 162, 170, 181, 187, 204, 208, 213, 218, 229, 284, 318, 351, 353, 362, 363, 393, 397, 398, 406, 431, 432, 435, 445, 447, 448, 450, 457, 458, 477, 485, 500, 528, 536, 537, 540, 541, 548, 557, 569, 585, 595, 610, 611, 612, 614, 615, 617, 621, 625, 661, 666, 669, 672, 674, 678, 682, 694, 699, 724, 728, 734, 739, 745, 746, 748, 757, 761, 765, 768, 771, 772, 782, 787, 788, 789, 797, 800, 801, 804, 805, 808, 820, 844, 857, 860, 867, 874, 875, 878, 880, 882, 888, 894, 895, 897, 918, 928, 929, 935

HEALTH ORGANIZATIONS—1, 3, 5, 6, 9, 10, 11, 13, 14, 15, 19, 21, 25, 26, 27, 29, 31, 32, 33, 34, 42, 43, 46, 49, 50, 54, 57, 58, 59, 61, 62, 68, 70, 71, 75, 76, 77, 82, 83, 88, 89, 91, 93, 94, 95, 99, 100, 101, 102, 103, 104, 107, 108, 110, 112, 113, 114, 115, 116, 117, 119, 120, 121, 123, 126, 127, 128, 129, 130, 133, 135, 141, 142, 143, 144, 146, 147, 149, 154, 158, 159, 162, 163, 165, 166, 167, 169, 170, 171, 172, 173, 175, 177, 181, 183, 185, 187, 188, 189, 190, 194, 195, 196, 199, 200, 201, 202, 203, 204, 205, 207, 211, 213, 214, 215, 221, 225, 227, 229, 232, 235, 237, 238, 242, 244, 245, 246, 249, 250, 251, 254, 259, 262, 264, 266, 268, 270, 271, 276, 278, 279, 280, 282, 290, 294, 296, 297, 300, 301, 307, 310, 313, 317, 320, 321, 322, 325, 326, 330, 335, 337, 338, 339, 345, 347, 349, 350, 352, 355, 356, 359, 360, 361, 363, 369, 371, 372, 373, 374, 375, 377, 380, 382, 383, 384, 385, 386, 387, 392, 393, 394, 395, 396, 397, 398, 399, 400, 401, 403, 404, 406, 407, 409, 410, 412, 413, 415, 418, 421, 423, 424, 427, 428, 438, 442, 443, 444, 449, 452, 453, 454, 455, 457, 458, 459, 463, 464, 467, 471, 473, 474, 475, 477, 479, 483, 484, 485, 491, 492, 493, 496, 497, 498, 500, 501, 505, 507, 512, 513, 514, 515, 516, 517, 518, 519, 520, 521, 523, 527, 528, 529, 530, 531, 534, 535, 536, 539, 541, 542, 543, 544, 545, 548, 549, 550, 551, 553, 556, 558, 559, 560, 561, 563, 564, 566, 569, 572, 575, 576, 577, 581, 582, 584, 587, 588, 591, 592, 593, 595, 596, 597, 598, 600, 601, 602, 603, 604, 605, 606, 608, 610, 611, 612, 613, 615, 616, 617, 619, 623, 624, 625, 626, 627, 628, 630, 631, 632, 633, 634, 635, 639, 645, 646, 647, 650, 651, 654, 655, 660, 663, 665, 667, 670, 671, 674, 675, 676, 677, 680, 684, 687, 689, 690, 691, 693, 695, 696, 701, 702, 704, 707, 708, 709, 710, 717, 718, 720, 722, 723, 725, 726, 728, 729, 730, 731, 732, 734, 735, 736, 737, 739, 741, 742, 744, 745, 746, 747, 748, 750, 751, 752, 753, 754, 755, 758, 759, 761, 762, 767, 770, 772, 773, 775, 778, 779, 782, 783, 784, 785, 786, 787, 789, 790, 791, 794, 795, 796, 798, 799, 800, 803, 806, 812, 817, 819, 820, 821, 827, 828, 831, 832, 836, 837, 838, 839, 841, 843, 844, 845, 846, 847, 851, 852, 853, 855, 856, 857, 859, 860, 861, 864, 865, 867, 871, 872, 874, 878, 879, 881, 882, 884, 885, 888, 891, 893, 894, 895, 899, 901, 902, 903, 906, 907, 908, 909, 912, 914, 915, 916, 917, 918, 923, 925, 926, 927, 930, 932, 935, 938, 939, 944, 945, 946

HIGHER EDUCATION—1, 2, 3, 5, 6, 7, 11, 12, 15, 21, 22, 23, 24, 26, 34, 43, 44, 52, 53, 54, 56, 57, 58, 59, 67, 71, 76, 79, 80, 85, 86, 87, 89, 92, 95, 97, 99, 108, 114, 120, 125, 126, 139, 162, 163, 170, 173, 175, 178, 182, 183, 187, 191, 197, 201, 204, 207, 209, 212, 226, 227, 242, 243, 244, 248, 250, 251, 254, 255, 257, 259, 261, 269, 270, 272, 273, 281, 282, 286, 287, 288, 294, 298, 309, 313, 314, 316, 317, 328, 330, 338, 340, 341, 342, 345, 346, 347, 348, 350, 351, 353, 357,

358, 359, 364, 366, 368, 369, 372, 373, 376, 377, 381, 383, 384, 385, 387, 388, 389, 390, 391, 393, 394, 395, 396, 398, 399, 400, 401, 402, 403, 404, 406, 407, 409, 410, 411, 415, 416, 417, 418, 419, 421, 422, 424, 425, 426, 428, 429, 430, 431, 433, 436, 440, 441, 442, 443, 445, 446, 447, 450, 451, 453, 455, 456, 459, 460, 461, 462, 463, 464, 467, 470, 471, 472, 473, 475, 476, 477, 478, 481, 482, 483, 484, 486, 488, 489, 491, 492, 495, 496, 497, 498, 499, 500, 501, 505, 506, 508, 509, 510, 511, 513, 514, 515, 517, 518, 520, 523, 525, 526, 528, 530, 531, 532, 534, 535, 536, 537, 540, 541, 542, 545, 547, 549, 551, 552, 554, 556, 558, 559, 561, 562, 563, 564, 567, 569, 573, 574, 575, 576, 577, 578, 579, 580, 581, 582, 583, 584, 585, 586, 588, 590, 591, 593, 594, 598, 599, 601, 602, 604, 605, 606, 607, 610, 611, 613, 616, 617, 618, 619, 620, 621, 622, 623, 626, 628, 630, 631, 633, 637, 638, 639, 640, 642, 643, 649, 652, 656, 658, 659, 660, 661, 662, 663, 664, 665, 668, 670, 671, 672, 673, 674, 675, 676, 679, 680, 681, 685, 686, 689, 690, 691, 692, 693, 697, 698, 700, 702, 703, 704, 705, 706, 707, 708, 710, 714, 715, 716, 719, 721, 722, 723, 725, 726, 727, 728, 729, 730, 731, 732, 733, 734, 735, 736, 738, 739, 741, 743, 744, 745, 746, 747, 748, 750, 751, 752, 753, 754, 755, 756, 757, 758, 760, 761, 762, 763, 764, 767, 768, 771, 772, 773, 774, 776, 777, 778, 780, 782, 783, 785, 786, 787, 789, 790, 791, 792, 795, 796, 797, 799, 801, 804, 805, 806, 808, 809, 810, 811, 813, 814, 815, 816, 819, 821, 822, 823, 825, 826, 827, 828, 829, 830, 833, 834, 835, 836, 837, 838, 839, 840, 841, 842, 843, 844, 845, 846, 847, 850, 851, 852, 853, 854, 855, 856, 857, 858, 859, 860, 861, 862, 863, 864, 865, 867, 868, 869, 870, 871, 872, 873, 878, 879, 880, 881, 882, 883, 885, 886, 892, 893, 894, 895, 896, 898, 899, 900, 901, 903, 911, 921, 923, 927, 933, 940, 942, 943, 947

HOSPITALS—3, 5, 15, 21, 26, 32, 34, 37, 39, 40, 42, 44, 54, 56, 57, 58, 60, 62, 65, 70, 71, 72, 77, 85, 86, 87, 89, 93, 94, 97, 99, 100, 101, 106, 107, 114, 118, 119, 125, 126, 127, 128, 131, 133, 137, 139, 141, 142, 145, 146, 147, 149, 150, 151, 157, 158, 159, 169, 170, 171, 172, 173, 175, 177, 181, 186, 187, 192, 195, 199, 200, 202, 205, 207, 208, 213, 215, 219, 221, 222, 225, 226, 227, 230, 232, 233, 239, 242, 245, 249, 251, 253, 254, 255, 256, 257, 258, 262, 265, 266, 272, 273, 277, 278, 281, 285, 290, 293, 295, 300, 301, 304, 305, 309, 310, 312, 313, 317, 323, 324, 325, 326, 329, 330, 338, 348, 352, 357, 363, 372, 377, 380, 381, 383, 386, 391, 393, 394, 399, 400, 401, 403, 406, 407, 409, 410, 413, 415, 421, 423, 425, 426, 436, 438, 440, 441, 444, 455, 458, 466, 467, 474, 476, 478, 486, 488, 489, 490, 496, 498, 502, 503, 505, 513, 518, 519, 526, 527, 528, 529, 530, 531, 533, 534, 535, 536, 538, 540, 541, 542, 544, 545, 549, 554, 556, 558, 559, 560, 561, 563, 564, 566, 569, 572, 573, 574, 575, 576, 577, 581, 584, 585, 586, 588, 589, 591, 593, 594, 595, 598, 600, 601, 603, 604, 605, 606, 607, 608, 609, 611, 613, 614, 615, 616, 619, 621, 623, 624, 627, 628, 629, 630, 631, 632, 637, 639, 640, 642, 647, 658, 664, 665, 671, 675, 676, 680, 681, 689, 691, 693, 694, 696, 697, 699, 703, 704, 710, 714, 716, 717, 718, 719, 720, 723, 725, 732, 734, 737, 740, 742, 743, 744, 745, 747, 748, 750, 753, 754, 757, 760, 762, 764, 765, 766, 767, 770, 772, 773, 779, 780, 781, 782, 783, 785, 786, 787, 879, 790, 791, 795, 799, 801, 804, 812, 815, 816, 817, 819, 821, 823, 824, 827, 828, 830, 831, 832, 834, 835, 836, 837, 839, 840, 841, 842, 843, 845, 846, 847, 848, 849, 850, 851, 852, 854, 855, 856, 859, 860, 863, 864, 865, 869, 870, 872, 877, 878, 879, 880, 885, 890, 892, 893, 894, 897, 899, 903, 907, 912, 913, 923, 925, 927, 932, 934, 935, 938, 940, 942, 944, 948

LIBRARIES—7, 30, 43, 51, 61, 65, 68, 80, 81, 83, 86, 87, 93, 105, 118, 126, 144, 160, 168, 170, 199, 255, 257, 272, 286, 292, 295, 300, 304, 309, 331, 332, 333, 387, 421, 428, 439, 505, 537, 561, 562, 568, 573, 579, 583, 585, 590, 597, 608, 617, 620, 630, 631, 633, 688, 701, 708, 720, 732, 738, 746, 753, 762, 773, 778, 781, 793, 829, 853, 855, 860, 869, 889, 893, 901, 914, 933, 935, 939, 940, 944, 947

MINORITIES—5, 9, 15, 23, 73, 74, 82, 83, 153, 175, 184, 254, 367, 382, 411, 415, 426, 428, 429, 434, 435, 447, 448, 449, 450, 454, 473, 485, 504, 526, 534, 542, 548, 551, 552, 556, 558, 563, 564, 569, 590, 592, 593, 594, 610, 611, 613, 619, 620, 626, 628, 638, 658, 662, 665, 666, 670, 683, 686, 687, 690, 702, 710, 714, 717, 733, 755, 772, 774, 779, 782, 791, 803, 848, 851, 855, 857, 870, 874, 893, 914, 945

898, 899, 900, 903, 904, 905, 906, 907, 908, 909, 910, 911, 912, 913, 914, 915, 916, 917, 918, 919, 920, 921, 922, 923, 926, 927, 928, 929, 930, 931, 932, 933, 934, 936, 937, 939, 942, 943, 944, 945, 946, 947, 948

WOMEN—8, 20, 35, 61, 70, 73, 76, 104, 117, 126, 152, 153, 162, 165, 166, 169, 177, 183, 184, 187, 189, 191, 199, 218, 232, 241, 250, 260, 267, 276, 287, 291, 304, 330, 331, 334, 340, 370, 371, 393, 397, 404, 407, 414, 429, 430, 436, 443, 450, 454, 472, 476, 479, 484, 493, 513, 520, 524, 526, 527, 535, 540, 548, 549, 550, 554, 558, 566, 575, 585, 589, 600, 605, 612, 642, 648, 650, 656, 657, 666, 670, 689, 723, 756, 769, 771, 772, 778, 779, 782, 787, 799, 806, 817, 838, 839, 847, 849, 865, 872, 878, 883, 884, 893, 915, 917, 920, 938

YOUTH ORGANIZATIONS—2, 3, 5, 8, 10, 11, 12, 14, 21, 23, 24, 26, 29, 31, 32, 33, 34, 35, 39, 40, 42, 45, 47, 49, 50, 54, 55, 56, 59, 61, 63, 64, 65, 66, 69, 70, 72, 73, 75, 76, 78, 79, 81, 82, 85, 87, 91, 93, 95, 96, 97, 98, 101, 102, 104, 105, 108, 110, 113, 115, 117, 118, 121, 124, 130, 132, 138, 140, 141, 143, 144, 146, 147, 153, 155, 157, 159, 164, 165, 166, 167, 169, 171, 173, 175, 177, 179, 180, 182, 183, 184, 185, 191, 192, 193, 194, 197, 200, 204, 206, 209, 211, 213, 215, 218, 224, 225, 228, 229, 231, 235, 236, 237, 238, 239, 240, 242, 244, 245, 247, 248, 250, 252, 253, 254, 255, 258, 260, 262, 264, 265, 268, 269, 273, 277, 279, 280, 281, 283, 285, 287, 290, 292, 293, 295, 296, 302, 303, 305, 306, 307, 309, 310, 311, 312, 317, 318, 320, 321, 322, 331, 335, 340, 345, 346, 347, 348, 351, 353, 354, 355, 359, 361, 362, 363, 366, 367, 369, 370, 371, 372, 373, 374, 376, 378, 379, 380, 382, 383, 387, 388, 389, 392, 393, 394, 395, 396, 397, 398, 399, 400, 402, 403, 404, 405, 406, 408, 410, 414, 415, 420, 421, 422, 424, 428, 429, 431, 432, 434, 435, 436, 439, 440, 441, 442, 443, 444, 446, 447, 448, 449, 450, 452, 453, 454, 458, 459, 461, 463, 464, 465, 467, 468, 471, 472, 473, 477, 480, 484, 485, 486, 487, 488, 489, 490, 492, 493, 494, 495, 496, 497, 498, 499, 504, 505, 506, 507, 508, 509, 511, 512, 514, 515, 516, 518, 520, 523, 524, 527, 529, 530, 532, 534, 537, 539, 540, 541, 542, 544, 545, 547, 548, 550, 552, 553, 554, 555, 556, 557, 558, 559, 563, 564, 565, 566, 567, 568, 569, 571, 573, 575, 578, 580, 582, 583, 585, 586, 587, 589, 590, 591, 592, 593, 594, 595, 596, 597, 599, 600, 601, 602, 603, 604, 605, 606, 608, 609, 610, 611, 612, 613, 614, 616, 617, 619, 620, 622, 623, 624, 626, 627, 629, 630, 631, 632, 633, 634, 635, 637, 640, 643, 645, 648, 651, 652, 653, 654, 655, 656, 657, 659, 662, 664, 666, 668, 669, 670, 671, 672, 673, 674, 676, 682, 683, 689, 690, 691, 692, 693, 694, 696, 697, 698, 701, 704, 705, 706, 707, 708, 711, 713, 715, 716, 717, 718, 722, 725, 726, 727, 728, 729, 730, 732, 736, 737, 738, 739, 740, 742, 743, 745, 746, 748, 750, 751, 752, 753, 755, 757, 758, 759, 760, 761, 762, 765, 766, 768, 769, 771, 772, 773, 774, 775, 778, 779, 780, 781, 782, 783, 789, 792, 793, 795, 796, 799, 800, 806, 809, 810, 815, 817, 819, 820, 821, 825, 826, 827, 829, 830, 831, 832, 833, 835, 836, 837, 838, 839, 840, 842, 843, 844, 847, 848, 849, 851, 853, 854, 856, 858, 859, 860, 862, 864, 865, 868, 869, 870, 871, 873, 876, 877, 878, 881, 883, 884, 887, 892, 893, 895, 896, 897, 898, 899, 900, 901, 902, 905, 906, 907, 910, 911, 912, 915, 917, 919, 920, 922, 924, 925, 927, 928, 930, 932, 933, 938, 940, 941, 944, 946, 948

Index to Federal Programs

(By Agency)

Comments

Thank you for purchasing the Third Edition of the *Directory of Building and Equipment Grants*. We welcome your comments (positive and negative). Please list funding sources that should be included in this *Directory*.

Thank you for your response.

Comments:

Name_____ Title _____

Organization _____

Address _____

City_____ State_____ Zip _____

Please send comments to: Editor
Research Grant Guides, Inc.
P.O. Box 1214
Loxahatchee, FL 33470